HUMAN RIGHTS

AND THE TRANSFORMATION OF PROPERTY

HUMAN RIGHTS

AND THE TRANSFORMATION OF PROPERTY

Stuart Wilson
MA (Oxon) LLB (with distinction) PhD (Wits)
Advocate of the High Court of South Africa
Member of the Johannesburg Bar
Visiting Adjunct Professor,
University of the Witwatersrand

juta

Human Rights and the Transformation of Property

First published 2021

© Juta and Company (Pty) Ltd
First Floor, Sunclare Building, 21 Dreyer Street, Claremont, 7708

Acknowledgment:
Front cover picture provided with permission to use by Jurgen Schadeberg.

ISBN: 978 1 48513 822 8

Production Specialist: Mmakasa Ramoshaba
Editor: James Ryan
Proofreader: Elisma Roets
Indexer: Lexinfo
Typeset in 11/13 Times Lt Std
Typesetting: Wouter Reinders

For Julian

ACKNOWLEDGEMENTS

Summing up your intellectual and personal debts is difficult and humbling. But it is not difficult *because* it is humbling. My connectedness with others – the fact that, however it felt at the time, I was never really alone in writing this book – is something in which I take great comfort.

My mother, Barbara, was a textile worker who had to run away from home to pursue her education. In my father, David, she was to meet a different kind of rebel – a man from a much more "respectable" class, who nonetheless managed to get himself expelled from school for refusing to accept that his teachers were perfectly entitled to assault him. I like to think that I have inherited at least some of their fierce intelligence, and their belief in the contingency of structures of authority. I am very sad that neither of them has lived to see this book being published. But I owe literally everything to them. My sister, Karin, and my brother, Robert, have loved and supported their precocious little brother more than he often deserved.

My undergraduate tutor, John Tasioulas, is an unmatchable combination of intelligence and generosity – and he personifies the lesson that those two things go best together. John's challenge to a bumptious undergraduate – to avoid separating action in the world from theory about the world – has done more than I can describe to shape my career as a writer and as a lawyer.

I started out that career at the Centre for Applied Legal Studies (CALS). There, I have Matthew Chaskalson and Salim Vally to thank for my job, Cathi Albertyn, Faranaaz Veriava and Theunis Roux to thank for their patience, and Sheeren Mills, Mike Nefale and Jackie Dugard to thank for their indulgence and friendship. Many of the ideas in this book owe a great deal to CALS, its researchers and its environment of experimentation in the early 2000s. I was allowed to do what was exciting to me, and to discover my interest in property law, housing and land tenure. Once discovered, CALS left me to pursue that interest to its logical – and often controversial – conclusions. In the first decade of this century, CALS was a place where everything felt urgent and possible, and the constitutional vision of a just and equal society always seemed within reach.

But it is to the staff, donors, directors, clients and allies of the Socio-Economic Rights Institute of South Africa (SERI) that this book owes the most. SERI, which Jackie Dugard and I co-founded, and which I directed for nearly seven years, has done at least as much as any other legal NGO to erode the structures of inequality and dispossession that lay at the heart of apartheid, and which still bedevil the constitutional project.

Today, SERI's work under Nomzamo Zondo remains as important and as impressive as it has ever been. I owe a special debt to Nomzamo. Her courage, insight and compassion keep me in awe. I also want to thank Zak Yacoob,

Khululiwe Bhengu, Thulani Nkosi, Maanda Makwarela, Dara Kell, Alejandra Anchieta, Osmond Mngomezulu, Teboho Moskili, Tiffany Ebrahim, Michael Clark, Kathleen Hardy, Michael Leonard, Amanda Duma, Princess Nkuna and Mami Molefe, whose work and comradeship I have particularly valued. Sanele Garane was a friend before she helped found SERI and remains a friend today. I have a profound sense of pride in Nkosinathi Sithole's work and achievements, and a real debt of gratitude to Lauren Royston, whose insight, advice and support were, and remain, essential to SERI's success. Sbu Zikode is the bravest person I know. He has sacrificed so much to Abahali baseMjondolo, whose work is discussed in this book. If SERI's support to Abahlali has lightened Sbu's load in any way, I am glad beyond imagination.

If the arguments in this book are right – or even just a bit right – SERI's contribution to the dismantling of apartheid and the achievement of an enduring social justice will be felt for decades to come, so long as the constitutional project can itself be sustained.

That project cannot be sustained without a skilled and independent legal profession. My colleagues at the Bar remain a source of advice, support and inspiration without which this book could not have been written. I want to single out Paul Kennedy, Heidi Barnes, Jacquie Cassette, Trish Ternent and Antony Gotz for encouraging and supporting me during the last 20 years, and for appearing in, and helping to conceptualise, many of the cases discussed in this book. Paul, in particular, has been a prudent counsellor, and a generous friend. Dumisa Ntsebeza, who spent many years as a director of SERI, has also been an important source of wisdom and encouragement. I am grateful to dozens of other colleagues whose commitment, work and skill have been exemplary to me. Chief among these is Anna-Marie de Vos. Advocacy is about explaining things convincingly to someone whose agreement cannot be presumed. I have never seen anyone do that better than her.

My closest friendship at the Bar has been with Irene de Vos, with whom I did pupillage, and whose intelligence, insight, irreverence and willingness to laugh out loud has sustained me through the many, many cases we have worked on together, some of which are discussed in this book. My pupils, Zweli Makgalemele, Ofentse Motlhasedi, Emma Broster, Mluleki Marongo and Maropeng Mpya are a constant source of friendship and pride.

Sandy Liebenberg is the world's most important and committed scholar of social and economic rights. She was SERI's first chairperson. She has provided unflinching support for, and exercised a great deal of influence over, my academic work. She is also my friend, and is in every way a class act. Marius Pieterse, who supervised the PhD dissertation on which this book is based, was patient, supportive and kind.

The front cover of this book features a photograph by Jurgen Schadeberg, the legendary photographer, whom I remember fondly from our work together documenting the conditions of people living in Johannesburg's inner city, and of African and Coloured people living on white-owned commercial farmlands in the early 2000s. That work can be seen in *Tales from Jozi* and *Voices from the Land*, two of his later books, which are well worth buying. I am grateful to Jurgen's wife, Claudia, and to his estate, for permission to use the photograph.

I am also grateful to the Bingham Centre for the Rule of Law in London, for awarding me a fellowship during which content from the early chapters of this book was presented, and to the MaxPo Institute at Sciences Po in Paris, which gave me a desk and a chair in my husband's office there, in which I wrote the bulk this book.

My husband is Julian Brown. There are simply no words to describe how much I love him. But let's try anyway. He is the funniest, cleverest, most delicious person in the world. He is my beginning and my end. My greatest supporter, and my most incisive critic. A successful writer himself, his work has made mine possible. It is the greatest joy of my life that we have been with each other for over a decade, and that we have several more decades of that delight to come. Io t'abbraccio mio tesoro.

Stuart Wilson
Johannesburg, March 2021

CONTENTS

ACKNOWLEDGEMENTS vii

FOREWORD xiii

PREFACE xv

CHAPTER ONE: MAKING SPACE FOR TRANSFORMATION 1
    1.1   *Penthouse Views*.. *1*
    1.2   *The Paradox of Law and Social Change* *4*
    1.3   *Towards a New Account of Law and Social Change* *7*
    1.4   *Property Law and Social Practice* *10*
    1.5   *Contemporary Struggles over Property Rights in*
           South Africa... *11*
    1.6   *The Way Forward*.. *14*

CHAPTER TWO: LAW AND TRANSFORMATION 16
    2.1   *The Ambitious Constitution*... *16*
    2.2   *Theorising Law and Social Change* *19*
    2.3   *The Classical Marxist Tradition: Law as Epiphenomenon* *21*
    2.4   *The Liberal Tradition: Law as Instrumentality* *24*
    2.5   *"Every Bloody Level": Law as Social Structurant* *27*
    2.6   *Structuring Transformation: South African Property Law*
           and Dispossession *33*

CHAPTER THREE: PROPERTY BARKS 36
    3.1   *The Common Law of Property and Social Exclusion*.............. *38*
    3.2   *How the Common Law of Property Treats Unlawful Occupiers,*
           Tenants and Debtors... *44*
           3.2.1 Unlawful Occupiers 44
           3.2.2 Landlords and Tenants 46
           3.2.3 Execution of Debts against a Debtor's Home 48
    3.3   *The Constitutional Property and Housing Rights Clauses*....... *52*

CHAPTER FOUR: TAKING BACK THE LAND 57
    4.1   *The Development of a Constitutionalised Law of Eviction* *60*
           4.1.1 Section 26(3) of the Constitution, the PIE Act and the
                 Common Law... 60
           4.1.2 The Construction of Equity in Eviction Proceedings..... 66

4.2   New Housing Rights Struggles   74
       4.2.1 Managing Relocations   75
       4.2.2 Taking Back the Land..   77
       4.2.3 We Won't Move   79
4.3   Changed Spaces   81

CHAPTER FIVE: JUST LETTING   82
5.1   The Rental Housing Act and Regulations...............................   84
       5.1.1 The Rent Control Act   84
       5.1.2 The Rental Housing Act   85
       5.1.3 The Rental Housing Act in Court..........................   88
5.2   The Tribunals in Action   92
       5.2.1 Rent Determinations   93
       5.2.2 The Plettenberg Cases   97
5.3   An Unreliable Resource?..   101

CHAPTER SIX: LOOSENING THE BONDS.....................................   103
6.1   Debtors, creditors and power...   103
6.2   Proportionality in the debt execution process   107
6.3   Resisting Execution   114
       6.3.1 The Arrear Amount or Overall Debt Claimed is
              Disproportionately Low   117
       6.3.2 Non-compliance with the National Credit Act 34
              of 2005   118
       6.3.3 The Qualified Right to a Reserve Price..........................   124
6.4   Debtors, Creditors and Social Change....................................   124

CHAPTER SEVEN: WHAT'S PROPERTY LAW GOT TO DO
              WITH IT?   126
7.1   The "Failure" of South African Land Reform..........................   128
7.2   Sustaining Transformation   130
7.3   Law in Action   131
7.4   Action in Law   135
7.5   The Structure of Law   138
7.6   Agent-centred Judges and Lawyers.......................................   140
7.7   The Many Faces of Law..   142

BIBLIOGRAPHY...   144
       Books and Articles   144
       Cases   149
       Statutes and Regulations..   152
       Research Reports and Media Articles.....................................   153

INDEX   154

FOREWORD

This is an important book. While an impressive work of scholarship, it also adopts an accessible tone. It will define debates on the meaning of property under the Constitution for years to come.

The book also tackles an important subject: property. Property ownership has been at the centre of the economic, political and social contestation in South Africa practically since the seventeenth century when the Europeans first arrived at the Cape and set forth to colonise the land of indigenous people. Since then, the history of the Cape has been characterised by violent conflict, reflective of the many episodes of dispossession and resistance.

The Europeans arrived with their own ideas of property, shaped and moulded in the violence of Europe of the earlier centuries. In displacing Africans from their land, Europeans also imposed new legal rules to define the relationship between indigenous people and the land – of the most important were laws relating to property ownership. The rules relating to what property is, who could own it, and the rights of non-owners were central to the colonial imagination of the Cape. As the European population grew and a need for expansion of the settlement beyond the Cape into the interior, their economic needs also increased. They needed people to labour, cattle to trade and more land.

Ideas of property also shifted to accommodate the economic and social needs of the settlers. People were once regarded as property, which could be acquired, exploited and sold in the open market, during the age of slavery. Land too was regarded by the Europeans, in contrast to African conceptions of land, as a commodity that could be bought and sold. Natural minerals such as gold and diamonds also entered the family of things that were subjected to ownership laws. The ideas of property and ownership helped to construct a society in which there were vast disparities in income, wealth and assets. These disparities defined the colonial age, and would be carried through to the apartheid period, in the twentieth century. One of the most notorious laws of the colonial period, which remained in the statute books for about 80 years, until 1991, was the Native Land Act of 1913, which prohibited ownership of land by Africans in designated European areas – which constituted 87% of the surface land area of South Africa. It ensured that Africans were effectively regarded as outsiders in the country of their birth.

Apartheid, as the successor to Empire, simply reinforced imperial prejudices. Its laws such as the Group Areas Act ensured that Africans remained a vast underclass, which was property-less and vote-less. Apartheid's collapse in the late 1980s addressed only the legal superstructure. The economic structure created under the colonial and apartheid period remained.

When the new Constitution came into effect in 1994, it faced formidable challenges. There were expectations that rather than establishing the legal foundations for reforms, the Constitution itself would bring about the reforms. In this way, the Constitution was perceived as a vector for political and economic changes. Thus, when that political expectation could not be fulfilled, the argument was that the Constitution had failed. This view persists.

What has been forgotten, perhaps, is the true role of the Constitution – laying the legal foundation for a new society founded on the values of equality, human dignity, and the achievement of freedom. To achieve this, the Constitution must serve a dual function of enabling transformation and simultaneously constraining political power.

It is accepted that property relations of the apartheid era which still persist should be transformed. However, the possibility of this transformation is constrained by politics and economics and the inherited legal culture which was hostile to notions of equality and dignity. It is in respect of legal culture that this book is particularly important. It traces the transformation of an idea of property in the constitutional era. It recognises the limits of transformation which are inherent in any legal system. But the book is bold, imaginative and insightful.

Another strength of this book is that its ideas are not imposed from the top; rather, it takes poor people, their concerns and their aspirations seriously. It seeks to transform our understanding of property by reimagining outdated modes of property and forging ahead to a new normative framework of property.

While ideas of property and ownership shall remain contested, Stuart Wilson's powerful message is never to stop imagining ways in which society could be fairer, better and more equal. The law will not achieve this on its own. But it will be an important foundation for this new, restorative project that this book calls upon all of us.

Tembeka Ncgukaitobi
March 2021

PREFACE

"… someone is hearing
The outcry and the birth-cry
Of new life at its term.
It means once in a lifetime
That justice can rise up
And hope and history rhyme."

Seamus Heaney
"The Cure at Troy"

If hope and history have ever rhymed, it was when South Africa ended 350 years of colonialism and apartheid by adopting the 1996 Constitution. But, Heaney says, justice rises up once in a lifetime. If we are lucky, we spend the rest of our days locked in struggle, trying to make sense of our need to commit to justice in theory, while regularly betraying that commitment in practice.

This book is about what happened after the ink dried on the Constitution, and we had to start deciding what it meant in practice. It concentrates on one of the Constitution's most ambitious commitments: to the right of access to adequate housing, and one of its most insidious foes: a common law of property designed to reflect the interests of wealthy merchants and landowners in early modern Europe, rather than landless black people in twenty-first century South Africa. The book argues that progress in achieving land reform, and access to adequate housing for all who need it, necessarily requires the restructuring of the common law of property, and the disruption of the hierarchies of power that lie at its core.

This argument has been honed through practice as much as through study. For twenty years, I have been involved in the defence of poor and vulnerable people against eviction, and in their legal struggles to secure access to better housing. At every turn, my colleagues and I have been met – by lawyers and laypeople alike – with the unexamined prejudices of property: the assertion of an owner's absolute power, the equation of landlessness with moral turpitude, and the fierce ideological commitment to neo-liberal economics and the smallest possible role for the state in the provision of basic social goods.

At first, I thought of all of this as a category mistake. These prejudices were political commitments that arose outside the law, and were simply not admissible against the Constitution's requirements that everyone has access to adequate housing. I was often frustrated, and not a little bemused, by the inability of otherwise intelligent people to understand that the Constitution must at least require some limitations on ownership rights, empathy and respect for landless people and a much larger role for the state in providing housing for those who could not afford to purchase it on the open market.

Then it dawned on me. The reactionary claims of property are not exclusively extra-legal. They spring from a deeply conservative common law tradition in which almost all lawyers have been trained, and which we have been encouraged to accept uncritically. Since that tradition reinforces many of the class privileges we can expect as affluent members of a propertied elite, there has never been any incentive, within the legal profession, to subject that tradition to much scrutiny. While a growing number of lawyers now accept that the Constitution requires the restructuring and adaptation of this tradition, the necessity, and terms, of this restructuring remain a subject of real controversy in the profession, and in the public at large.

It has taken twenty years of grinding litigation – and statutory and policy reform – to begin to place limits on the prejudices of property, and to begin to transform the law of property into a set of rules fit to implement the Constitutional vision of access to land and adequate housing for all who need it. This book is, in no small measure, a memorial of that process.

Chapter 1 posits the central tension that animates this book: the coexistence of a constitutional commitment to an egalitarian society in which power and wealth are radically redistributed, with a set of legal rules and process that often tend to the opposite result. It outlines a theory of property law and social change that explains this tension, and can help to begin to resolve it.

Chapter 2 theorises the way in which this is possible. It argues that what is socially important about the law is its capacity to shape the spaces in which ordinary men and women think and act to meet their needs and give effect to their aspirations. It argues for an "agent-centred" theory of law and social change: one that focuses not so much on law as an instrument of policy reform, but as a part of the social framework that structures the opportunities open to ordinary men and women in their everyday lives.

Chapter 3 discusses the state of South African property law at the end of apartheid. It argues that property law was designed to maximise the power and agency available to people with common law ownership rights, and deny power and agency to those without them. This made the common law of property particularly amenable to colonial and apartheid projects of conquest, racism and dispossession.

Chapters 4, 5 and 6 argue that the Constitution has, over time, allowed poor and vulnerable people to create and occupy new spaces of power and agency that would not have been possible within the discursive framework of the common law alone.

Chapter 4 charts the legal developments that have established a rule against evictions that lead to homelessness. It argues that the development of this rule has permitted unlawful occupiers to stake powerful claims to urban land rights, including the rights to trigger and control the upgrading of shack settlements. Chapter 5 charts the development of a rule against unfair termination of residential leases, and assesses the performance of rental housing tribunals charged with ensuring that residential landlords comply with their duty to act fairly. Chapter 6 sets out the constitutional limitations that have been placed on the rights of banks to foreclose on residential mortgage bonds. By requiring the act of foreclosure to be proportionate to the nature and extent of a mortgagor's default, the Constitution has created an important space in which debtors can resist foreclosure and challenge unfair conduct by creditors.

By way of conclusion, Chapter 7 draws together the strands common to each of these developments, and sums up what an agent-centred theory has to say about the role of property law in a project of social transformation.

CHAPTER ONE

MAKING SPACE FOR TRANSFORMATION

1.1   PENTHOUSE VIEWS

Sometime in late April 2003, I hauled myself up the sixteen floors of "San Jose", a derelict building in Johannesburg's inner city. I was a young researcher working with the Centre on Housing Rights and Evictions (COHRE) to document the living conditions of very poor people now living in once fashionable high-rise tenements. Despite being derelict, and having no water or electricity supply, San Jose was home to well over 300 people. Some had been evicted from other buildings and moved into empty units long abandoned by their owners or tenants. Others were people who had bought units in San Jose when it was a sought-after place to live. But they had been unable to move on to better housing as the building started to deteriorate when capital took flight from Johannesburg's inner city in the late 1980s and early 1990s.[1]

At the same time that money left Johannesburg to follow more lucrative property investments to the north of the city,[2] the influx controls that had kept South Africa's majority African population out of its major urban centres under apartheid collapsed and were eventually repealed. This meant that large numbers of relatively poor people were looking for a foothold in Johannesburg's urban core. High vacancy rates, coupled with the willingness of slum landlords to pack their buildings full of tenants who were willing to pay over the odds for substandard accommodation, meant that living conditions in the inner city gradually deteriorated over the course of the 1990s. The Johannesburg inner city gently slipped beyond the control of the state and private landlords, and became the site of a large number of often overcrowded and unhealthy slum properties.[3]

On the sixteenth floor of San Jose, there was the shell of a stylish penthouse. Its large, open-plan hallway was now home to several young men, sleeping on foam pallets and old base sets, with curtains and cardboard partitions put up for privacy. This was the antechamber of their urban dream. They had come to Johannesburg from KwaZulu-Natal, on South Africa's east coast, to find work – any work – that would allow them to support parents, wives, girlfriends and children back in rural homesteads hundreds of miles away. These young men were petrol pump attendants,

---

[1] Centre on Housing Rights and Evictions *Any Room for the Poor? Forced Evictions in Johannesburg, South Africa* (2005) 6.

[2] See S Goga "Property Investors and Decentralisation: A Case of False Competition?" in R Tomlinson, RA Beauregard, L Bremner and X Mangcu (eds) *Emerging Johannesburg: Perspectives on the Post-apartheid City* (2003) 71–84.

[3] See, generally, A Morris *Bleakness and Light: Inner City Transition in Hillbrow, Johannesburg* (1999).

security guards, cleaners and scrap collectors. The lucky ones were waiters or shop assistants. Few earned more than R2 000 a month, most significantly less. But their wages were, for them, small fortunes. Wages represented access to a cash economy and to consumer goods that were beyond their reach in the homes they had left behind.

Here, in the ruins of a 1960s modernist daydream, new plans and aspirations were being formed. A new life was being imagined and built on the fumes of capital.

As I interviewed the penthouse crew, and most of the other residents of San Jose, it became clear that these dreams and aspirations were under threat. Few people of any means were keen to live in central Johannesburg in the mid-to-late 1990s. However, by 2003, that was changing. The City of Johannesburg Metropolitan Municipality was embarking on a series of slum clearances. The idea was to have San Jose, and hundreds of other buildings like it, declared unfit for habitation, and to obtain court orders evicting their residents on to the streets, apparently for the sake of their safety.[4] Once empty, the buildings could be handed over to private property developers who would renovate them and let them out at a profit, taking advantage of the now renewed demand for middle- and upper-income housing. Of course, this housing would be beyond the means of the people who had to be evicted to make way for it.[5]

The trigger for this process was the service of hundreds of urgent eviction applications in each building. In San Jose, and in every other inner-city building where I conducted my research, these eviction applications were produced by the dozen. The applications would all make the same, standard form allegations about the absence of utilities and poor sewage reticulation. They would all play on the same prejudices about urban slums, and insinuate – without ever actually demonstrating – that the building was a hideout for violent criminals and sex workers.

The eviction applications were instituted in terms of section 12(4)(b) of the National Building Standards and Building Regulations Act 103 of 1977. That provision permits a municipal building control officer to issue a notice demanding someone leave their home if, in the building control officer's opinion, this is necessary for their safety. Once the notice was issued, the municipality would generally apply to court to give effect to it. These applications invariably presented the current occupants of the buildings they targeted the same "choice": leave their homes in compliance with the notice, go to court to try to defend themselves against eviction, or be violently removed.[6]

Of course, few people living in these buildings – most of them fairly recent migrants from rural South Africa – could hope to marshal the legal and financial resources necessary to oppose their eviction in court. The result, for most, was their prompt dispossession. Between 2000 and 2006, 122 eviction orders were obtained from the Johannesburg High Court, and approximately 10 000 people lost their

---

[4] Centre on Housing Rights and Evictions (note 1 above), 41–2.
[5] Ibid 59.
[6] Ibid 80.

homes when these orders were executed.[7] Most, if not all, ended up moving on to another derelict property in the same area.[8]

The speed with which the law was able to dispossess so many people was all the more remarkable, given that, just three years before Johannesburg's inner-city regeneration programme kicked in, South Africa's final post-apartheid Constitution had sought to draw a line under mass evictions of African people by the state.

The Constitution, which came into effect on 4 February 1997, was perhaps the most ardent statement of faith in the law's capacity to bring about egalitarian social transformation in human history. It was a product of an improbable compromise between the rulers of the racist apartheid state and the leaders of the African National Congress (ANC) committed to apartheid's destruction, by revolutionary violence if necessary. The Constitution ceded political power to the African majority by introducing universal adult suffrage and a common voters' roll. This replaced a racially stratified voting system where Indians and Coloured people were junior partners in a white-dominated polity, and in which Africans were given no vote and no national political representation at all.

The price of the political kingdom, though, was a much weaker commitment to economic transformation than the African majority had initially aspired to. In the Freedom Charter,[9] South Africa belonged to all who lived in it, and the land was to be shared among those who worked it. The Constitution postponed this dream. Racial patterns of property ownership were preserved, and expropriations of property were subjected to compensation requirements. Beyond the Constitution, the ANC committed itself to a neo-liberal economic orthodoxy.[10]

Economic transformation was not abandoned, however. The Constitution made provision for the adoption of laws authorising land restitution and redistribution.[11] It also provided for an apparently generous list of socio-economic rights: not to be arbitrarily evicted, to be provided with adequate housing, to healthcare, to education, to social security, to a healthy environment and to fair labour practices. The task of giving content to these rights, though, was almost invariably deferred to future legislative intervention, or jurisprudential developments based on the evaluation of policy through the prisms of "reasonableness" and "progressive realisation".

Perhaps most importantly, all existing law was left intact.[12] This included the common law of property, which had lent itself so easily to the project of colonial and apartheid dispossession of the African majority.[13] Much of the colonial and

---

[7] S Wilson "Litigating Housing Rights in Johannesburg's Inner City 2004–2008" 27 *South African Journal on Human Rights* (2011) 137.

[8] Centre on Housing Rights and Evictions (note 1 above) 43.

[9] The Freedom Charter (1955) was a declaration of principles to govern a post-apartheid state adopted by a mass meeting organised by the Congress of the People – an alliance of anti-apartheid organisations, including the African National Congress – at Kliptown in Johannesburg on 26 June 1955. It is acknowledged as one source of inspiration for the South African Constitution, 1996.

[10] P Bond *Talk Left, Walk Right: South Africa's Frustrated Global Reforms* (2004).

[11] Section 25(7) of the Constitution.

[12] Section 2 of Schedule 6 to the Constitution, 1996.

[13] A van der Walt "Tradition on Trial: A Critical Analysis of the Civil Law Tradition in South African Property Law" (1995) 11 *South African Journal on Human Rights* 169. For an engaging account of "how the land was lost"

apartheid legal regime would have to be carefully unpicked by the development of a strongly egalitarian, transformative constitutional project in the months and years to follow.

The net result of all of this was that the intricate relationship between property and prejudice that sustained a racist state for over 300 years remained substantially intact. It was, however, placed on notice that constitutionally driven social change was in the offing.

1.2   THE PARADOX OF LAW AND SOCIAL CHANGE

This book is about how far and to what extent the South African Constitution has been able to unpick the powerful connection between property and prejudice that underpinned colonialism and apartheid. In making this evaluation, I confront the paradox embedded in the faith South Africans have placed in constitutional and legal forms to achieve social transformation, and engage the long-standing debate about the extent to which law can structure and direct social change.

The engagement of law and legal processes to evict 10 000 people from their homes so soon after the passage of a Constitution meant to bring mass evictions to an end is both paradoxical and entirely unremarkable. The South African Constitution's aspirational content notwithstanding, the power structures that sit at the heart of South African property law remained intact. Within those power structures, poor people were vulnerable to eviction, at the hands of rich people and the state.

This paradoxical quality to the law has long been an object of study, along with the contradictions inherent in using law and legal forms and processes to achieve social change. "We use the law though we are terrified of it, contemptuous of its Janus face." We ask the law for "what we need, hoping [it] will not kill us before we have finished stating our claims".[14] The law promises emancipation, yet requires obedience. It insists on its own equal application, but can seldom be engaged except by those with the resources necessary to deploy lawyers, their expertise and the money to pay for it. It promises justice, but its institutions, processes and ideology everywhere sustain injustice, in the form of the wrongful deprivation of liberty, the infliction of state and corporate violence and the dispossession of the poor and vulnerable.

Yet the use of the law as a means of securing progressive social change remains attractive. We celebrate when the law exonerates the innocent, when it curbs the overweening state and corporate power, and when it compensates those who have been wronged. Over the past 50 years, since at least the birth of the civil rights movement in the United States, we have praised litigants, and their lawyers, as they

---

in the complex process of colonial dispossession, see T Ngcukaitobi *The Land is Ours: South Africa's first Black Lawyers and the Birth of Constitutionalism* (2018) 11–38.

[14] E Bruce-Jones "Black Lives and the State of Distraction" *Los Angeles Review of Books* <https://lareviewofbooks.org/essay/black-lives-and-the-state-of-distraction> last visited 4 March 2016.

have sought redress through the legal system – often against terrible odds – even where they have ultimately failed.

Except in perhaps the most particular of circumstances, failure has been the easiest interpretation of what has happened when litigants have pressed for broad social change through the law. The civil rights movement desegregated the United States in law, but not in fact.[15] In South Africa, the adoption of socio-economic rights has coincided with greater economic inequality.[16] Across the world, even as human rights protections have been enhanced, global poverty and inequality remain overwhelming. Governments and courts have curtailed civil liberties in the name of security against terrorism.

And yet, at least in South Africa, faith in seeking change through creating and enforcing legal rights appears to be stronger than ever before. Our Constitutional Court is celebrated for its decisions on the rights of access to adequate housing,[17] healthcare,[18] freedom of expression,[19] children's rights,[20] and a slew of criminal procedure rights.[21] Political disputes between parliamentary factions regularly end up in court.[22] The courts themselves are perceived as a key arena of dissent in our dominant-party democracy. Social movements, such as Abahlali baseMjondolo, the Anti-Privatisation Forum and the Treatment Action Campaign, together with labour unions, regularly turn to the courts to advance and defend their interests – as do thousands of other individual and group litigants where they can marshal the resources necessary to do so.[23]

Where does the truth lie? Are we profoundly mistaken about the law and its capacity to achieve social change? Or can struggles about the law, in some non-trivial sense, actually drive social change? In this book, I want to suggest that we are not mistaken in assigning value to law as an agent of change, but that the available theories of law's role in social change are not adequate to account for what happens when people – whether organised political groups or ordinary men and women – turn to the law and lawyers to advance their social interests. I want to suggest that law and social change are most intimately and powerfully linked, not on the grand scale of elite political struggle, but in more modest, everyday struggles about the terms on which ordinary men and women respond to and shape the limits placed on

---

[15] Howard Zinn *A People's History of the United States* (2005) 466–77.

[16] J Seekings and N Nattrass *Class Race, and Inequality in South Africa* (2005) 3–4. On the general lack of an association between the adoption of socio-economic rights and reductions in inequality see B Ray *Engaging with Social Rights: Procedure, Participation and Democracy in South Africa's Second Wave* (2016) 330; J King *Judging Social Rights* (2012) 2.

[17] *Government of the Republic of South Africa v Grootboom* 2001 (1) SA 46 (CC).

[18] *Treatment Action Campaign v Minister of Health* 2002 (5) SA 721 (CC).

[19] *Laugh It Off Promotions CC v South African Breweries International (Finance) BV t/a Sabmark International and Another* 2006 (1) SA 144 (CC).

[20] *Christian Education South Africa v Minister of Education* 2000 (4) SA 757 (CC).

[21] *S v Zuma* 1995 (2) SA 642 (CC); *S v Makwanyane and Another* 1995 (3) SA 391 (CC).

[22] *Democratic Alliance v Speaker of the National Assembly and Others* 2015 (4) SA 351 (WCC).

[23] J Brown and S Wilson "A Presumed Equality: State and Citizen in Post-apartheid South Africa" (2013) 72 *African Studies* 86; J Brown *South Africa's Insurgent Citizens: On Dissent and the Possibility of Politics* (2015) 127–47.

their range of autonomy. Struggles about the scope and content of property law are a paradigmatic example, because they shape the terms on which men and women access the resources necessary to sustain a dignified, autonomous existence.

If the relationship between law and social change is conceptualised in this way, the apparent paradox of trust in the law's emancipatory potential in the face of its oppressive realities can be resolved. Because law helps structure the terms on which dignity, autonomy and resources are available to everyday agents, influence over the shape and content of laws tends to decide whether the law is experienced as repressive or emancipatory.

The standard accounts of the role of law in social change have yet to capture this complexity. At their most basic, they either reduce law to an epiphenomenon of the balance of political and social forces, or, at best, an instrumentality through which social change is effected by people who have the specialist knowledge necessary to integrate it into an effective political strategy. The "law as epiphenomenon" account simply misconstrues the nature of law and the role it plays in social practice. The "law as instrumentality" account correctly assumes that law is at least partially autonomous from the power relationships to which it can be applied, but fails to ask why this is so, and what flows from law's status as a structurant of social practice.

Something beyond the standard accounts is required. In this book, I offer an account of law as a social structurant that shapes the spaces within which agency is possible. Law constitutes a fundamental form of social practice. It is woven into the background attitudes and constraints within which ordinary people negotiate the terms of their interactions with one another: "inherited legal conventions shape the very terms of citizen understanding, aspiration and interaction with others".[24] Law also helps shape the contours of possible action. It often places "effective inhibitions on the exercise of power",[25] whether by direct coercion or by moulding an agent's perceptions of what is permissible action, and therefore what is possible. Law accordingly plays an important part in defining the spaces within which agency is possible.

But, the law is also malleable, subject to interpretation and change, and the validity and application of particular laws can be challenged and reshaped in particular circumstances. Law, as well as being a key structurant of the spaces within which agency is possible, is also a tool with which it is possible to refashion those spaces.

By way of illustration, I offer an account of the development of South African property law since the end of apartheid. Property law – and the "ownership model"[26] on which it is based – shapes the terms on which ordinary people access the basic resources which are essential not only to their survival and material comfort, but also to the terms on which they interact socially. Property law also expresses class relationships which structure some of the most fundamental forms of social and economic inequality in present day South Africa. If property law can

---

[24] M McCann (note 5 above) 6.

[25] EP Thompson *Whigs and Hunters: The Origins of the Black Act* (1975) 266.

[26] JW Singer *Entitlement: The Paradoxes of Property* (2000) 3.

be reshaped, then so, in a non-trivial sense, can the class relationships which sustain ongoing inequality.

In this book, I argue that this is precisely what is happening in key areas of property law. Litigants, courts, the state and Parliament have embarked on a sustained process of reimagining the nature and purposes of South African property law. The ownership model has been repeatedly challenged as a way of structuring property relationships, and groups of people traditionally denied rights in the South African property regime have been granted a degree of legal recognition. This recognition has created and expanded the spaces within which it is possible for these "property outsiders"[27] – those who lack existing property rights, or whose property rights are subordinated to the will of those who hold stronger property rights – to reshape the terms on which property is distributed. Through everyday practices of negotiation and challenge, property outsiders have begun to interfere with the legal processes of dispossession which sustain inequality.

The particular areas in which this reshaping has taken place are the law applicable to unlawful occupation of land, landlord and tenant law and debtor/creditor law. In each of these areas, the processes of dispossession which give effect to the rights and expectations of "property insiders" – owners, or those whose property rights give them a dominant position in legal relationships about property – have been limited, qualified or challenged by reference to the social needs of the property outsiders who are at risk of dispossession. Evictions that lead to homelessness have been declared generally unlawful.[28] Landlords seeking to terminate residential leases have been required to show that the termination is fair.[29] Creditors seeking to execute against defaulting debtors must now show that alternatives to execution have been offered[30] and, where execution would lead to loss of the debtor's home, that execution is a proportionate response to the default.[31] These legal innovations have often been developed as limitations on a property insider's ordinary common law rights to dispossess an outsider.[32] It is within the spaces created by these limitations that everyday challenges to economic power can begin to effect powerful social change.

1.3   TOWARDS A NEW ACCOUNT OF LAW AND SOCIAL CHANGE

Forty years ago, in a now-famous dissent from the standard Marxist analysis, EP Thompson observed that "the rhetoric and rules of society are something a great

---

[27] The term "property outsiders" is inspired by the terms "property outlaws" in E Penalver and S Katyal *Property Outlaws: How Squatters, Pirates and Protestors Improve the Law of Ownership* (2010). Penalver and Katyal argue that the reform of property law is at least partly driven by challenges to the concepts of ownership presented by illegal incursions upon them.

[28] *Occupiers, Shulana Court v Mark Lewis Steele* [2010] 4 All SA 54 (SCA) para 16.

[29] *Maphango v Aengus Lifestyle Properties* 2012 (3) SA 531 (CC).

[30] *Sebola and Another v Standard Bank of South Africa Ltd (Socio-Economic Rights Institute of South Africa and Others as Amici Curiae)* 2012 (5) SA 142 (CC).

[31] *Jaftha v Schoeman; Van Rooyen v Stoltz* 2005 (2) SA 140 (CC).

[32] I have appeared as an advocate in many of the cases I will describe in seeking to make this argument. I have represented unlawful occupiers, tenants and debtors involved in them. I have sometimes appeared as a friend of the court. The cases in which I appeared are marked with an asterisk in the table of cases at the end of this book.

deal more than sham".[33] In his path-breaking study of the implementation of the Black Act 1723 – a piece of legislation which sought to protect the property rights of a prosperous commercial elite against petty crime and civil disobedience, by rapidly and substantially enlarging the use of the death penalty – Thompson suggested that in clothing the enforcement of their interests in the rule of law, that commercial class had to accept significant limitations on the exercise of what would otherwise have been an irresistible force. Although the English propertied class of the early eighteenth century was "a political oligarchy inventing callous and oppressive laws to serve its own interests" it cannot be concluded that "the rule of law itself was humbug". He went on, "the rule of law itself, the imposing of effective inhibitions upon power and the defence of the citizen from power's all-intrusive claims, seems to me to be an unqualified human good". To overlook this "is to throw away a whole inheritance of struggle *about* law, and within the forms of law, whose continuity can never be fractured without bringing men and women into immediate danger".[34]

Thompson's observations about the way in which legal forms curb the exercise of power in wicked legal systems were taken up in South Africa under apartheid as a way of explaining the participation of lawyers and judges in the apartheid legal system. Apartheid was presented as a legally regulated and sanctioned system of social ordering that was implemented in a fair and predictable manner. Ideas of fairness, freedom and equality embedded in the law could accordingly be turned against the system to ameliorate some of its most pernicious effects in specific contexts, and, perhaps more importantly, to expose apartheid as a system of government that was anything but fair, predictable and law-governed.[35]

For Thompson, law is able to limit and direct power because, at least in modern capitalist societies, law is imbricated in every important social and economic relationship. It exists at multiple levels and is embedded in a range of different social contexts. There is no meaningful separation, for example, between "law" and "economics", because economics can only be studied as a set of predefined normative relationships between people, resources, capital, commodity and labour. In other words, social power relationships are "simultaneously economic, social and moral".[36] Law plays a vital role in structuring these relationships precisely because it is a set of normative claims about the right forms of social order that is backed up by authority.

If law structures social relationships in the way Thompson suggests it does, then it also shapes the opportunities for action available to ordinary men and women in everyday contexts. Based on Thompson's insight, I want to suggest that the power of law as an agent of social change lies in its ability to create or destroy spaces in which socially subordinate groups – the poor, racial minorities, women, sexual

---

[33] EP Thompson (note 25 above) 265.
[34] Ibid 266.
[35] R Abel *Politics by Other Means: Law in the Struggle Against Apartheid, 1980–1994* (1995).
[36] EP Thompson *The Poverty of Theory and Other Essays* (1978) 289.

minorities and indigenous populations – can think and act to give effect to their plans and aspirations.

Conceiving of the law in this way requires us first to recognise the inherent limits of the use of law as a political strategy. If law creates, expands and/or contracts opportunities for action, then its role in bringing about social change is at best secondary. It is the agents that act within the spaces law carves out that actually change things. However, without the space in which to act, the changes that can follow on an effective legal strategy are not themselves possible. It seems to me that this way of understanding legal strategies for change makes sense of, but places appropriate limits on, the critiques of the law's capacity to bring about change. It suggests that it is not enough to make the simple (and often irrefutable) observation that changes in the law following legislative reform or progressive court victories have not always been commensurate with changes in practice. That is true of almost all social change lawyering. Judgments and statutes do not magically produce change (although they are often no more or less effective than a range of other more traditional political strategies). At the same time, however, real social change is seldom possible without an alteration in the background rules people create to govern their everyday behaviour. While it is correct to point out, for example, that the civil rights movement has hardly succeeded in desegregating the US, it is equally unlikely that such desegregation that has taken place would have been possible without the legal victories of the civil rights movement.

The second advantage of thinking about the space-creating, agency-enhancing potentials of legal strategies for social change is that it honours our common-sense intuitions about in whose hands social agency actually lies. It does not lie primarily in the hands of lawyers and judges – or even legislators – exercising their legally endowed powers. Law shapes the terms on which agents act, form relationships and adopt social practices. But it does not in itself constitute the changes in behaviour and social practice that it sometimes brings about. This observation is a particularly important antidote to the liberal tradition of social change lawyering, which tends to privilege lawyers, elite activists and their specialist capacities to "strategise" about the law and persuade judges and legislators to adopt particular dispositions. Too much of the writing in that tradition discusses the formulation and execution of elite strategy, and stops when a change in the law has been achieved. Little is said, or thought, about how the way in which lawyers and litigants frame their arguments promotes or retards the spaces in which ordinary people will subsequently act, once the law has been changed. However, if we are serious about drawing convincing links between law and social change, we cannot avoid placing this relationship at the centre of our inquiry.

A third advantage of this way of conceiving of law and social change is that it accords with powerful accounts of the conceptual foundations of legal rights. James Griffin's account of human rights helps illustrate the point. Griffin locates the philosophical justification of rights in their capacity to protect the conditions necessary for the exercise of agency.[37] Rights, in other words, create spaces in which humans can act to pursue their goals, to realise themselves and forge a path through life. If, as Griffin urges, rights protect and enhance human agency, then we cannot ignore the extent to which particular laws, through which general rights are protected, limited or realised in particular contexts, constrain or expand the spaces in which ordinary men and women think and act.

It is against this background that we should, in my view, be considering the relationship between law and social change in contemporary South Africa. Law can neither be reduced to the handmaiden of base economic and social interests nor instrument in the hands of the "savvy" activist.[38] Law is embedded in the fabric of everyday social practices. It shapes perceptions, expectations, moral world-views and concrete action – not just on the operatic terrain of political struggle, but in the mundane interactions that constitute everyday life. Changes in the law shape these everyday practices by helping to define the boundaries of the possible.

1.4   PROPERTY LAW AND SOCIAL PRACTICE

Nowhere is this account of the relationship between law and social change more obviously illustrated than in the rules and practices of property law. Property law defines the scope of access to material goods. It embodies "how we, as a society have chosen to reward the claims of some people to finite and critical goods, and to deny the claims to the same goods by others".[39] It not only shapes important terms of social participation; it affects the ways men and women exist in space. The rules of land tenure define where ordinary people may live and the terms on which they can stay there. The rules applicable to consumer credit define the extent of the monetary resources they can deploy to meet their material wants and needs. The rules of consumer credit also provide for the forfeit of homes, cars and other goods which are necessary to chart a course through everyday life.

In short, the rules of property law form part of the social fabric. They are deeply immersed in the background noise of everyday life. Often without conscious thought, they shape basic social expectations and behaviour. For that reason, the rules of property law are often thought to be static. But they are not.

We live in the grip of a pervasive "ownership model" of property.[40] This model posits property as tangible goods or incorporeal rights over which individuals or corporations have exclusive control. The world is carved up into domains of ownership – exclusive control of a right or an object, and freedom to do with it as one wishes. We have lived with this ownership model since at least the late

---

[37] J Griffin *On Human Rights* (2008) 32–33.

[38] For a careful and sensitive contextual study of socio-economic rights in the hands of what he calls "rights savvy" activists, see T Madlingozi "Post Apartheid Social Movements and Legal Mobilisation" in M Langford, J Dugard, B Cousins and T Madlingozi (eds) *Socio-Economic Rights in South Africa: Symbols or Substance?* (2014) 92. See also J Dugard, T Madlingozi and K Tissington "Rights-compromised or rights-savvy? The use of rights-based strategies by Abahlali baseMjondolo, the South African shack-dwellers' movement" in H Alviar-Garcia, K Klare and L Williams (eds) *Social and Economic Rights in Theory and Practice: Critical Inquiries* 23.

[39] L Underkuffler-Freund "Property: A Special Right? (1996) 71 *Notre Dame Law Review* 1033, 1046.

[40] JW Singer (note 26 above) 2–3.

Roman Republic.[41] And, although we accept that an owner's complete freedom to use his property entirely as he wishes is a fiction (ownership of a shotgun does not entitle its owner to use it to kill people), social claims on ownership interests have been carved out as exceptions to a general rule: that property is something controlled, dominated, and from which other social claims are excluded in favour of the personal use and enjoyment of its owner.[42] To be sure, an owner can enter into various contracts alienating one of the incidents of his ownership. He can lease his property to a tenant. He can encumber it as security for a debt. He can sell it. He can even lay waste to it on a whim. But, these limitations on ownership rights are granted by the consent of the owner, and are usually revocable, on notice, more or less at the owner's will.

Redistributive claims, concerns about inequality, poverty and social needs have always been located outside property law. It has seldom been accepted that the structure of property rights themselves is affected by concerns about inequality. Rather, it is the distribution of property rights on the ownership model that has traditionally been the concern of the state, not the nature of those property rights themselves. Welfare states have generally aimed to enhance the capacity of individual men and women to purchase property rights on the open market through welfare payments, or to provide goods to individual men and women by establishing relationships modelled on traditional property law categories. For example, the state may provide housing by paying out a rent voucher, renting out its own public housing, or transferring ownership of land and a house to an individual. In each case, the ownership model of property rights is reinforced, or at least left unchallenged.

1.5   CONTEMPORARY STRUGGLES OVER PROPERTY RIGHTS IN SOUTH AFRICA

What if that changed? I want to argue that, at least in South Africa, some of the most basic structures of property law have undergone substantial alteration since the end of apartheid, and that these alterations have created spaces in which ordinary people have begun to reshape the terms on which they access land, tenure, and credit.

At the end of apartheid, South African property law was a substantially unreformed artefact of the law of the Province of Holland in the seventeenth-century Netherlands. The property regime inherited from seventeenth-century Holland was itself heavily influenced by legal concepts and principles dating back as far as the late Roman Republic. Apart from planning law, land administration, and statutes providing for expropriation[43] and limitations on prescription,[44] this Roman-Dutch common law of property was largely free from statutory interference. This 'common law' of property is a system of largely inflexible rules which created a hierarchy of rights in property. At the top of the hierarchy sits ownership – complete

---

[41] D Graeber *Debt: The First 5000 Years* (2001) 200.

[42] JY Stern "What is the right to exclude and why does it matter?" in J Penner and Michael Otsuka (eds) *Property Theory: Legal and Political Perspectives* (2018) 38.

[43] Prescription Act 68 of 1969.

[44] Expropriation Act 63 of 1975.

control or 'dominium' over a thing, defined as the freedom to deal in one's property entirely as one wishes. Without limiting the generality of the concept of dominium, common law writers have sought to develop the concept of ownership as a "bundle" of rights and powers over a thing.[45] The usual list includes the right to use, exclude others from, enjoy the fruits of, consume, possess, dispose of, vindicate and defend the owned property.[46]

Although the common law does place some internal limitations on the rights of owners, for example through the law of nuisance (governing the circumstances under which a landowner can be interdicted from using their land to the prejudice of their neighbours) and the law of estoppel (which potentially limits an owner's right to vindicate property they have negligently represented is in fact the property of another), these limits are relatively slight and highly specific. In particular, except to the extent that an owner chooses to limit or sell one or more of their ownership rights, the common law does not limit ownership rights to achieve redistributive ends, or to meet perhaps urgent and pressing social needs of non-owners. So, for example, the *rei vindicatio*, which is the common law action through which an owner recovers possession of their property from another, does not recognise the social consequences of dispossessing a holder of an owner's property as any reason not to permit the owner to repossess it. Potential homelessness, for example, would never have been recognised as a reason not to allow a property owner to repossess their land from a person living on it. Only the existence of a countervailing common law right is sufficient to defeat an owner's vindicatory action.[47]

The common law accordingly parcels the world off into a series of (almost) absolute domains within which, in the absence of their agreement to limit their rights (for example, by leasing his property or putting it up as security for a debt) an owner has exclusive rights to possess and deal in his property as they see fit, without regard for the economic needs or well-being of others.

The common law regime accordingly lends itself to the creation of at least two classes of person. First there is the 'property insider'. A property insider is a holder of a recognised common law right in property. The ultimate property insider is a common law owner, with their virtually unfettered rights to possess and use their property as they see fit. But property insiders are also lessees, mortgagees, holders of servitudes, usufructuaries and so on: people who hold rights against the owner of a thing because the owner has chosen to encumber their property by creating a subordinate right in it. These subordinate rights can sometimes be quite extensive. Leases can be very long. A mortgagee can have extensive rights to sell an owner's property in execution of a debt. A usufructuary has a lifetime right to use and take the fruits of the relevant property. However, these rights are all conceptualised as a "subtraction from the dominium"[48] of the owner. In other words, subordinate

---

[45] AM Honoré "Ownership" in A Guest (ed) *Oxford Essays in Jurisprudence* (1961) 370. JY Stern (note 42 above) 38.

[46] G Willie and G Bradfield *Willies Principles of South African Law* 9 ed (2007) 470.

[47] *Chetty v Naidoo* 1974 (3) SA 13 (A).

[48] *Ex parte Geldenhuys* 1926 OPD 155.

common law rights are held from the owner, are always temporary, and will revert to the owner once the conditions necessary for their termination are satisfied.

A 'property outsider' is someone who uses property without any common law rights to do so. Although the common law acknowledges the existence of property outsiders by, for example, recognising precarious occupation,[49] and the possibility that prescription may turn an ostensibly unlawful possessor of property into an owner after 30 years,[50] it assigns them no substantive rights. The *mandament van spolie* accords thin procedural protection to a possessor – even an unlawful possessor – who is dispossessed of property without due process of law.[51] Before the advent of the Constitution, however, even this protection was fairly easy to oust by statute.[52] Fundamentally, a property outsider is, at best, tolerated, and at worst, subject to prompt dispossession, more or less at the will of the property owner. Property outsiders include people who once had common law rights, but who no longer do so – for example, tenants who are holding over and debtors whose loans have been called up. They are outsiders because the common law provides no protection for them from the moment their common law rights have been terminated at the will of the owner – whether by the exercise of what has been called a landlord's "bare power"[53] to terminate a lease on notice, or because of the consequences that follow on a debtor's default on a credit agreement. The common law affords property outsiders no positive right to acquire property, and tacitly assumes that property outsiders will have sufficient resource endowments to acquire some form of property right, and become an 'insider' again.

However, in the conditions of extreme inequality that characterise the South African economy, this assumption simply cannot be made. A large proportion of the South African population is unemployed, unable to access credit and in effect locked out of urban rental land and housing markets.[54] In these circumstances, neither the common law of property itself nor the economy provide an easy route between property outsider and property insider status.

Accordingly, models of property law that address the rights and obligations of owners and holders of lesser common law rights have begun to look increasingly anachronistic. Traditional legal analysis tends to be focused on relationships between owners, holders of other common law rights and, where relevant, the state. What contemporary property law writing has all but ignored is how the law deals with people who have no common law rights at all.[55] Relationships between

---

[49] *Malan v Nabygelegen Estates* 1946 AD 562 573.

[50] Section 6 of the Prescription Act 68 of 1969.

[51] As Voet famously put it, even a thief can bring a spoliation application: see Voet 41.2.16.

[52] Prevention of Illegal Squatting Amendment Act 42 of 1975.

[53] *Maphango v Aengus Lifestyle Properties* 2012 (3) SA 531 (CC) para 10.

[54] SERI, *Minding the Gap: An Analysis of the Supply of and Demand for Low-Income Rental Accommodation in Inner City Johannesburg* (2013).

[55] For exceptions, see A van der Walt "Exclusivity of Ownership, Security of Tenure and Eviction Orders: A Critical Evaluation of Recent Case Law" (2002) 18 *South African Journal of Human Rights* 372; A van der Walt (note 13 above); and WJ du Plessis "Protection of traditional knowledge in South Africa: does the 'commons' provide a solution?" in DA Frenkel (ed) *Public Law and Social Human Rights* (2013).

people with and without common law property rights is one of the most contentious political debates in contemporary South Africa. Yet, this debate is not a mainstream concern of property law.

It clearly should be. The study of a system of law that does not ask questions about the interests that system tends to exclude or subordinate is, at best, incomplete. More fundamentally, however, it is important to recognise that, in the last 20 years, there have been many constitutional, statutory and jurisprudential developments that have attempted to address the needs of property outsiders. In doing so, these developments have not only punctured the ownership model of property law, but they have begun to carve out spaces in which the processes of dispossession that help sustain rampant economic inequality can be challenged.

1.6   THE WAY FORWARD

As it turned out, the residents of the San Jose penthouse were to play a critical role in this process. They were able to oppose the eviction applications brought against them by the City of Johannesburg with the help of human rights NGOs and public interest lawyers at the Johannesburg Bar. San Jose's residents resisted their eviction by explaining their social circumstances. They had come to Johannesburg to look for work, and they had found it. But the income they were able to earn was insufficient for them to be able to simply leave San Jose and find accommodation elsewhere, except in another derelict building, from which they would be vulnerable to eviction again in terms of the same slum clearance programme that was being used to challenge their right to stay at San Jose.

It accordingly made no sense to evict the residents of San Jose in the interests of safety, since doing so would leave them markedly less safe. They would be on the streets, with no option but to look for another derelict building to occupy elsewhere. This did not so much as solve the underlying problem of unsafe living conditions at San Jose as move these conditions elsewhere.

On the strength of this argument, and relying on the right of access to adequate housing in section 26 of the Constitution, the residents resisted their eviction, and were eventually able to compel the municipality to provide them with better accommodation a few blocks away, in which most of them still live.[56]

It is clear that South Africa's new Constitution did not immediately stop unjust evictions that led to homelessness – there were 122 such evictions before the City of Johannesburg got around to San Jose – but latent in the Constitution was the discursive opportunity to push back the processes of gentrification and dispossession that would have been impossible to resist without it.

The rest of this book is about how the Constitution, and legislation adopted to give effect to it, has provided similar discursive opportunities in a variety of other contexts, and has enabled the poor and the dispossessed to challenge the power structures set up by South Africa's common law of property. The ways in which

---

[56] The eviction application was eventually refused in *Occupiers of 51 Olivia Road, Berea and 197 Main Street, Johannesburg v City of Johannesburg* 2008 (3) SA 208 (CC).

these opportunities have been exploited, and the restructuring of property relations that has resulted, says a great deal about the role law can play in a project of social transformation.

CHAPTER TWO

LAW AND TRANSFORMATION

2.1 THE AMBITIOUS CONSTITUTION

"Ours is a transformative Constitution." It "provides a mandate, a framework and, to some extent, a blueprint for the transformation of our society from its racist and unequal past to a society in which all can live with dignity".[1] The social change desired in the Constitution is the dismantling of all the forms and effects of colonialism and apartheid, and the construction of a society based on human dignity, equality, freedom, non-discrimination, constitutional supremacy and universal adult suffrage.[2] Colonialism and apartheid excluded and subordinated 80% of South Africa's population to the needs and desires of the other 20%. The forms and methods of this exclusion were manifold. To a substantial extent, these forms and methods were stitched intricately into the deep social and economic structure of South African society. Black people were excluded from most of the professions; from the legal right to acquire, generate or own most businesses; from almost all urban and rural land tenure rights in the 80% of the country reserved for white occupation; from South African citizenship; from decent education; and from decent healthcare. They were denied the right to vote; the right to seek office outside the "self-governing territories"; and the right to freedom of expression. They were disproportionately subject to arbitrary arrest; detention without charge; police brutality; forced labour and torture.

The list goes on, but the point should be clear. The South African Constitution is an unabashed statement of faith in the capacity of law and legal forms to bring about social change. And the social changes required are not simply limited to the removal of formal discrimination based on race, but extend to the reshaping of economic and social forms that have grown up to support that discrimination. These forms are often deeply embedded, not just in distinctions of race, but of class, social origin, gender, sexual orientation, language and ethnicity. Not only does all of this have to be undone, but a new social order, which is, essentially, a negation of almost

---

[1] *Rates Action Group v City of Cape Town* 2004 (5) SA 545 (C) para 100. The Constitutional Court speaks in equally lavish terms in *S v Makwanyane* 1995 3 SA 391 (CC) para 262: "What the Constitution expressly aspires to do is to provide a transition from these grossly unacceptable features of the past to a conspicuously contrasting ... future."; *Du Plessis v De Klerk* 1996 (3) SA 850 (CC) para 157: "[The Constitution] is a document that seeks to transform the status quo ante into a new order"; *Soobramoney v Minister of Health, KwaZulu-Natal* 1998 (1) SA 765 (CC) para 8: "a commitment ... to transform our society into one in which there will be human dignity, freedom and equality, lies at the heart of our new constitutional order".

[2] Section 1 of the Constitution, 1996.

everything that has come before, is to be constructed in its place. Law has never been given so daunting a task.[3]

The conditions under which the law must achieve this transformation are unpromising. There has seldom been agreement about how best to govern a just society, and even where there is, vested economic interests tend to trump lofty social aims. Although only an isolated fringe of South Africans would speak up for apartheid today, apartheid still underpins much of the economic structure, and it patterns South Africa's gross racial and economic inequality.

Disrupting these patterns requires interference with economic structures and forms of inequality that were born or entrenched under apartheid, but which are jealously guarded by those who benefit from them today.

The distribution of property rights, particularly the rights to land and housing, is probably the most important example of these structures of inequality. The exclusion of the majority of South Africans from access to land and adequate housing is the result of patterns of property ownership and access to land which were developed under colonialism and apartheid. The Constitution itself did not directly interfere with the distribution of land and property rights at its inception. Its effect was, in fact, to respect existing property rights, but to leave room for reforms of property law that might lead to redistribution of property rights through statutory reform,[4] so long as the laws passed were non-arbitrary,[5] and expropriations were accompanied by just and equitable compensation.[6] In addition, the Constitution entrenched a right of access to adequate housing, which provided formal protections against "arbitrary eviction",[7] and against interference with existing access to adequate housing.[8] The Constitution also required the state to "take reasonable measures within its available resources to progressively realise" everyone's right of access to adequate housing.[9]

Accordingly, although a major part of the task of transformation must be to redistribute rights to property and land, the Constitution is impressionistic about how this particular task must be carried out. Existing large-scale property owners,

---

[3] There is extensive literature on the challenges of transformative constitutionalism, insofar as they concern legal culture and legal reasoning. That is not my chief concern here, but see, for example, K Klare "Legal Culture and Transformative Constitutionalism" (1998) 14 *South African Journal on Human Rights* 146; P Langa "Transformative Constitutionalism" (2006) 17 *Stellenbosch Law Review* 351; K van Marle "Transformative Constitutionalism as/and Critique" (2009) 20 *Stellenbosch Law Review* 286; D Davis and K Klare "Transformative Constitutionalism and the Common and Customary Law" 2010 (26) *South African Journal on Human Rights* 403; M Pieterse "What do we mean when we talk about transformative constitutionalism?" (2005) 20 *South African Public Law* 155.

[4] Section 25(5) to 25(9) of the Constitution.

[5] Section 25(1) of the Constitution.

[6] Section 25(2) of the Constitution.

[7] Section 26(3) of the Constitution.

[8] Section 26(1) of the Constitution; *Jaftha v Schoeman; Van Rooyen v Stoltz and Others* 2005 (2) SA 140 (CC) para 34.

[9] Section 26(2) of the Constitution.

who hold the key to the redistribution of property rights, are unlikely to volutarily relinquish their economic advantages.

Many of them would ask why they should do so, given that the Constitution is at best ambiguous in its attitude to existing rights. Purely from a layperson's perspective, what is 'arbitrary', 'reasonable' or 'just and equitable' is a value-laden inquiry that depends very much on the political and moral instincts of the person giving those terms meaning, and the context in which those terms are deployed. A lawyer giving meaning to those terms must, to be sure, take account of the text in which they appear, and the purpose of that text, but the Constitution is itself fairly general, and does very little to specify the circumstances under which the imperative to 'transform' society means limiting or redistributing property rights, or leaving them undisturbed.[10]

Accordingly, few would have predicted, when the final Constitution was adopted, that it would generate a number of very specific principles: that evictions leading to homelessness are not to be permitted;[11] that landlords must demonstrate that the termination of a residential lease is fair in all the circumstances;[12] that a bank has to demonstrate that executing against a person's home was fair and proportionate, even though its contractual rights permitted execution merely on default.[13] These changes in the law were worked out through practice, as the broad purposes and open text provisions of the Constitution and subordinate legislation were applied by judges and legislators in specific contexts.

These changes are not redistributive in the sense that they authorise the direct transfer of property rights. Rather, they alter the existing law-governed distribution of power in three basic economic relationships, which are fundamental to the property law regime: the relationship between owner and occupier; the relationship between landlord and tenant; and the relationship between debtor and creditor. By doing so, they create and reshape spaces for action that did not exist before those changes took effect. The changes enhance the position of the weaker party in each of those relationships, by providing some protection against coercive action by the more powerful party. They create conditions under which an owner cannot evict, a landlord cannot take away rights, and a bank cannot call up a debt. In this way, each of the alterations is transformative, not in the sense that society suddenly re-orders itself because of them, but in the sense that they change the nature of the

---

[10] In S Woolman *The Selfless Constitution: Experimentalism and Flourishing as Foundations of South Africa's Basic Law* (2013), Stuart Woolman draws attention to the Constitution's potential to support ongoing democratic experiments meant, presumably, to tend towards a broadly transformative vision. But Woolman calls attention to the fact that constitutional values underdetermine the nature and extent of the transformation required. He places emphasis on the Constitution's potential to foster an at least partly path-dependent trajectory of transformation towards ends that are constructed through trial, error and experimentation.

[11] *Occupiers, Berea v De Wet* 2017 (5) SA 346 (CC) para 57.

[12] *Maphango v Aengus Lifestyle Properties* 2012 (3) SA 531 (CC) para 51.

[13] *Gundwana v Steko Development* 2011 (3) SA 608 (CC) para 44.

relationship between important categories of people embedded in critical economic relationships with each other.

What happens once the formal legal relationship changes is contingent on a range of other social factors. Reasonable people might disagree about whether changes in the law, expressed through the alteration of these relationships, are truly significant, transformative, progressive or reactionary. But my argument is that no one can reasonably deny that the changes in the law alter the terms of human relationships, and, as a result, lead to social change.

2.2   THEORISING LAW AND SOCIAL CHANGE

In this chapter, I want to suggest that law brings about social change by altering relationships between agents with unequal power. These alterations almost inevitably affect the boundaries of either party's agency. As the range of available courses of action open to either party expands or contracts, there are knock-on effects for deeply embedded social power structures. To give a landlord a wider range of rights and powers over tenanted property – by, for example, making it easier to terminate a lease – is automatically to weaken the position of the tenant in that relationship. On the other hand, to expand the range of rights and powers available to the tenant– by, for example, making it harder to increase rents by imposing rent controls – is to strengthen the position of the tenant, and expand their range of action.

I also want to suggest that existing theories of the relationship between law and social change have overlooked this aspect of the way the law operates in society. In later chapters, I will argue that the particular changes in property law brought about in the areas of unlawful land occupation, landlord and tenant law, and debtor and creditor law have, in fact, led to some progressive, transformative social change. In this chapter, however, I will restrict myself to a review of the available theory on the relationship between law and social change, and to argue for what I consider to be the autonomy-shaping space-creating potential of law that they overlook.

It is important to acknowledge, at the outset, that there are at least two well-known theories of the role of law in social change which I will set aside. The first is the basic conservative theory that the primary function of law is to preserve rather than alter existing social relations. Dealing with constitutional law, Antonin Scalia famously remarked that "I do not worry about my old Constitution 'obstructing modernity', since I take that to be its whole purpose".[14] The idea that the purpose of law is to preserve rather than transform existing social relationships – often because this is said to be the will of a divine being – is as old as the law itself. Law has deep roots in religion and the preservation of ideal social orders based on it. These roots are not about changing society, but about preserving it by codifying, consolidating

---

[14] A Scalia "Modernity and the Constitution" in E Smith (ed) *Constitutional Justice Under Old Constitutions* (1995) 313–14.

and enforcing what are taken to be its existing customs, mores and distributions of power.[15]

The second theory arises from a strong current of literature about the proper relationship between law and market exchange. This theory has its origins in the writings of Fredrich Hayek,[16] and has latterly developed into the sub-discipline of "Law and Economics". The Law and Economics literature posits a role for law in ensuring the most efficient forms of economic exchange possible.[17] "Efficiency" in this sense almost always means the sense given to that word by classical economic theory, and deals with the interaction of rational, utility-maximising contracting parties with perfect information, striking bargains on the open market.

The reason for not considering these theories is the same in each case. Both accept a powerful – if very specific – causative social role for law, and proceed to make far-reaching normative claims about what that role should be. In both cases these claims are incompatible with the values and transformative purpose of the South African Constitution. The Constitution seeks the very opposite of the preservation of an existing social order, and so conservative theories of the role of law will not assist in understanding it. The Constitution is not primarily interested in the facilitation of efficient market relationships, except, perhaps, insofar as this can be demonstrated to be consistent with, or to promote, the plurality of values that the Constitution entrenches, or the protection and fulfilment of Constitutional rights. Indeed, many of the amendments to property law I shall describe later in this book are decidedly inefficient, at least from the perspective of classical economics. They distort apparently efficient economic exchange because they seek to promote other values and interests that are inconsistent with that exchange. They weaken traditional property rights, which are asserted, by classical economists, as being necessary for efficient economic exchange and growth.[18]

Conservative and economic theories of law accordingly present no obstacle to my argument that laws lead to social change, because they both accept that proposition. Their normative claims about what sorts of change law should lead to are at odds with, and accordingly irrelevant to, the changes in property relationships brought about by the South African Constitution.

The main focus of this chapter will instead be on two political traditions that seek social transformation of a broadly redistributive sort, and from within each of which claims have been made about the extent to which law, and changes to it, lead to social change. These traditions are the classical Marxist tradition and the radical liberal tradition. I will outline their features and limitations. I will then argue that each overlooks the embeddedness of law in social practice. I will argue that it is

---

[15] A Schiavone *The Invention of Law in the West* (2012) 4–7.

[16] FA Hayek *The Constitution of Liberty* (1960).

[17] R Posner *Economic Analysis of Law* (1973); G Calabresi "Some Thoughts on Risk Distribution and the Law of Torts" (1961) 70 Yale Law Journal 499; R Coase "The Problem of Social Cost" 1960 (3) *Journal of Law and Economics* 31.

[18] World Bank *South Africa Systematic Country Diagnostic: an incomplete transition – overcoming the legacy of exclusion in South Africa* (2018) iv. See also R Epstein *Takings: Private Property and the Power of Eminent Domain* (1985).

only by examining the relationship between law and agency in a social context that it is possible to assess the role and limits of law in effecting social change.

Finally, I outline what I will call an "agent-centred" approach to law and social change.

2.3   THE CLASSICAL MARXIST TRADITION: LAW AS EPIPHENOMENON

The Marxist tradition has historically ignored or been actively hostile to the idea that changes in law could contribute to social transformation. Yet Marx never gave a comprehensive treatment to law's role in social structures and social change. His views on law have to be derived from asides in discussions of other subjects. What Marx did say about law in those asides seemed to discount the idea that law could be treated as autonomous from the economic relationships in which it is embedded. In *Capital*, Marx treated law merely as the outcome, and perhaps memorialisation, of class struggle, not as having any causative role itself to play in determining the contours of, and opportunities open to, those waging that struggle. For example, Marx's discussion of the legal struggle to shorten the working day, and to eliminate child labour, treats legislation as no more than the record of the changing frontlines of class struggle in mid-nineteenth-century England.[19] The aphorism "between equal rights, force prevails"[20] appears in that discussion, and is often cited as an example of just how unimpressed Marx was with lawmakers and legal forms.[21] In the *Grundwisse*,[22] Marx appears to make explicit what was implied in *Capital*: that "every form of production creates its own legal relations, form of government, etc". Economic relationships of exploitation are dressed up as legal relationships and, even in constitutional republics, law serves simply to ensure that "the right of the stronger prevails".

The observation that law follows on, but does not constitute basic economic relationships has been pursued in secondary treatments of Marx's work. In GA Cohen's *Karl Marx's Theory of History: A Defence*,[23] Cohen advances a reading of Marx that affirms law's character as being entirely explained by the basic economic structure.[24] Cohen sought to explain an ambiguity in Marx's thought: his use of 'rights' and 'law' to describe both fundamental relationships between capital and labour constituting the economic 'base' of society *and* the legal forms these relationships take in the social 'superstructure'. Cohen explains that what Marx really means when he talks about 'rights' as between capital and labour, and as between capitalists, property and commodities, is 'powers'. These are simply the ability to do with labour and property what the capitalist wills. It does not mean the normative or moral or legal right to exploit these resources. Rights and laws in their ordinary, normative, sense are part of the superstructure: the way in which political

---

[19] K Marx *Capital Volume 1* (1976) 340–416.
[20] Ibid 344.
[21] C Miéville *Between Equal Rights: A Marxist Theory of International Law* (2005) 8.
[22] J Elster *Karl Marx: A Reader* (1986) 7.
[23] GA Cohen *Karl Marx's Theory of History: A Defence* 2 ed (2001).
[24] Ibid 217–25.

structures place an ideological stamp of approval on relationships determined by class struggle or economic bargain, and authorise the use of force to preserve the basic character of those relationships.

Pashukanis makes the same point but in the context of legal theory. Legal relationships between subjects are just the "reverse side of relations between products of labour that have become commodities".[25] Laws are not built on pre-existing norms, but are merely the memorialisation of relationships that develop through commodity exchange. To consider the law as a body of norms divorced from the relationships that generate it is to reduce it to a "lifeless abstraction". Transactions involving the exchange of commodities are "the cell-form of the legal fabric: only there does the law accomplish its real movement".[26] The forms and content of law are simply the result of the way in which commodities are produced and exchanged.

Accordingly, the whole edifice of property and contract law, for example, simply reflects the particular mechanism through which commodity exchange takes place and the relationships of production that are required to sustain it. As a result, even in a transformed communist society, Pashukanis thought that law could only ever play a purely technical role, regulating and controlling the distribution of resources in a planned economy. The idea of a constitutional state, in which law plays a role in the distribution and control of wealth and power is a "mirage".[27]

This is a grim picture for anyone who wants to stake a claim for the capacity of legal struggles to bring about anything but the most temporary and minimum change to economic and social structures, at least in a capitalist society. If a particular mode of capital accumulation requires a particular legal regime, then that regime will grow up around it, unless, of course, there is a countervailing social force, such as the organised working class, to stop it. Law plays no part in shifting the basis on which that struggle takes place.

But this base–superstructure relationship, in which economy is action and law is consequence, has fairly clear limits. To the extent that Marx ever thought that law was only consequence and never cause (he said far too little about it to be sure either way), he could not have had in mind every legal relationship that actually exists. It is difficult to deny that contract and property law, as presently constituted, owe much of their content to the mercantilist needs of the capitalist class, particularly the need to promote the ease of commodity exchange. But move beyond contract and property, and the economistic reduction of law to whatever relationships of production need it to be becomes far less convincing. It fails to account for the existence of public law: the body of rules that shapes the interaction between state and citizen.[28] This body of law, which encompasses everything from the writ of *habeas corpus* to complex environmental legislation, tax laws, competition law, and securities and exchange controls, owes little to commodity exchange, and is in

---

[25] EB Pashukanis *Law and Marxism: A General Theory* (1976) 85.

[26] Ibid.

[27] Ibid 146–8. B Fine *Democracy and the Rule of Law: Marx's Critique of the Legal Form* (2002) 164–5.

[28] B Fine (note 27 above) 211.

fact founded on the need to regulate or frustrate some of the social consequences of that exchange.

Unless one accepts that this is all part of a complex strategy of mystification, in which capital strategically makes small concessions solely in order to maintain its overall domination of social and economic life, then the existence of public law poses a strong challenge to the classical Marxist account. In order to dismiss public law as a mystification, one would have to suppose that capital is centrally organised and directed, and that manifold corporate attempts to influence and change public laws to more easily facilitate commodity exchange were not seriously undertaken. Neither of these things is plausible, or consistent with Marx's overall theories about the nature of capital.

Law cannot be assigned to an easily defined subsidiary role in the social structure. Law does not "keep politely to a 'level'". It is imbricated within the mode of production and productive relations themselves (as rights in property).[29] It occupies a liminal space, between and placing limits on various spheres of action. It forms part of the arena of class and broader social struggle. It influences the ways in which those struggles are waged, together with their aims and outcomes. It is not simply the ideological expression of one or other economic structure.

Wherever the law admits ends that are not simply commercial in character, the neat relationship between economic 'base' and legal 'superstructure' breaks down. Struggles about family law during the past century have promoted gender equality, the right of divorce, the autonomy of women,[30] and, latterly, the extension of marriage to persons of the same gender. It is far from clear that any of the rules of family law, or the massive changes that have been wrought in them, can be reduced neatly to the changes in the rules of commodity exchange or the needs of capitalism during this time. They must have some other source.

That source is likely to be the non-commercial ideas and actions of ordinary men and women, reflected in changes to the structures of their moral economy; their vision of what is just, proper, and what is possible; their pursuit of their everyday and longer-term goals; social ideologies; their decisions about how to live, and who to love. In other words, besides being a commercial protuberance, law emerges from the sum total of relationships that are not primarily economic, or those strands of economic relationships that are not about commodity exchange, but about affection, culture, language and community. These ideas and actions, when aggregated into *loci* of agency, test the boundaries of existing social structures, and can change them. Those structures produce and are themselves produced by, at least in part, legislation and the accretion of other legal norms, and the manner in which they are sought to be altered will be, in part, an alteration in the law. In other

---

[29] EP Thompson The Poverty of Theory and Other Essays (1978) 96.
[30] S Fredman *Women and the Law* (1998). See also C Albertyn "Gender and Public Interest Litigation in Post-Apartheid South Africa" in J Brickhill (ed) *Public Interest Litigation in South Africa* (2018) 185.

words, law does not on its own explain social change, but nor does social change explain law.

If this is accepted, then there is room to consider a stronger, more efficacious role for law in explaining social change.

2.4   THE LIBERAL TRADITION: LAW AS INSTRUMENTALITY

The liberal tradition of law and social change accepts the autonomy of law, but only conditionally, and to a limited degree.[31] In this account, law tends to be presented as a tool to achieve specific public policy goals.

The liberal tradition accepts that changes in legal forms do not, in themselves, lead to changes in the social structure. It rejects the idea that social change in a constitutional state starts with the adoption of a new law, whether through legislation or court decision, from which automatically follows the implementation of a new set of social arrangements and behaviours.[32] The liberal tradition suggests instead that this ideal-typical account of how the law acts on society is a powerful "myth",[33] which is rooted in social values that can be appealed to change behaviour and restructure social relationships over time. In the liberal tradition, law leads to social change largely because of its aspirational and symbolic content. Changes in law, especially through litigation, signal symbolic recognition of the ends they embody, which must then be made 'real' through other forms of political struggle. The law, in other words, is a "landing force" of change. But it requires a "breakthrough" led by "forces from behind which take the advantage of the opening to go the rest of the way".[34]

Accordingly, the liberal approach to law and social change amounts to a qualified endorsement of rights as instruments of social action. Rights are less established social facts than potentially useful "political resources".[35] Constitutional rights and progressive jurisprudence provide authoritative statements of public policy goals. But their articulation and assertion is never the end, and often comes at an early stage, of more wide-ranging social struggles. They signal that political claims have achieved a partial and often insecure official recognition. Declarations of rights must be made real by other forms of political action, such as lobbying bureaucrats and legislators, or campaigning for public support, or protest and other forms of direct action. While textual formulations of constitutional rights may be fairly immutable, concrete interpretations are always contingent. The "politics of rights" refers to the manifold forms of political action through which declarations of rights (whether or not they are made by courts) are pursued as sometimes useful tools of

---

[31] Parts of this section are borrowed from my earlier article "Litigating Housing Rights in Johannesburg's Inner City: 2004–2008" (2011) 27 *South African Journal on Human Rights* 127.

[32] S Scheingold *The Politics of Rights: Lawyers, Public Policy and Political Change* (1974).

[33] Ibid 13–15.

[34] W Chafe *The Unfinished Journey* (1995) 153.

[35] S Scheingold (note 32 above) 84.

lobbying and protest, while nonetheless recognising this contingency and plotting out political strategies accordingly.[36]

One of the aims of a politics of rights could be to develop what Michael McCann has called a "jurisprudence from below", in which constitutional rights are defined and internalised through an assessment of their meaning and import to a particular social struggle, by people directly engaged in that struggle. The interests of the rights-claiming group are thereby transformed and universalised into statements of entitlement, rather than expressions of interests or preferences.[37] Whether or not these claims secure recognition depends on the outcome of a broader social struggle, which may or may not employ legal forms.

In this tradition, law becomes a means to an end. It is an instrument through which goal-directed political action might achieve certain specified political designs. Much of the literature in this tradition tends to set out detailed case studies of change-oriented lawyering, together with more or less systematised attempts to set out the conditions under which law can be "leveraged" to one or other political end.[38] The leading examples of this literature are Stuart Scheingold's *The Politics of Rights*,[39] which drew the distinction between rights as social facts and rights as political resources set out earlier, and Michael McCann's *Rights at Work*,[40] which charts the role of law in the American pay equity movement in the 1980s and 1990s. These two profoundly important works stand out in a much larger field of work on law and social change in the liberal tradition, which varies from scholarly studies of legislative impact,[41] to almost biographical treatments of particular lawyers and litigation strategies.[42]

The idea of the law as an instrumentality also appears to be the dominant mode of thinking about the role of law in social change in South Africa. Particular case studies of litigation-intensive social struggles adopt a critical distance from the law, and emphasise the need to "make shape and break"[43] it to bring about desired public policy goals. Looking across a range of different cases, legal practitioners have tried to identify a series of strategies for 'using' rights and the law, such as the dissemination of legal information to the general public, the provision of legal advice, legal advocacy and mobilisation, and litigation. They have gone so far as to attempt to identify a list of factors that maximise the prospect of ensuring that litigation leads to social change. These factors include ensuring one's clients are

---

[36] S Wilson "Taming the Constitution: Rights and Reform in the South African Education System" (2004) 20 *SAJHR* 418, 421.

[37] This process may be akin to what Sally Engle Merry calls "naming" injustice in S Engle Merry *Getting Justice and Getting Even: Legal Consciousness Among Working-Class Americans* (1990).

[38] DA Schultz *Leveraging the Law: Using the Courts to Achieve Social Change* (1998).

[39] S Scheingold (note 25 above).

[40] M McCann (note 5 above).

[41] DM Engel and FW Munger *Rights of Inclusion: Law and Identity in the Life Stories of Americans with Disabilities* (2003).

[42] O Fiss *Pillars of Justice: Lawyers and the Liberal Tradition* (2017); D Cole *Engines of Liberty: The Power of Citizen Activists to Make Constitutional Law* (2016).

[43] M Heywood "Shaping, Making and Breaking the Law in the Campaign for a National HIV/AIDS Treatment Plan" in P Jones and K Stokke *The Politics of Socio-Economic Rights in South Africa* (2005) 181.

"properly organised"; having an overall, long-term strategy; ensuring that there is a co-ordinating movement able to share information between activists engaged in a particular struggle; having access to effective and accurate social research; bringing legal challenges at the right time; framing a case in a manner that is most likely to meet with judicial approval; and following up legal precedents, once they are obtained, to ensure that they are effectively implemented.[44]

The problem with this instrumentalist approach – at least as it had been developed and articulated in South Africa – is that it often fails to fully account for the ways in which law itself constitutes and structures social action. While often claiming critical distance from the law, it overlooks the way in which those who are wielding law as an instrument, or implementing legal strategies, are themselves enmeshed in legalistic ways of thinking about social action and carrying it out, and the ways in which the law itself subtly imposes values and attitudes on the person who wields law as an instrument.

This is what makes the instrumentalist approach peculiarly liberal. It posits an epistemological scheme within which law is wielded by a fundamentally asocial individual standing outside the field to which the legal instrument is to be applied. The possibility of making judgements about desirable social goals from an "Archimedean point" – that is, a point outside of society from which basic features can be evaluated – is a central theme of modern liberal thought, within which the structures of a fundamentally just society are said to be capable of identification *a priori*, or at least pre-socially.[45]

But the Archimedean perspective clearly has its limitations. Laws do not just help compose the foundations of society in a clearly identifiable and objectively ascertainable way. Laws permeate social practice. They shape agency and language. They often play a critical role in constituting personal identity.[46] In these senses, laws are inextricably linked to the social material to which they are meant to be applied. It seldom makes much sense to think about law as an instrument that is applied by an agent to a society from the outside. Law forms part of the arena of social struggle.[47] To use an Archimedean metaphor, law is not a lever with which it is possible to move the world from the outside. Law is the lever, the world and the person who pulls it all at once. Any theory of law's role in social change must be able to account, at the bare minimum, for how law structures and directs both the agent, the world in which they act, and the content of the legal principles being deployed. The conception of law as an instrumentality to achieve clearly defined political goals is not able to capture this level of complexity.

The urge to characterise law as an "instrument" is no doubt born of a justified caution. Those who do so want to maintain a critical distance from the law, not to be taken in by its myth. They may also want to assert their identities as professionals,

[44] G Marcus, S Budlender and N Ferreira *Public Interest Litigation and Social Change in South Africa* (2014) 109–26.

[45] J Rawls *A Theory of Justice* (1971) 260–3, 584.

[46] M McCann (note 5 above) 230. See also Engel and Munger (note 41 above) (2003).

[47] EP Thompson (note 29 above) 96.

detached from, and disinterested in, the content of the law, and merely describing its application in specific contexts. But it does not seem to me to be an abandonment of critical distance or professional ethics to assert that law is enmeshed in the fabric of the society in which it plays a role in changing. Nor is it incompatible with asserting that law nonetheless has a degree of autonomy within those social arrangements. Law is shaped by, and shapes, social structure and social action.

Recognising that law and those who wield it as an instrument are embedded in society has at least one important consequence: it calls attention to the privileged class position of lawyers and legal activists, and the biases and distortions in social change activism that this position might bring with it. To consider law as an instrumentality is almost necessarily to assign an unearned objectivity to the instrument and the person who wields it. Both, at least notionally, stand outside society, with the bird's eye view that implies. The lawyer or legal activist rationally and dispassionately applies the law (of which they have specialist knowledge), to achieving the social objectives on which they have a privileged perspective, because of the position from which they wield the legal instrument.

It is not possible to get caught up in this fiction if law is understood to be imbricated in the milieu of other influences on the thoughts, actions and consequences of lawyers and legal activists and their clients themselves. The class position of the lawyer or legal activist must then be faced head-on. At what goals has legal action been directed, and who has selected them? What counts as "success", and from whose perspective is success determined? How does the selection of particular cases and policy goals influence the capacity of change-oriented lawyering to make a practical difference in the lives of ordinary men and women? Except when the goals are clear and simple – the abolition of the death penalty, the desegregation of schools, the recognition of gay marriage – these questions will be difficult to answer. They will require a clear understanding of the social context in which the relevant legal rules operate, together with a view from the inside of how the rule operates on the person or class that is subject to it.

The liberal instrumentalist view is accordingly at once too sceptical and not sceptical enough of the law's role in social change. It is too sceptical because it fails to account for how law works within and through other social structures and practices. It is not sceptical enough because it fails to account for the unstated attitudes and prejudices that lawyers and legal activists bring to the table, and the insufficient regard it has to the context in which law must operate. Law is not simply a political tool to be applied in the struggle towards specific public policy goals – just one more string to the bow of a movement for change. It both constitutes and shapes the values and attitudes that lawyers and legal activists bring to their mission. This requires a way conceptualising law in society that goes beyond mere instrumentality.

2.5   "EVERY BLOODY LEVEL": LAW AS SOCIAL STRUCTURANT
The classical Marxist critique of the role of law in social change, based on Marx's somewhat aphoristic writing on the subject, too strongly denies any causal role for

law in social change. It tends to focus too narrowly on the common law of contract and property law, where economic power relations tend to influence the content of law most strongly, and on international law,[48] where the realities of power imbalances between nations often override the observance of the norms intended to ameliorate them. It is perhaps easy to provide examples of law simply reflecting the balance of economic and social power if attention is only paid to these areas of law. But treating law as merely reflective of, rather than acting on, those power relations fails to account for, among other things, the existence of public law, and for the radical transformation of family law.

The liberal instrumentalist account tends to see the value of law as not much more than a way of clothing pre-existing political goals in normatively useful terms, which can then be deployed by interest groups, lawyers and activists to achieve social change. This account abstracts both the law as an 'instrument' and the lawyer or activist wielding the instrument, from the social context in which both are embedded. In this way, the liberal instrumentalist tradition cannot make sense of the subtle and overt ways in which law operates through manifold social structures and practices, beyond the particular goals articulated by a lawyer or legal activist's programme.

In some respects, the classical Marxist and the liberal traditions share the same fundamental limitation. They tend to stand outside social practice while at the same time being hopelessly embedded in it. They then try to decode the role of law in social practice from a perspective that cannot account for the way in which law acts on the individual agents that are subject to it. The classical Marxist critique sees, from the outside, that the most fundamental structures of society are essentially economic. But it cannot, from the outside, account for the ways in which law is at least partially autonomous from economic power. The liberal tradition sees law simply as another set of political norms that can be applied to achieve specific political goals by those with specialist knowledge necessary to do so. It fails to account for the ways in which law structures the everyday opportunities and constraints placed on those in whose name the instrument is to be wielded.

I want to propose a change in perspective. I want to suggest that an agent-centred approach allows us to ask a more sensitive and complex set of questions about how law shapes social change. How does the law operate, together with other social forces, to shape the constraints on and opportunities open to the human agents that are subject to it? What influence does the law have "from the inside"?

There is some support, in the existing literature, for such a change in perspective. Loose collections of "post-Marxist" or "New Left" theories have accepted the role of liberal democratic institutions, such as the rule of law, in securing the conditions of modest forms of individual freedom and equality. They have sought to face head-on the unresolved contradiction on the Left between hostility to the idea of the rule of law as a mystifying ideology, and the actual practice of a Left politics, which

---

[48] See C Miéville (note 21 above) (2005).

has often demonstrated a real concern for legality and liberty.[49] Instead of rejecting legal institutions as mere expressions of capitalist productive relations, generative of little more than ideological modes of domination,[50] they have accepted, to some degree, the need to engage with and attempt to restructure these forms, as means of securing social change. They have contrasted their position with the standard Marxist theory of social change: viz. that the contradictions of capital will eventually become so acute as to enable the revolutionary overthrow of liberal institutions and their replacement with formations of proletarian control.[51]

These theories have rarely engaged with the law and its capacity to facilitate and direct social change.[52] Nor do they explore law's mechanism of action, or the relationship between the structure of legal concepts and reasoning, and the promise and limitations of legally structured social change.

Yet, they contain fertile insights. In *The Poverty of Theory*, EP Thompson argued against the Marxist tendency to isolate and confine law to part of the economic 'superstructure' and treat its efficacy, or lack of it, on that basis. It is simply not possible, Thompson argued, to understand law as separate from economic or productive relationships, or from politics or ideology. Law does "not keep politely to a 'level'" but is "at every bloody level". It is "imbricated within the mode of production and productive relations themselves". It is present in philosophy. It appears "bewigged and gowned in the guise of ideology". It is "an arm of politics and politics is one of its arms". It is an academic discipline "subjected to the rigour of its own autonomous logic". It contributes "to the self-identity of both the rulers and the ruled". It "affords an arena of class struggle, within which alternative notions of law were fought out".[53]

Developing these insights, it is possible to conceive of law in social practice as a fluid structure with a marbleised form, shading in and out of social relationships. It thickens and fades at different times, places and social locations. Some activities and social processes are almost exclusively dominated by the direct application of law; others by simply the faint echo of an old legal norm that has been encrusted in morality or local *mores*. In order to consider the role of law in social change, attention must be paid to the particular arena in which law is being deployed or which it constitutes, and how law acts on the behaviour and consciousness of the agents involved. Consciousness, experience and behaviour will find simultaneous expression in politics, religion, morality and law. The task must be to identify

---

[49] H Collins *Marxism and the Law* (1982) 146.

[50] Ibid 17–34.

[51] C Mouffe *For a Left Populism* (2018) 46; N Bobbio *The Future of Democracy: A Defence of the Rules of the Game* (1984).

[52] D Mitchell *The Right to the City: Social Justice and the Fight for Public Space* (2003) 26–9 is a possible exception.

[53] EP Thompson (note 29 above) 96.

where the law is in any particular set of social relationships and what role it plays in shaping and changing them.

This does not mean that studies of law in social practice can only ever be highly particularised and centred on one or a small number of agents, although ethnographic studies of legal consciousness provide a rich seam of thinking about the agent-centeredness of law, and how it interacts with morality, ideology and political consciousness.[54] What it does mean is that attention should be paid to how law shapes the opportunity structure facing ordinary men and women embroiled in critical social processes and institutions, and how changes in the law affect that opportunity structure. The way in which a law shapes an opportunity structure can be fairly direct, by giving or taking away rights, or indirect by influencing the scope of morally, politically or socially permissible action. For example, the law on gay marriage can change to directly provide for the right of gay people to marry. But it can also, whether or not it makes that direct provision, influence the ways in which ordinary men and women feel about, and respond to, gay marriage by acting on agent-centred impressions of morality or social propriety, making gay marriage more or less acceptable as an idea, whether or not it is actually legally permitted. It can also influence institutional behaviour, whether by encouraging or discouraging state and private institutions to make gay marriage practically accessible. The way that the law acts directly and indirectly on these social structures will influence, but obviously not determine, the range of action available to a gay person over time.

This agent-centred approach to the study of law and social change accords with important legal-theoretical and philosophical accounts of the content, purpose and social role of legal rights. In *On Human Rights*, James Griffin sets out and defends an account of human rights which is grounded in what he calls "personhood". Griffin argues that human rights are grounded, primarily, in the need to protect our "human standing" as agents. This standing has three components: autonomy, liberty and the minimum provision of certain basic resources and capabilities. Autonomy is the ability to "choose one's own path through life"; to choose our own conception of what is good and worthwhile about life; and not to be dominated or controlled by someone or something else. Having chosen, "one must be able to act" and, the choices made by a human agent must be real: the result of some meaningful, informed deliberation. This requires a minimum level of resources and capabilities, which enable us to access and evaluate information, and act on it. Finally, we must be free to act on these choices without someone forcibly preventing us from doing so. That requires the protection of our liberty. The rights to which we are

---

[54] S Engle-Merry *Getting Justice and Getting Even: Legal Consciousness Among Working Class Americans* (1990); P Ewick and S Silbey *The Common Place of Law: Stories from Everyday Life* (1998). There is also a body of European philosophical and sociological literature that confronts the way that the theory and practice of law construct the legal subject itself – in other words, how the law shapes ideas of the self and the social world. See, in particular, P Bourdieu "The Force of Law: Towards a Sociology of the Juridical Field" (1987) 38 *Hastings Law Journal* 814. See also B Latour *The Making of Law: An Ethnography of the Counseil d'Etat* (2010). This book maintains a neutrality about exactly how law constructs the subject or shapes consciousness. My argument is that, *however* the subject is constituted, the subject has agency, and, whatever role the law plays in constituting the subject, it also plays a role in expanding and contracting the spaces in which the subject acts.

entitled are those which are necessary to protect and facilitate the development of our personhood: to allow us to decide autonomously, to be free to act on our decisions without outside restriction, and to have the resources and capabilities necessary to do so.[55]

It does not matter whether Griffin's account of personhood and the agency that underpins it strikes us as correct, or too extensive, or incomplete. What requires attention is his conceptual scheme: rights are justified because they protect human standing and human agency. They create the normative context in which we are (or should be) free to act to pursue our goals. Although Griffin was only concerned with the moral and conceptual underpinnings of human rights, it seems to me that the role that legal rights play is no different. They create, or at least form part of, the framework within which agency is possible. That framework may be indirect and subtle, such as when legal principles influence the content of ideology or morality that guides individual deliberation or action. It might also be direct and coercive, such as when a person acts in a particular way simply because the law commands it. It may also be facilitative, whether directly or indirectly, such as when a law creates an opportunity for action, or a space for deliberation, whether by requiring that one exist, or by influencing another person or institution to facilitate it.

A similar scheme can be found in Sandra Liebenberg's work on dignity and human rights. Liebenberg calls attention to the value of human dignity in interpreting the socio-economic rights in South Africa's Constitution. Human dignity is not possible without "access to basic social services". Such access "is crucial not only to people's physical survival, but also to enable the development of their potential to shape their own lives and to be active agents in the shaping of our new society". Socio-economic rights must protect this agency, and, in adjudicative contexts, the focus should be "on the actual impact of the state's actions or omissions on the life chances of disadvantaged groups". Again, Liebenberg posits legal rights as protective or facilitative of human agency. Her focus is on the extent to which rights enable people to act to bring about the ends that are important to them.[56]

The agent-centred approach to law as a social structurant also accords with Robert Nozick's theory of moral rights. Nozick's book *Anarchy, State and Utopia* forms the theoretical underpinnings of modern libertarianism – one that emphasises the smallest possible role for the state and maximum possible protection for existing property rights. Both of these ends have a deep incompatibility with the social transformation project encoded in the South African Constitution. It is nonetheless important to call attention to Nozick's theory of rights as "side constraints".

Nozick rejected the idea that rights ought, properly construed, to be concerned with particular social outcomes. Rather, the purpose they ought to serve is in placing "side constraints upon the actions to be done" or to be refrained from.[57] Nozick's insight is that rights structure actions as well as ends. His view was that rights

---

[55] Griffin *On Human Rights* (2008) 33.

[56] S Liebenberg "The Value of Dignity in Interpreting Socio-Economic Rights" (2005) 21 *South African Journal on Human Rights* 1.

[57] R Nozick *Anarchy, State and Utopia* (1974) 29.

should *only* prescribe minimal constraints on actions, and not say anything about social ends at all. Nozick's theory of rights was that only a minimal number of side-constraints to permissible action should be accepted, and that these derived from what is strictly necessary protect the property holdings (including what Nozick called "self-ownership") of others.

One need not accept this theory to agree with Nozick's basic conceptual insight: that part of the utility of moral (and hence legal) rights is to structure action, even if no particular end is prescribed. Rights affect process as well as substance. Legal rights structure and shape agency as well as often specifying ends towards which that agency ought to be directed. Nozick would reject anything so flamboyant as Griffin's idea of "personhood" as the end to which a system of moral or legal rights should be directed. But he would accept that rights were nonetheless capable of structuring the exercise of agency, and the conditions under which personhood is meaningful.

There is accordingly a fairly wide spectrum of agreement about the agency-structuring function of human rights. And if human rights find the protection of agency as the primary ground for their justification, then it seems to me that the extent to which legal rights promote or retard agency ought to be central to assessing the role of law in bringing about social change. The focus, I suggest, ought not to be so much on the role of law in a static social "superstructure", or its functional role in achieving specific policy goals, but on the part it plays in shaping the conditions of agency of ordinary men and women. This widens the scope of the law and social change enquiry considerably, and allows it to make sense of the social life of areas of law such as property, contract, delict and other areas of private law that have, until now, received relatively little critical attention beyond an economistic reductionism. I will explore the critical literature on property law in general, and South African property law in particular, in the next chapter. For now, the only points I seek to make are that an account of the role of law and social change would be incomplete without an exploration of the ways in which law structures the basic choices people make in everyday life, especially the way that it structures access to material goods; that changes in those laws are an appropriate focus for the study of law and social change; and that assessing how those laws affect the exercise of human agency is a sound method of charting the causal relationship between particular laws and particular social outcomes.

It is important to recognise that those social outcomes are not simply the changes in the law themselves. The social outcomes that an agent-centred theory of law and social change will ultimately be concerned with are what happens after a law is changed. In other words, the action will be in the way that law actually restructures the spaces in which normative agency is exercised, how that agency is actually èxercised, and the role that law plays in determining the path that is actually taken.

In this book I only intend to call attention to the ways in which changes in property law have restructured the spaces in which different forms of agency are possible. I will also provide illustrations of where developments in the law have been exploited by poor people exercising agency. But it is important to emphasise that the empirical part of the work – characterising the way in which people act in the spaces that have been restructured by changes in the law – is as important as being able to describe the way in which law shapes the opportunity structure for ordinary men and women. The agent-centred theory I want to advocate for tells us where to look and what to look for. It does not necessarily entail any particular vision of what will be found.

2.6   STRUCTURING TRANSFORMATION: SOUTH AFRICAN PROPERTY LAW AND DISPOSSESSION

Adopting an agent-centred approach to law, and emphasising the role of law in structuring the spaces in which ordinary men and women face opportunities and constraints in giving effect to their goals and aspirations, underscores the substantial potential law has to re-stitch the social fabric. It also emphasises the far-reaching work South African law and the South African Constitution have to do in bringing about the social transformation the Constitution encodes. It calls attention to the significant choices left unmade about exactly how South Africa is to facilitate and constrain the agency of those who live here, in the achievement of the Constitutional vision. But it also permits us to think in fairly fine-grained ways about the direction of law and social change in South Africa, and particularly the transformational path that the Constitution is taking. It allows us to develop a grasp, not just of the ends that the Constitution seeks, but the legal principles and techniques that are required to achieve them.

An agent-centred approach also allows us to understand the law's dynamic role in specific social processes, not just its static place in the social structure. Adjustments to those processes – and to the role law plays in them – can strengthen or weaken the position of those who are subject to them. This is a particularly important observation for this book. One of the main objectives of the Constitution is to widen access to land and property. The state is specifically enjoined to "foster the conditions which enable citizens to gain access to land on a progressive basis"[58] and to "take reasonable legislative and other measures, within its available resources, to achieve the progressive realisation" of the right of access to adequate housing.[59] In the context of South Africa's history of widespread racially-based dispossession of land and housing, these objectives cannot be achieved without a thorough examination of the legal processes through which people can be dispossessed of land and housing, and the extent to which those processes can be adjusted to more effectively secure people against dispossession.

At the beginning of this chapter, I noted that the Constitution has been referred to as a 'framework' or a 'blueprint' for social transformation. But even this characterisation is too ambitious. If it is accepted that one of the key arenas of social transformation in contemporary South Africa is the distribution of land and property,

---

[58] Section 25(5) of the Constitution.
[59] Section 26(2) of the Constitution.

then the Constitution itself gives relatively little guidance on how transformation is to be achieved. Its text leaves far too many unanswered questions for that. The Constitution is really a set of undeveloped opportunities for, and constraints on, the range of actions available to the agents to which it is applied. It is flexible enough to restructure and shape those opportunities and constraints in a way that promotes or retards the redistributive ends that are espoused on its behalf. But exactly how that happens depends on the way in which ordinary people, their lawyers and judges understand the law to operate, and affect their everyday exercise of their agency.

Most theories of law and social change overlook this aspect of law's social life. Classical Marxists more or less deny that it exists. Liberal instrumentalist theories place little trust in ordinary people's capacity to achieve social change, and tend to assume that change happens when lawyers and legal activists formulate and pursue specific policy goals. But it is only by examining the extent to which law is interleaved in specific social processes, and the opportunities for action that it advances or denies to ordinary people, that it is really possible to understand how law leads to social change. In the remainder of this book, I intend to illustrate this point by reference to three transformations in property law that have taken place since the end of apartheid: in the law of landlord and tenant; the law regulating unlawful occupation of land; and the law regulating the relationship between debtors and creditors.

These transformations have taken place against the historical background of widespread dispossession of property rights for most South Africans. Contemporary property law debates, especially those about expropriation of land with or without compensation, tend to focus on distributive outcomes. Under apartheid, roughly 80% of the population (African people) were consigned to 20% of the land. Even today, 72% of farmland is still owned by white people.[60] As of 2011, white people constituted only 9% of the population.[61] Some 49% of urban freehold land is owned by white people.[62] And 45% of all individually owned sectional title units are owned by white people.[63]

In the face of these statistics, the focus on the distributional problems is understandable. But ignoring the processes of dispossession that led to them, almost all of which were legally regulated, means that there can be little discussion of how these mal-distributions came to be, and what sort of legal regime is required to prevent them from getting worse, or from re-occurring once a programme of accelerated land redistribution has run its course. Although the distributive statistics are stark, the available statistics on land dispossession after the end of apartheid are of even more concern: well over one million people were evicted from South African commercial farmlands between 1994 and 2004.[64] In five years

---

[60] Department of Rural Development and Land Reform *Land Audit Report: Phase Two: Private Land Ownership by Race, Gender and Nationality* (2017) 8.

[61] Statistics South Africa *Census 2011*.

[62] Department of Rural Development and Land Reform (note 60 above) 12.

[63] Ibid 17.

[64] M Wegerif *Still Searching for Security: The reality of Farm Dweller Evictions in South Africa* (2005) 46.

between 2003 and 2008, in the Johannesburg inner city alone, a further 10 000 people were evicted from their homes to make way for inner-city regeneration.[65]

It is only by focusing on processes of dispossession, asking what they look like from the inside, examining the role of law in those processes, and asking questions about what forms of agency the regulation of those processes permits and limits, that it is possible to fully account for the role the law plays in changing the distribution of land and property in South Africa. It is only once that question is answered that it is possible to ask whether the transformation of the property regime through law is a realistic goal, and what would be required to achieve such a thing. Before exploring these possibilities, however, it is necessary first to sketch out the state of property law at the end of apartheid. That is the focus of the next chapter.

---

[65] S Wilson (note 31 above) 137.

CHAPTER THREE

PROPERTY BARKS

"There are property rights. The dog is my property. My property barks. There you have it." So says Gilbert Longabaugh, in the Coen Brothers' film *The Ballad of Buster Scruggs*. Mr Longabaugh is brushing off complaints from other travellers in a caravan traversing the prairies somewhere between Iowa and Oregon. The complaints are about the noise his Jack Russell Terrier "President Pierce" makes barking at "animals larger than himself". As Mr Longabaugh's sister points out, "almost all animals" are larger than President Pierce. Mr Longabaugh's remarks are meant to come off as priggish and absurd. He is a pathetic character of many schemes but no accomplishment. We are not meant to take him seriously.

Yet Mr Longabaugh's casual assertion of an absolute property right that entitles him to cause a nuisance to others is a familiar feature of the common law of property. It strikes at a tension. On the one hand, at the core of the common law of property lie far-reaching, individualist claims to total control over the use and enjoyment of one's own things. On the other hand, the practical reality is that property is a fundamentally social institution, which has to reconcile the assertion of property rights with the public good. The real questions that lie at the core of property law are what the public good is, whose rights will have to yield to it, and in what circumstances.

These questions are often obscured by the way that the common law of property structures itself, and the manner in which it has developed in the two millennia since the late Roman Republic. At the core of the common law of property lies the Roman concept of 'dominium' – absolute control over a thing to the exclusion of all other claims over it. Anyone who has a passing familiarity with Roman history and society will find it easy to draw links between the concept of 'dominium' over a thing, and the power the Roman *paterfamilias* had over the women, children and slaves in his household. This connection has been pointed out, probably most famously, by Orlando Patterson.[1]

The influence of 'dominium' as a founding idea – perhaps the most fundamental conceptual foundation – of modern property law is pervasive, especially in South Africa. In *Geldenhuys*,[2] a case that still forms the staple of every first or second lecture in the undergraduate property law courses taught throughout South Africa, limited real property rights, other than ownership itself, are described as "subtractions from the dominium"[3] of the owner. The common law of property, we are told, starts with the acquisition of absolute control over a thing, and is then

---

[1] O Patterson *Slavery and Social Death: A Comparative Study* (1982) 31. See also David Graeber *Debt: The First 5000 Years* (2011) 199–200.

[2] *Ex parte Geldenhuys* 1926 OPD 155.

[3] Ibid 164.

complicated by the carving out of subsidiary rights, such as usufruct, mortgage securities, and lease.

This, André van der Walt remarks, is "the normality assumption". Property is owned by a person, and that person has the right to exclusive possession or control of the thing he owns. That is the "normal state of affairs", that will most likely be upheld in the absence of good reason for not doing so. "Good reason" at common law, is a statutory right that limits the right of the owner, or a countervailing common law right that can rarely come into existence without the express consent of the owner.[4]

In this way, the common law of property accepts and attempts to account for the common-sense notion that property law cannot only concern itself with the rights of an individual owner.[5] It also makes some room for the notion that ownership rights have to be balanced against the public good. The problem, however, is that this balancing takes place in a legal framework that is fundamentally skewed in favour of existing owners. If property should normally be with its owner, and the only good reasons we have for taking it away from an owner, or at least limiting their rights over it, are countervailing common law rights or statutory limitations, then the prospect of bringing about social change through adjustments to property holdings seems particularly grim. Non-owners are placed in a fundamentally subordinate social position.

In a state inhabited exclusively by existing property owners, or where it is easy to acquire property, this need not be so worrisome. But in South Africa, the vast majority of the population does not own any significant property. The acquisition of significant property – land, housing, motor vehicles, and financial instruments such as credit and pension funds – is close to impossible for most people. In these circumstances, a property law that is skewed towards the protection of owners, and the respect for their 'dominium', starts to look not just inappropriate, but downright oppressive.

Some of the problem might be solved, it is true, by simply redistributing ownership rights more widely. But, in this chapter, I want to argue that something more is required. The inherent inequality of property in South Africa is not just a feature of skewed distribution: it is a feature of the structure of the common law of property itself. If the common law of property is not itself restructured, the development of significant inequality over time is almost inevitable, no matter how effective programmes of redistribution might be. The common law of property must be remodelled in order to replicate equality, fairness and recognition of the public good, and limit absolutist conceptions of ownership.

In the rest of this chapter, I will first set out in greater detail the extent to which the common law of property is hobbled by what Joseph William Singer calls its central "paradox": its inability to make sense of the tension between ownership

---

[4] A van der Walt *Constitutional Property Law* (2005) 412. See also S Wilson "Breaking the Tie: Eviction from Private Land, Homelessness and the New Normality" (2009) 126 *South African Law Journal* 270.

[5] A van der Walt "Tradition on Trial: A Critical Analysis of the Civil Law Tradition in South African Property Law" (1995) 11 *South African Journal on Human Rights* 169, 178.

and the public good.[6] Singer has argued, persuasively, that this limitation of the common law of property arises when trying to reconcile competing claims between owners themselves, as well as when trying to mediate the clashing claims of owners and non-owners to the same property.

Secondly, I will briefly survey the state of the common law of property as it stood at the end of apartheid, insofar as it relates to the central themes of this book: ownership of, and eviction from, land, relationships between landlords and tenants, and relationships between debtors and creditors. I will show that each area of law sets up a strict hierarchy, sometimes between owners and non-owners, and sometimes between holders of strong or weak common law rights. In the case of debtor and creditor relationships, one kind of ownership right trumps another. But the common feature of those relationships is hierarchy. Weaker rights always give way to stronger ones. People without common law rights always give way to those with common law rights. They all give way to ownership, and some forms of ownership trump others. These hierarchies sometimes, but not always, suited the purposes of the apartheid state. Where they did suit those purposes, by reinforcing racial division of power, the apartheid state tended to reinforce common-law-created inequalities. Where they did not – for example, where they created unsustainable or undesirable inequalities between classes of white people – the apartheid state legislated fairly aggressively to regulate and reshape common-law proprietary relationships.

Thirdly, I want to suggest that the constitutional regulation of property law after the end of apartheid provided a framework within which the necessary remodelling of the common law of property is possible. Sections 25 and 26 of the Constitution have created a fundamental break with the idea of ownership as dominium. It is true that the Constitution sets out to provide recognition to property rights existing at the time of its promulgation. However, sections 25 and 26 also create a framework within which property rights can themselves be restructured in a non-arbitrary manner that promotes the concept of property as a social good, and recognises that competing claims over the same property ought not automatically to be settled in favour of an existing owner, or the party with stronger common law rights.

These developments have opened up social and economic spaces in which individuals and communities can act for themselves to achieve social change. The following three chapters will give concrete examples of those spaces and the manner in which law has developed to open them up.

3.1   THE COMMON LAW OF PROPERTY AND SOCIAL EXCLUSION

At the heart of the common law of property lie stubborn conceptions of power and exclusion. To be a property owner is to control property to the exclusion of all others. In Roman law, to have property was simply to have 'dominium' over a thing.[7] William Blackstone described "property" as "that sole and despotic

---

    [6] JW Singer *Entitlement: The Paradoxes of Property* (2000) 1–9.
    [7] RW Lee *An Introduction to Roman Dutch Law* 2 ed (1925) 120. The entry for "dominium" in the index to Aldo Schiavane *The Invention of Law in the West* (2012) 589, simply states "See *Property*".

dominium which one man claims and exercises over the external thing of the world, in total exclusion of the right of any other individual in the universe".[8] The same basic idea appears, in more demure terms, in fairly recent South African law. In *Chetty v Naidoo* the Appellate Division recapitulated the common sense idea of ownership as power and exclusion. The court held that although "it may be difficult to define *dominium* comprehensively … one of its incidents is the right of exclusive possession of the *res*, with the necessary corollary that the owner may claim his property wherever found, from whomsoever holding it". Accordingly, "it is inherent in the nature of ownership that possession of the *res* should normally be with the owner, and it follows that no other person may withhold it from the owner unless he is vested with some right enforceable against the owner".[9]

It follows from this that common law property rights really only engage two kinds of person: owners, and those who hold rights against an owner. Rights against an owner are almost always held because the owner has created them. Leaving aside the right to delivery created by an agreement of sale, most are terminable, if not at the will of the owner, then on conditions that the owner will have determined by agreement in advance. Ordinarily, at least at the time of their creation, the owner is confident that they will be able to fulfil those conditions and regain unencumbered ownership. Accordingly, the extinction or limitation of an owner's rights must usually be, in some non-trivial sense, voluntary – for example, by putting up the ownership right as security for the repayment of a debt, or willing the right to someone else after their death. The same applies to temporary limitations of an owner's right to possession, such as a lease, where an owner voluntarily loans the use of the thing to someone else for a defined period. Non-owners, or those without subordinate common law rights granted by owners, are completely out of the picture.

A related problem is the internal hierarchies that the common law of property sets up. It is not just the needs of those without any property rights that are unaccounted for. As James Stern points out, property law is really an "authority structure, in which control or domination over a defined subject matter is the basic conceptual currency".[10] Within the hierarchy of power that ownership as dominium sets up, the social needs of existing holders of subordinate property rights often receive inadequate protection. These hierarchies sometimes redound to the prejudice of owners themselves, where ownership rights compete with each other. Real security rights, for example, make powerful inroads into ownership rights by making the continued ownership conditional upon the repayment of a debt. The rights of the owner of the debt have to compete with the rights of the owner of the thing taken in lieu of repayment of the debt. The common law of property tends to enhance the power of money lenders by placing few limitations on their right to take and realise the property of a debtor. The power imbalance between debtor and creditor

---

[8] W Blackstone *Commentaries on the Law of England Book 2* (1776) 2.
[9] *Chetty v Naidoo* 1974 (3) SA 13 (A) 20A-D.
[10] JY Stern "What is the right to exclude and why does it matter?" in J Penner and M Otsuka (eds) *Property Theory: Legal and Political Perspectives* (2018) 38.

is particularly severe where an owner has put up a valuable personal asset, such as a house or a car, as security for a debt. In that sort of case, the common law has no way of evaluating the fairness of a creditor taking that asset in satisfaction of a debt.

Outside the voluntary limitation or extinction of ownership rights, the common law of property makes few concessions to social claims that compete with ownership. The doctrine of estoppel sometimes works to deprive an owner of a thing which they have negligently allowed to be represented as the property of another.[11] Acquisitive prescription allows the involuntary transfer of ownership from the owner to another person, if that person has used the property openly as if it were their own for a period of thirty years.[12] Nuisance law places limitations on what an owner can do with their own land where the owner's chosen use causes an unreasonable interference with the rights of others. Those rights are normally the competing property rights of neighbouring owners.[13]

Beyond this, however, limitations on ownership rights tend to be imposed from outside the common law of property. The most obvious are statutory limitations on ownership rights, such as the power of expropriation, and a range of regulatory limitations on the use and enjoyment of ownership rights. These regulatory limitations are often extensive, and are primarily concerned with abating public nuisances and ensuring the ability of the state to install infrastructure on privately owned land.[14] At their most extensive, they include statutory limitations that directly serve redistributive purposes, such as rent control legislation.[15]

The fundamental point, however, is that social claims on property tend to be located outside the common law of property itself. Property is about the power of owners, and subordinate rights holders, over things, not about how things can be used fairly to meet competing social needs. From a purely common law perspective, it matters not, for example, whether an owner's vindication of their property would extinguish its use for an important social purpose which is not itself embodied in a property right. So, for example, the mere fact that a piece of land may be occupied residentially by hundreds or thousands of people, or used to grow food for the population of a town, makes no difference to the owner's entitlement to possess the property and exclude the occupiers or farmers from it, unless the property is expropriated, or the occupiers and farms can rely on a countervailing property right.

The problem is not limited to land used for residential purposes. In *Governing Body of the Juma Musjid Primary School*, the Constitutional Court had to deal with an application to evict a school. The court acknowledged that some way had to be found to place limits on individual ownership where it clashed with other constitutionally protected interests. The court held that "... normal ownership

---

[11] *Quenty's Motors Ltd v Standard Credit Corporation* 1994 (3) SA 188 (A).

[12] *Malan v Nabygelegen Estates* 1946 AD 562 574. Given legislative effect in section 1 of the Prescription Act 68 of 1969.

[13] *Gien v Gien* 1979 (2) SA 1113 (T).

[14] See, for example, *Reflect All 1025 CC v MEC for Public Transport, Roads and Works, Gauteng Provincial Government* 2009 (6) SA 391 (CC).

[15] See, for example, the Rents Act 80 of 1976.

rights are not counterposed only to constitutional housing rights, but also, as this case shows, to other fundamental rights. What must be weighed against the right of ownership, in each case, will depend on the content of each specific countervailing right".[16] The court acknowledged that the common law idea of ownership was not just inimical to competing habitation rights sourced outside the common law, but to any social claim located outside an owner's direct interests.

The upshot is that common law ownership, conceived of as almost unfettered power over a thing, creates widespread social problems. Historically, these problems have generally been resolved in favour of the owner, at the cost of substantial hardship for non-owners.

Legal realism has presented a partial challenge to this account of ownership. Rather than the exercise of "power by owners over things", realism says, property law is really about "relations among people with respect to things".[17] Ownership is not just an undifferentiated power over things, but a set of specific entitlements, each of which subsists in a relationship between the owner and another person. The power to exclude a person from one's property, for example, implies a specific kind of relationship with those to be excluded. Once this is understood, the justice or efficiency of the right to exclude can be evaluated in a specific context. So it goes for all the other standard incidents of ownership in the "bundle" of rights that accrue to the owner.[18] The right to raise capital against property, for example, is embedded in a complex set of financial arrangements and networks, which create claims and interests in the property put up as security. The business of the common law of property, insofar as it relates to real security, is to work out how these claims and interests are, and ought to be, reconciled in a range of contexts.

The insights of legal realism provide much-needed complexity to the basic idea of ownership as power over things. But they do not address the fundamental presumptions associated with ownership. While the ownership right can usefully be defined and limited with respect to its incidents, the owner still retains his power over those incidents. In addition, where the incidents of ownership do not themselves seem to fully describe the totality of possible relationships between owners, things and other people, or where ownership rights are exercised in a new context, the assumption tends to be that any resulting social competition for rights over a thing will inevitably be resolved in favour of the owner.[19]

So seeing ownership as a "bundle of rights", each of which implies a correlative set of duties and relationships with others, does not in itself resolve the difficulty that the common law of property has in recognising the interests of those without pre-existing property rights. Rather, it emphasises that difficulty. It helps us acknowledge that property is fundamentally a social institution, but one which sets up an often pernicious hierarchy between owners and holders of subordinate rights

---

[16] *Governing Body of the Juma Musjid Primary School and Others v Ahmed Asruff Essay NO and Others* 2011 (8) BCLR 761 (CC) para 70.

[17] JW Singer (note 6 above) 10.

[18] AM Honoré "Ownership" in AG Guest (ed) *Oxford Essays on Jurisprudence* (1961) 107, 114.

[19] JW Singer (note 17 above) 10.

derived from ownership, on the one hand, and those who have neither kind of right, on the other.

The problem is compounded once property rights are provided with philosophical pedigree and constitutional protection. The concept of ownership as dominium predates the standard philosophical justifications now given for it by at least 1 500 years. For Locke and Nozick, property rights arise from original acquisition, and the mixing of one's labour with an object.[20] Once acquired, property rights are absolute and can only be extinguished by voluntary transfer or limitation.[21] These decidedly *ex post facto* justifications for an institution that grew up to reinforce patriarchal control of Roman society tend to deepen rather than resolve the difficulties that the common law of property has in responding to social needs.

The common law conception of ownership as *dominium* has become remarkably entrenched. It has spread through colonial conquest, first by the Romans and most recently through the imperial expansions of the late nineteenth and early twentieth centuries. Once entrenched, it has survived a wide variety of attempts to alter legal relationships to recognise a wider variety of social claims. It has been constitutionalised across a range of jurisdictions. Perhaps because of its social utility as a means of control, and its inherent friendliness to the mercantile interests behind Enlightenment revolutions in England (in 1649 and 1689) and the United States (in 1776), it has grown with the modern state, and remains, despite its obviously anachronistic nature, at the core of modern law. Gretchen Carpenter has drawn attention to the durability of old habits of legal reasoning well after they appear to have been overtaken by social and legal developments incompatible with them.[22] The law of ownership has done more than survive as a ghost of legal reasoning, however. It has been continually repurposed and grafted into successive legal regimes across a wide variety of social and historical contexts.

This durability is crystallised in the way that modern constitutions have entrenched protection for property rights. Property rights in modern constitutions tend to be purely defensive protections of an individual owner's dominium against an overweening state. Social claims, and the claims of people without property rights, tend to be characterised as "expropriations" or (at least in the United States) regulatory "takings" made by the state, for public purposes.[23] No modern constitution affords a positive right to own property.[24] The effect is to give constitutional protection to a pre-existing notion of property rights which is, at best, in profound tension with public welfare[25] – at least in the overwhelming

---

[20] John Locke *Two Treatises of Government* (1689).

[21] Robert Nozick *Anarchy State and Utopia* (1974).

[22] G Carpenter "Constitutional interpretation by the existing judiciary in South Africa — can new wine be successfully decanted into old bottles?" (1995) 28 *Comparative and International Law Journal of Southern Africa* 322.

[23] JP Byrne "What we talk about when we talk about property rights – a response to Carol Rose's Property as a Keystone Right?" (1995) 71 *Notre Dame Law Review* 1049, 1053.

[24] In J Waldron *The Right to Private Property* (1988) 423 – 445, Jeremy Waldron considers whether there could be a right general right to acquire private property.

[25] J Ryan Collins, T Lloyd and L Macfarlane *Rethinking the Economics of Land and Housing* (2017) 10–13.

majority of jurisdictions with substantial inequality of resources, a problem with resource poverty, or in customary law property regimes where property ownership as dominium is not widespread, or has little purchase, as a conception of property.

One answer to these difficulties with the common law of property has been to deny that takings of property for redistributive or welfarist purposes are legitimate at all, and assert the economic efficiency of strongly protected absolutist conceptions of property rights. It is often argued that allowing owners and holders of other property rights to interact freely in a substantially unregulated marketplace is the best way to increase aggregate welfare.[26] But few could accept such an extreme view today. In the aftermath of the sub-prime mortgage crisis, and the deepening inequality that has attended on the substantially *laissez-faire* economic policies of Western and South African governments over the last forty years,[27] the idea that a high level of aggregate social welfare can be achieved by leaving property owners to themselves seems quaint.

The problem of the common law of property's failure to respond to the needs of people who do not hold ownership rights, or rights derived from them, remains. Ownership as dominium is a central feature of South African property law. It presents a substantial obstacle to social change in South Africa by sustaining the processes of dispossession which characterised colonialism and apartheid. As Lucy Williams warns, legal structures "create and perpetuate income imbalances ... law constructs poverty".[28] If South African property law remains unreformed and unchallenged, severe limits are imposed on the possibility of law bringing about meaningful social change.

Whether common law hierarchies of power redound to the prejudice of non-owners (as is mostly the case), or owners themselves (as is sometimes the case), the fundamental problem is the zero-sum game of domination and subordination that the common law of property infuses into social relationships about property. That power game is derived from, but does not always serve, the enhanced protection the common law gives to owners' rights through the concept of dominium.

In the next section, I set out how, in the areas of law to which this book addresses itself, the common law of property sets up those hierarchies and relationships. I show that, under colonialism and apartheid, the state sought to reinforce and deepen the inequalities created by common-law-inspired hierarchies of power where they suited the state's purposes. However, the state was prompt to regulate the common law, if the common law had undesirable consequences for the racial division of power.

---

[26] R Epstein *Takings: Private Property and the Power of Eminent Domain* (1985).

[27] See T Piketty *Capital in the Twenty-First Century* (2014) 15–16.

[28] L Williams "Introduction" in L Williams A Kjonstad and P Robson *Law and Poverty: The legal system and poverty reduction* (2003) 1.

3.2   HOW THE COMMON LAW OF PROPERTY TREATS UNLAWFUL OCCUPIERS, TENANTS AND DEBTORS

3.2.1   Unlawful Occupiers

"Any shack or house that is built on land that has not been hired or purchased is illegal and will be removed." Wayne Minnaar, a Johannesburg Metropolitan Police Commander, said this in justification of the demolition of 1 000 families' homes at Rabie Ridge, Johannesburg, on 30 April 2019.[29] As a statement of post-apartheid law, it is inaccurate and misleading, but as a statement of what the common law of property allows to be done to people without common law rights acquired by "purchase", "hire", or otherwise, it is telling. It is a fair indication both of the profound vulnerability faced by people who unlawfully occupy their homes, and of the deep-rooted social attitudes sustained by absolutist conceptions of ownership.

The mere fact that 1 000 families have to live on land to which they have no common law rights ought to raise profound questions about the common law itself. Instead, it generally results in a categorisation, based on the absence on common law rights. The occupiers are "unlawful". They ought not to be where they are, and the owner of the property has the right to remove them. It does not matter that to do so would make the occupiers homeless, might result in the destruction of the little property they do own, or would severely disrupt the livelihoods, health and education of thousands of people. All that matters is the 'unlawfulness' of their occupation.

This categorisation, though obviously harsh to the point of callousness, is simply the logical result of accepting that an owner of land has dominium over it. Part of that dominium is the right to exclude all others from it. André van der Walt says that the common law takes the view that "existing land rights should be entrenched and protected against unlawful intrusions, without first having to assert or prove their socio-political legitimacy".[30] It is not just that the common law does not assign weight to the consequences for those excluded; it is that the common law has no way of capturing or analysing those consequences at all.

This is plain from the basic logic underpinning the *actio rei vindicato*, which is the procedural mechanism that gives effect to an owner's right to exclusive possession. "It is", the Appellate Division tells us in *Chetty v Naidoo* "inherent in the nature of ownership that possession of the *res* should normally be with the owner, and it follows that no other person may withhold it from the owner unless he is vested with some right enforceable against the owner (eg, a right of retention or a contractual right)". Accordingly, "the owner, in instituting a *rei vindicatio*, need, therefore, do no more than allege and prove that he is the owner and that the defendant is holding the *res* – the onus being on the defendant to allege and

---

[29] Z Postman "Huge Shack Demolition in Johannesburg" *GroundUp* (30 April 2019) <https://www.groundup. org.za/article/huge-shack-demolition-johannesburg> last visited on 2 May 2019.

[30] A van der Walt "Exclusivity of Ownership, Security of Tenure and Eviction Orders: A Critical Evaluation of Recent Case Law" (2002) 18 *South African Journal of Human Rights* 372, 373.

establish any right to continue to hold against the owner".[31] The owner need only go to the trouble of proving that the occupier had no rights if the owner had already acknowledged the occupier once had a right at some prior point in time. Otherwise, there is no need to demonstrate this – as the absence of occupiers' rights over land is ordinarily assumed.

Accordingly, one person's ownership of land necessarily implies another's dispossession. Such is the logic of the common law. The common law does not balance the social consequences of the dispossession against the rights and privileges of ownership. Nor does it advance a reason why such a balancing exercise is unnecessary. Ownership just is. As a result, dispossession just follows.[32]

One is often encouraged to consider these forms of deductive reasoning as being value-neutral and applied primarily in the context of the need for certainty in commercial settings. Just like contract law and maritime law, what property law does is assign commercial benefits and burdens in a more or less predictable, value-neutral manner. Secure property rights and enforceable contracts are the cornerstone of a well-functioning economy. The law exists primarily to provide certainty in commercial transactions between roughly equal parties, where the worst that can happen is the loss of commercial premises or money.[33] The law is blind to the identity of the parties or the content of the transaction. Given these purposes, so the argument goes, introducing value-based reasoning in areas like property and contract can be destructive of the rule of law itself.[34]

But the resolution of commercial conflict is plainly not the only or even the most important function of property law. Nor is property law value neutral. The common law of property, as we have seen, sets up a series of complex social hierarchies, which tend to favour and entrench an absolutist conception of ownership. While the rules that give rise to these hierarchies can be expressed in fairly innocuous terms, that does not mean that, taken together, they are 'value-neutral'.

Nor is the impact of property law actions like the *rei vindicatio* felt only, or even primarily, in commercial contexts. As André van der Walt has argued, "the marginalisation of non-ownership rights" was the "foundation stone" of apartheid land law,[35] which was enlisted in a highly political project to crystallise and entrench South Africa's racial hierarchy in public life, and in every significant area of private life. The apparently apolitical content of the common law of property facilitated

---

[31] *Chetty v Naidoo* 1974 (3) SA 13 (A), 20B-D.

[32] In the words of André van der Walt, people without rights are not just excluded, "they are never even allowed to enter the race". See A van der Walt "Tradition on Trial: A Critical Analysis of the Civil Law Tradition in South African Property Law" (1995) 11 *South African Journal on Human Rights* 169, 179.

[33] A view of contract law cast in these terms has been strongly defended by Lewis ADP in *Oregon Trust v BEADICA 231 CC* 2019 (4) SA 517 (SCA), and just as strongly rebutted by Theron J in *Beadica 231 CC and Others v Trustees for the time being of the Oregon Trust* 2020 (5) SA 247 (CC). Both judges reached the same conclusion on the facts, however.

[34] *Bredenkamp v Standard Bank of South Africa Ltd* 2010 (4) SA 468 (SCA) para 39.

[35] A van der Walt (note 30 above) 400.

the eviction and relocation of millions of people, in aid of the implementation of apartheid land settlement policy.[36]

Much of that work was done, not by explicitly racial legislation, such as the Group Areas Act 41 of 1950, but by enhanced eviction legislation such as the Prevention of Illegal Squatting Act 52 of 1951 (PISA). In addition to providing enhanced powers to local authorities to address unhealthy or unsafe living conditions through eviction,[37] PISA sought to build upon and strengthen an owner's rights, sourced in the *rei vindicatio*, to remove an unlawful occupier from their land. Unlawful occupation became a criminal offence,[38] and eviction became a remedy granted on conviction.[39] Land owners and "lawful occupiers", too, were given powers to seek the eviction of occupiers of their land on the basis of health and safety concerns.[40] The PISA regime reached its apotheosis in 1976, with the insertion of section 3B, which allowed an owner of land to summarily destroy any home erected on their land without their consent.

By the end of apartheid, therefore, the common law's already strong protection of an owner's right to exclusive possession of their land had been supplemented by enhanced statutory rights to evict a person and demolish their home without having to obtain a court order. The common law hierarchy of power had, perhaps, never been so extreme as that between owners and occupiers of land at the dawn of constitutional democracy.

3.2.2   Landlords and Tenants

When people cannot become the owner of a thing they need, they try to rent it. Residential tenancy is perhaps the primary means by which people secure their residential tenure when they are unable to buy a home outright or obtain a mortgage. In doing so, they enter into a contract of lease that allows them to obtain temporary possession of a home for the period set out in the lease. In return, the owner of the property receives rent and accepts the limitations on their use and enjoyment of the property. Their right to exclusive possession of the leased property is temporarily suspended on the conditions and to the extent set out in the lease.

Contracts of lease for residential property are rarely freely made agreements between parties of equal bargaining power. Residential accommodation, especially in urban areas, is a scarce commodity. Owners of residential property are able to negotiate terms as to rent and conditions of termination that are favourable to them.[41] Leases routinely limit the power of tenants to withhold rent in cases where the condition of the property has deteriorated,[42] make short or late payment of rent

---

[36] See C Walker and L Platzky *The Surplus People* (1985) and C Murray and C O'Regan *No Place to Rest: Forced Removals and the Law in South Africa* (1990).

[37] Section 5(1)(b).

[38] Section 1 of the Prevention of Illegal Squatting Act 52 of 1951.

[39] Section 3.

[40] Section 5(1)(a).

[41] S Maas "Rent Control: A Comparative Analysis" (2012) 15 *Potchefstroom Electronic Law Journal* 41, 43.

[42] Many residential leases require payment of rent "without set off", or specifically require the tenant to contract out of the right to remit rent against a landlord's failure to adequately maintain the property.

when in financial distress,[43] or remain in occupation of the property for longer than the owner wants. It has long been understood that it is inherent in the nature of a lease that it comes to an end, and that a landlord can terminate the lease at any time and for any reason, once the initial period expires, by providing reasonable notice.[44]

The fundamental point is that, save to the extent that they specifically contract it out in the lease, the owner's power of dominium remains unaffected. That tends to affect the way in which leases are interpreted. The presumption that an owner's eventual right to repossess the property always trumps the lessees' rights to remain in it (except as specifically contracted for) has generally defeated any attempt, using the conceptual resources of the common law itself, to temper a common law owner's right to terminate a lease on the grounds that to do so would be disproportionate or otherwise unfair. Even after the adoption of the Constitution, the Supreme Court of Appeal held that the termination of a lease on residential property could never constitute a breach of the right to housing, because merely entering into a lease necessarily curtailed that constitutional right to the extent of the benefits enjoyed by the tenant in the contract itself. Those rights that the lease do not specifically assign to the tenant remain with the owner of the leased property.[45]

Even the colonial state and the apartheid state recognised that the combination of absolutist conceptions of ownership, inequality of bargaining power between landlords and tenants, and the scarcity of residential property, meant that the residential property market had to be regulated. It was acknowledged that "[i]n view of the fact that housing is one of the basic necessities of life, the state was forced to interfere in the market-place and to introduce legislation protecting the economically weaker party, the lessee, against exploitation by the lessor".[46]

Tenant protection legislation was first introduced in South Africa with the Tenants Protection (Temporary) Act 7 of 1920. That Act stipulated that, so long as the tenant paid the rent due and performed all of their other obligations in terms of the lease, the lessor could not evict the lessee unless the property was required for their personal accommodation.[47] This, the Appellate Division acknowledged, constituted "a drastic interference with the common law rights of lessors".[48] In addition, later rent control legislation[49] limited rent increases, and created Rent Boards that would set rents at a level that ensured that scarcity of accommodation did not result in rent increases that the tenant could not reasonably sustain.[50] The legislation also widened the bases on which a lease could be terminated, to include

---

[43] Some leases automatically terminate on non-payment, or short payment of rent, without a formal notice of cancellation or call to remedy the breach.

[44] WE Cooper *Landlord and Tenant* 2 ed (1994) 61–5.

[45] *Maphango (Mgidlana) v Aengus Lifestyle Properties (Pty) Ltd* [2011] 3 All SA 535 (SCA) paras 28 and 29. The Constitutional Court later overturned this decision. The Constitutional Court's treatment of the relationship between leasehold rights and the Constitution will be discussed further in Chapter 5.

[46] See "Tenant Protection" in WA Joubert (ed) *The Law of South Africa* (1986) volume 23 para 373.

[47] Rosenow and Diemont *The Rents Act in South* Africa 2 ed (1950) 1.

[48] *Herison v South African Mutual Life Assurance Society* 1942 AD 259 263.

[49] The Rents Act 13 of 1920; the Rents Act 43 of 1950 and the Rent Control Act 80 of 1976.

[50] S Maas (note 41 above) 59.

the need to reconstruct or renovate the property,[51] or where the lessee agreed in writing to vacate the property and the property had previously been used for the lessor's personal accommodation.[52] However, these conditions were still substantial limitations on a lessors "bare power" of termination.[53]

The Rent Control Act 80 of 1976 froze rents at 1949 levels, unless Rent Boards specifically authorised another "reasonable rental", sufficient to provide an owner with an annual return of 8.5% of the value of the rented property.[54] The Rent Control Act 80 of 1976 was eventually repealed by the Rental Housing Act 50 of 1999. This was largely in response to arguments that rent control itself contributed to the scarcity of residential accommodation.[55] Whether these arguments are sound is not a question it is necessary to address,[56] but the regime brought into effect by the Rental Housing Act, and the impact it has had on relations between landlords and tenants, will be explored in Chapter 5.

The apparently generous provisions of rent control legislation must, of course, be evaluated in the context of the full range of apartheid law and policy. It is unlikely that anyone other than white people who could not afford to buy their own homes benefited much from rent control. Other pieces of apartheid legislation ensured that the majority of the population could not live in urban South Africa at all, and ensured that residential accommodation for black people was scarce. Black people living in rural areas were subject to different legal regimes that did not involve rent control, or the need for it. Black people only became part of a multi-racial urban tenant class once influx controls collapsed, and even then, their status as tenants was precarious until group areas legislation was repealed in the early 1990s.

Be that as it may, it is noteworthy that, for almost 100 years, the common law of landlord and tenant has been considered so inappropriate to the social needs of those hiring residential accommodation that it has been heavily controlled by legislation. It has long been acknowledged that, left to its own devices, the common law has no way of taking account of the complex social field that it is supposed to regulate, because it sets up a strong but inappropriate hierarchy between lessor (owner) and lessee (non-owner).

3.2.3   Execution of Debts against a Debtor's Home
The hierarchies of power that lie at the core of the common law of property generally favour the right of ownership. But there are a few exceptions. The most important of these is where ownership rights compete with the rights of creditors. The common law provides multiple routes through which ownership rights can be extinguished

---

[51] Section 21(1)(f) of the Rents Act 43 of 1950.

[52] Section 21(1)(e) of the Rents Act 43 of 1950.

[53] *Maphango v Aengus Lifestyle Properties (Pty) Ltd* 2012 (3) SA 531 (CC) para 29.

[54] Sections 1 and 6 of the Rent Control Act 80 of 1976.

[55] See "Rental Housing" in WA Joubert (ed) *The Law of South Africa* 2 ed (1997) volume 23 para 163.

[56] The dominant perception is that rent control reduces both the quality and quantity of rental housing. But, as a general proposition, this is probably untrue. Much depends on the form rent control takes, and how, if at all, rent control regimes can respond to changes in market structure. See R Arnott "Time for Revisionism on Rent Control?" *Journal of Economic Perspectives* (1995) 9 (1) 99.

to satisfy the debts of the owner. These debts are often extraneous to the ownership right over the thing owned, in the sense that there is often no connection between the debt owed and the thing owned. Accordingly, it is possible to lose ownership of a home, a car or another valuable possession for the failure to pay debts that are not specifically secured on them, or indeed on any of the owner's property.[57] At least one common law authority deals extensively with the process for execution of debts that can be executed against an owner's property, whether or not the debt is specifically secured against it.[58]

It would be wrong, however, to see the collection of debt as an anomalous weakness in the right of ownership. The right to collect a debt has long been considered a thing that is itself capable of ownership.[59] The right can be ceded to another, sold on and even bundled together with other debts, all of which can be bought and sold as a package.[60] Debt generates interest (in the way that corporeal property sometimes generates other residual income). Debt can also, like much corporeal property, be destroyed at the will of the owner (through debt forgiveness). It is better, therefore, to see the extinction of ownership through execution of debt as the outcome of a competition between two different kinds of ownership rights – one over the thing executed against, and the other over the debt executed. In this way, it becomes easier to understand why the common law of property extends such power to owners of debt. The primary value of a debt is the confidence that the debtor will repay it, with the necessary interest. If the debtor does not or will not meet his obligations to pay, then the value of ownership over the debt is significantly diminished. The common law of property protects the value of owning the debt by permitting the creditor, as an ultimate sanction, to execute the debt against the debtor's property. This expedient is as much a way of encouraging the debtor to repay the debt (thereby enhancing the confidence of others that he will do so) as it is a way of compensating the creditor in the event that the debt is not repaid.

The law of debtor and creditor is accordingly a field of regulation that seeks to balance the rights of owners of different kinds of things, where the holders of the ownership rights have a debtor/creditor relationship. It seeks to set out the conditions under which one kind of ownership right may trump another.

In this book, I am primarily concerned with real security. That is, the relationship established where a debtor places a specific ownership right at the disposal of the owner of the debt. The owner of the debt, the creditor, can claim the right to take and liquidate the thing against which the debt is secured, usually by selling it and applying the proceeds of the sale to the outstanding balance on the debt. The creditor's claim over the proceeds of the sale of the property on which the debt is secured receives preference over unsecured creditors. The creditor can ordinarily claim 'special execution' against the specific property on which the debt is secured,

---

[57] *Gerber v Stolze* 1951 (2) SA 166 (T) 171–2.

[58] A Mattheus *De Auctionibus* (1680).

[59] See, for example, J Voet *Commentary on the Pandects* (translated by J Buchanan) volume 1 book 1 131 para 28.

[60] R Skidelsky *Money and Government: The Past and Future of Economics* (2018) 324–5.

without first having to realise the value of any of the debtor's other property. This is 'real security'. It is 'real' because it is enforceable against the owner, all his successors in title and anyone who possesses or uses the property against which the debt is secured, right up until the point that the debt is satisfied. In this way, the security for the repayment of the debt attaches to the property itself: "the right to continued ownership" of the thing against which the debtor is secured "depends on repayment". Real security "curtails the right of property at its root, and penetrates the right of ownership". The creditor's rights "are fused into the title itself".[61]

The particular kind of real security at issue in this book is the mortgage bond secured over residential property. The mortgage bond is perhaps the primary vehicle used to acquire a home. In consequence, most people acquire their homes and their biggest lifetime debt at the same time. The purchase of residential property is usually arranged through most – sometimes all – of the purchase price being advanced to the seller by a bank. The purchaser then becomes the owner of the property, but the property is subject to a real security right in the form of a mortgage bond, which can be called up in the event that the owner of the property fails to meet their payment obligations. The mortgagee's right to call up the bond is accessory to the mortgagor's failure to fulfil their payment obligations.[62]

Execution against mortgaged property is only possible because of the debt collection machinery provided by the state. The state provides the courts system through which the contractual right to execute against the mortgaged property is transformed into a court-sanctioned right to take and sell the property. It also provides the Sheriffs who actually take possession of ('attach') and sell the property, and the police force that can provide the Sheriff with the force of arms they may need to ensure that the order for attachment and sale is carried out, and, ultimately, that the mortgagor vacates the property.

As soon as a mortgagor falls behind in the fulfilment of their payment obligations, the mortgagee has at least three options: tolerate the default, while encouraging the mortgagor to bring his payments up to date, restructure the mortgagor's payment obligations, or set in motion the process of execution. The manner in which the state regulates the execution process – the ease or hardship with which the property may be executed against – is likely to materially influence which of these options the mortgagee selects, and at what time. Accordingly, the easier it is to execute against mortgaged property, the more likely the mortgagee is to resort to that option, and to do so quickly.

The execution process contains three stages. First, the debt is accelerated. This means that the mortgagee exercises his right to call up the entire principal debt against which the mortgaged property is secured. So, for example, a mortgage bond may secure a debt of R1 million, payable in instalments of R10 000 per month (including interest) over 20 years. In June of the tenth year of the term of the loan, the

---

[61] *Standard Bank v Saunderson* 2006 (2) SA 264 (SCA) para 2. These remarks were made in the context of evaluating the effect of a mortgage bond on ownership rights, but they apply equally to all real security.
[62] *Kilburn v Estate Kilburn* 1931 AD 501.

mortgagor defaults. He pays R9 000 instead of R10 000. In response to the default, the mortgagee may accelerate the debt, meaning that they can demand immediate repayment of the remaining capital amount. For argument's sake, imagine that this is R500 000.[63] Accordingly, even though the mortgagor only short paid R1 000, they immediately become liable for payment of an amount five hundred times that. Interest is added to the principal amount (often at a higher rate than the interest rate on the loan) from the date of demand. Penalty charges and other bank charges may also be added.

Assuming that the mortgagor cannot immediately produce the rest of the principal debt, the mortgagee may then proceed to the second stage of execution. The second stage involves obtaining judgment for the total outstanding amount (plus interest and costs), and the court's leave to specially execute against the mortgaged property.

The third stage of the process is the sale itself, which must be conducted by the Sheriff of the court by public auction.

The common law position immediately before the advent of the South African Constitution, 1996, both encouraged and rewarded prompt execution. In the first place, a mortgagee could accelerate the bond and execute against the mortgaged property immediately upon any default. It did not matter how little or large the default was. Any breach of any payment obligation was sufficient to enable the mortgagee to accelerate. This aspect of the mortgagee's power, which is still technically extant,[64] has led to some fairly absurd situations, even after the end of apartheid. Mortgage bonds have been called up for as little as R18 owing at the time execution was sought.[65]

Second, the process of obtaining judgment was almost entirely administrative. The questions before a court were whether there had been a default, and whether the acceleration clause had been properly engaged. Once those questions had been answered in the affirmative, an order for special execution followed, no matter the size or circumstances of the default or the impact of execution on the mortgagor. Execution itself was said to be an "executive matter which is dealt with by the Registrar",[66] that did not require court oversight. In 1994, the Rules of Court changed to take the process of both judgment and execution beyond the purview of judges altogether. Rule 31(5) of the Uniform Rules of Court was amended to allow the whole of the process of judgment and execution to take place outside the courtroom. So long as the mortgagee provided a certificate of the balance

---

[63] In reality, it is not, because of the way mortgage repayments are structured. The debtor repays the capital portion of the loan much more rapidly towards the end of the term of the loan. At the beginning of the loan term, interest takes up almost all of the repayment instalments.

[64] Although unlikely to be ratified by a court, for the reasons set out in Chapter 6.

[65] *ABSA Bank v Ntsane* 2007 (3) SA 554 (T).

[66] *Gerber v Stolze* 1951 (2) SA 166 (T) at 171E.

outstanding, a registrar of the court – not a judge – could grant both judgment and leave to execute against the mortgaged property.[67]

The third and final part of the process was the sale of the property at public auction supervised by the Sheriff. This process was exhaustively regulated in order to ensure that the auction itself was transparent and well-advertised. Non-compliance with the formalities prescribed for advertising and conducting a sale generally invalidated it.[68] Be that as it may, the sale was not a forum in which the substantive fairness of the execution could be raised. Only payment of the judgment debt was generally enough to stop it altogether.

Accordingly, the process of execution against mortgaged residential property before the advent of the Constitution was swift, could follow on the smallest default, and presented few opportunities for the mortgagor to raise the substantive fairness of the sale of their home. The common law had no way of weighing the proportionality between the size and circumstances of the default, and the consequences to the debtor of the execution of the debt. As a result, it placed mortgagees (usually very large banks) in an extremely powerful position, and made the prompt exercise of the right to execute much more likely.

3.3   THE CONSTITUTIONAL PROPERTY AND HOUSING RIGHTS CLAUSES

The adoption, in 1996, of the final Constitution's property and housing rights clauses significantly revised the conceptual foundation of the common law of property. Latent within the final text of sections 25 and 26 of the Constitution was the potential to substantially restructure the common law hierarchies of power outlined above. At stake in the negotiations leading to the interim and final Constitutions' property and housing rights clauses was the very structure of post-apartheid property law.

The importance of the negotiations about the property clause was widely acknowledged at the time. It was sometimes argued that part of the task of post-apartheid legal reform was to free the common law of apartheid-era interference, and restore it to a pristine, non-racial state. It was less often acknowledged that the internal hierarchies created and reproduced by the common law of property had a number of affinities with the racial division of power, and are problematic for any attempt to build a just society after the end of apartheid. [69]

On the other hand, André van der Walt wrote of nothing less than the common law tradition itself being placed "on trial".[70] Van der Walt criticised what he called the "private law conceptualism"[71] inherent in property law, which depended on

---

[67] *Gundwana v Steko Development CC* 2011 (3) SA 608 (CC) para 53.

[68] *Messenger of the Magistrate's Court, Durban v Pillay* 1952 (3) SA 678 (A), although the decision in *Todd v First Rand Bank Ltd and Others* [2013] 3 All SA 500 (SCA) was somewhat more equivocal.

[69] A van Aswegen (ed) *The Future of the South African Private Law* (1994) quoted in A van der Walt (note 32 above [tradition on trial]) 170, said that "the apartheid era cannot be attributed to Roman Dutch law – the blame must be placed squarely on the shoulders of the ruling minority who introduced the system of apartheid by way of legislation, and there were primarily enable to this end by the doctrine of parliamentary sovereignty which derives from English constitutional law".

[70] A van der Walt (note 32 above).

[71] Ibid 178.

establishing abstract networks of rights and obligations between subjects and objects, or persons and things. These networks gave rise to "a strict conceptual logic deriving from what is seen as abstract, universal and essential relations between the concepts themselves". Accordingly, the right of ownership, for example, is defined in the abstract as including the right to exclude others from access to the owner's property. The argument begins and ends within the very concept of ownership itself: "persons without any rights at all … have no chance against an owner: in fact, they are never even allowed to enter the race".[72]

Van der Walt argued for an approach to property law that replaced this dry conceptualism with a more supple structure of legality that emphasises "property as a medium of participation in the collective".[73] This is, in other words, a conception of property law that is capable of reconciling competing historical and social needs and claims about property. It involves appreciating the nature and context of these needs and claims, deliberating between them and choosing an outcome that gives due recognition to each of the interests at play in a particular case. It is to be emphasised that this implies no particular set of values or outcomes. It simply suggests a process of reasoning that recognises what is really at stake in property disputes, rather than applying a pre-existing, ossified logic to a set of facts, and generating a rights-holding "winner", and a "loser" whose status is marked by the absence of rights.

A separate but related debate influenced the negotiation of the constitutional text itself. The National Party (NP) and the African National Congress (ANC) were the two most important players in the multi-party negotiating process that led to the interim Constitution, and in the Constituent Assembly, that led to the adoption of the final Constitution. The ANC was "anxious that a constitutional right to property should not impede legislative programmes addressing the massive disparities of wealth which were the legacy of apartheid".[74] The NP aimed to entrench constitutional protection for property holdings as they stood at the end of apartheid. The NP also wanted to ensure that state interference with existing property holdings was always subject to compensation. Its initial position was to demand that even taxes that had what it called a "confiscatory effect", should be constitutionally invalid.[75]

In relation to socio-economic rights, the major fault line, both between the ANC and the NP, and within the ANC itself, was between those in favour and those against entrenching socio-economic rights in the Constitution at all. The NP was naturally hostile to constitutionalising rights that might require the redistribution of resources. The ANC was split. On the one hand, there were those who felt that socio-economic rights would hamper the implementation of large-scale redistributive programmes, and interfere with the state's ability to prioritise and allocate resources

---

[72] Ibid 179.

[73] Ibid 204.

[74] M Chaskalson "Stumbling Towards Section 28: Negotiations Over the Protection of Property Rights in the Interim Constitution" (1995) 11 *South African Journal on Human Rights* 222, 223.

[75] Ibid 223.

between different social programmes by granting too much power to judges in the resource allocation process. On the other, some believed that entrenchment of socio-economic rights would enable the state to be held accountable for implementing those programmes, and that, in a country as unequal as South Africa, there was little point in entrenching civil and political rights without also entrenching socio-economic rights.[76]

The final text of the property clause and the housing rights clause was, in effect, a compromise struck between these competing concerns. The text of both clauses also represents a move away from abstract conceptualism in legal reasoning to a socially situated, value-based approach to reconciling the interests at play when enforcing property and housing rights. The text of both provisions represents a move towards "a politically infiltrated legality".[77]

Section 25(1) of the final Constitution protects existing property holdings, but also subjects those holdings to regulatory interference, so long as this is non-arbitrary and is authorised by law. The state can, therefore, non-arbitrarily deprive a person of a property right or interest, without compensation, so long as the deprivation is not so extensive as to amount to an extinction or expropriation of property rights. In that event, section 25(2), (3) and (4) of the Constitution provides that the expropriation must be for a public purpose or in the public interest, and must be accompanied by just and equitable compensation determined by agreement or calculated by a court, having regard to a range of factors, only one of which is market value. Section 25(5) and (6) of the Constitution authorises a legislative programme of land reform. Section 25(7) provides for a process of restitution of specific land to individuals and communities deprived of it as a result of racial discrimination after 19 June 1913. Section 25(8) affirms that the property clause cannot "impede" the state from taking steps toward land and water reform aimed at addressing historical racism.

Section 26(1) of the Constitution grants a general right of access to adequate housing. Section 26(2) places a positive obligation on the state to take reasonable legislative and other measures within its available resources to achieve the progressive realisation of that right of access. The positive obligation to take "reasonable steps" towards implementing the right, rather than providing housing on demand, mollified those who were worried about authorising too much judicial interference in social programmes, or entrenching entitlements that were not practically realisable. Section 26(3) provides a right against arbitrary eviction. The core aspect of that right is a prohibition of evictions from, or demolitions of,

---

[76] C Heyns and D Brand "Introduction to Socio-Economic Rights in the South African Constitution" (1998) *Law Democracy and Development* 2 153. See also D Davis "The case against the inclusion of socio-economic demands in a bill of rights except as directive principles" (1992) 8 *South African Journal on Human Rights* 475.

[77] F Michelman "Possession v Distribution in the Constitutional Idea of Property" (1987) 72 *Iowa Law Review* 1319, 1340.

a person's home unless a court order is first obtained. A court, before granting an eviction order, must consider "all the relevant circumstances".

What matters here is not the detail of the text itself. It is the structure and purpose of both provisions. In the first place, section 25(1) of the Constitution is a particularly finely balanced provision. On the one hand, it freezes property holdings as they were on the day the Constitution came into effect.[78] On the other, however, it creates the conditions under which they can be radically interfered with, through a legally authorised, non-arbitrary deprivation. The extensive claims of ownership to power and exclusivity are checked by the authorisation of legislative action to deprive a person of property in a manner that is non-arbitrary.

The Constitutional Court has held that "non-arbitrary" deprivation is one that takes place with "sufficient reason" and in a procedurally fair manner. Whether there is "sufficient reason" for a deprivation is a highly context-sensitive inquiry, which embraces, all at once, the purpose of the deprivation, the means used to achieve that purpose, the relationship between the means and the purpose, and the proper evaluative standard against which that relationship should be tested.[79]

Expropriation is also permitted "for a public purpose" or "in the public interest", subject to compensation. The range of purposes and interests that can animate a deprivation or an expropriation are not hard to guess: they are at least the social and economic reform purposes listed in the remainder of section 25, and the legislation enacted to give effect to it.

The advancement of the section 26 right to housing is also a purpose for which deprivation may well be permitted, but section 26(3) of the Constitution itself authorises a deprivation of property, to the extent that it allows a court to decline to grant an eviction order, once it has taken into account the relevant circumstances. Although the Constitution does not spell out what circumstances are "relevant", the language of "relevant circumstances" is at least supple enough to encompass the social consequences following on eviction. It is precisely these kinds of consequences that the common law rules out.

Accordingly, the Constitution authorises a wide range of interferences with existing common law property rights, while at the same time allowing those rights to subsist so long as action to limit or interfere with them is not actually taken. In determining the scope and limits of that interference, regard is to be had, not to abstract ideas of exclusivity, power and dominium, but to the social purposes and ends spelled out in the Constitution itself. The text of sections 25 and 26 of the Constitution accordingly creates significant potential to reshape property rights in a manner that would conform to a more just and inclusive society. It subjects common law presumptions about who should have power over property, and about whose rights should prevail in property disputes, to searching questions about the

---

[78] 4 February 1997.

[79] *First National Bank of SA Ltd t/a Wesbank v Commissioner South African Revenue Service 2002* (4) SA 768 (CC) para 100.

underlying hierarchies of power that the common law serves, and whether those hierarchies are consistent with pressing social concerns.

Accordingly, respect for individual "dominium", power and control over property was, at least formally, replaced as the foundation of property law. In its place was put, a multi-faceted framework which recognises existing common law rights, concepts, and relationships, including those implicating dominium, but which also creates the space in which those concepts, rights and relationships can be interrogated, tested and reshaped to serve social needs. Sections 25 and 26 themselves outline what those social needs are, and provide for the passage of legislation to spell them out in greater detail. This new framework is inimical to the strict hierarchies of power established by the common law of property.

Far from merely asserting itself, ownership would now have to justify its claims by reference to a plurality of ends specified in the Constitution itself. In practice, though, the ideological hold of the common law of property, dominium and ownership over the judiciary, the legal profession and academia has not been easy to break. But sections 25 and 26 of the Constitution set the stage for a radical rethinking of common law presumptions insofar as they apply to processes of dispossession – processes of eviction, extinction of leasehold tenure, and processes of execution against residential property. In the remaining chapters of this book, I map out the ways in which these processes have been reshaped through constitutional reform, and constitutionally mandated legislation. This reshaping has opened up new spaces of agency and action that were foreclosed by the hierarchies of power sanctioned by the common law. As a result of the creation of these new spaces, those previously subject to the exercise of the ownership power are not only back in "the race", as André van der Walt might have put it, they are making at least some of the rules.

CHAPTER FOUR

TAKING BACK THE LAND

The relationship between the property and housing rights clauses of the Constitution took some time to begin working itself out. It was, in fact, ten years before the Constitutional Court found the opportunity to state what ought to have been obvious the moment the text was settled. In *Port Elizabeth Municipality*,[1] the Constitutional Court pointed out that the Constitution "imposes new obligations on the courts concerning rights relating to property not previously recognised by the common law. It counterposes to the normal ownership rights of possession, use and occupation, a new and equally relevant right not arbitrarily to be deprived of a home".[2] In place of the hierarchies between rights holders and unlawful occupiers set up by the common law, the Constitution recognises that "[t]he expectations that ordinarily go with title could clash head-on with the genuine despair of people in dire need of accommodation".[3] The Constitution accordingly recognises that the question of whether an unlawful occupier ought to be dispossessed of land is fraught with social complexity and potentially devastating human cost.

For that reason, section 26(3) of the Constitution places the burden of considering whether and when a person is to be evicted from their home on the courts. In discharging their duty to decide whether to evict a person from their home, the courts must avoid establishing "a hierarchical arrangement between the different interests involved, privileging in an abstract and mechanical way the rights of ownership over the right not to be dispossessed of a home".[4] Rather, a court must "balance out and reconcile the opposed claims in as just a manner as possible, taking account of all the interests involved and the specific factors relevant in each particular case".[5]

This flattening of the common law hierarchy between owner and unlawful occupier displaced hundreds of years of legal authority. It widened the range of admissible facts in a residential eviction application from an almost purely conceptual determination of the parties' common law rights, to the full range of social benefits and burdens that might follow on the grant or refusal of an eviction order. Accordingly, "[t]he way in which the courts are to manage the process has … been left as wide open as constitutional language could achieve, by design and not by accident, by deliberate purpose and not by omission".[6]

In this chapter, I will argue that this opening up of legal and conceptual space brought with it a wide social and economic space in which poor and vulnerable

---

[1] *Port Elizabeth Municipality v Various Occupiers* 2005 (1) SA 217 (CC).
[2] Ibid para 23.
[3] Ibid.
[4] Ibid.
[5] Ibid para 18.
[6] Ibid para 22.

people could, and did, act to expand the range of options available to them to secure their tenure and enhance their access to adequate housing.

Initially, the Constitution was understood to make no more than a decidedly procedural commitment to simply considering the needs of poor people before an inevitable eviction takes place. But that has now matured into a process through which people under threat of eviction can obtain substantive housing and tenure rights. These rights materialise through the practical or formal legal recognition of unlawful occupiers' rights to resist eviction altogether, and to remain where they are, or they arise in accommodation provided by the state in the aftermath of an eviction, or they take the form of limitations on the state's capacity to coerce a particular set of development solutions. The social consequences of these rights for the people who acquire them are the enhancement of their agency, through the widening of the range of life choices that are realistically open to them. In this way, the reform of eviction law has led to real social change.

In the first part of this chapter, I consider the text of section 26 of the Constitution, the legislation enacted to give effect to it, and the trajectory followed in the courts' at first uncertain, and then fairly confident, strides towards providing substantive tenure protections to people under threat of eviction. The lower courts were initially reluctant to embrace the impact of the Constitution and subordinate legislation on common law relationships between owners and unlawful occupiers. It was not until the Constitutional Court's decisions in *Grootboom*[7] and *Port Elizabeth Municipality*,[8] and the Supreme Court of Appeal's decision in *Modderklip*,[9] that the consequences of the new constitutional dispensation were clearly understood. Even then, it took the follow-up litigation that eventually led to the Constitutional Court's decision in *Blue Moonlight*[10] to complete an outline of the new substantive protections available to poor people who face homelessness on eviction.[11]

In the second part of the chapter, I set out the respects in which these protections have widened the range of options available to poor and vulnerable people seeking to secure a home. I show how the development and implementation of these protections support my overall argument about property law's role in social change. I show that eviction applications have precipitated a range of new claims on behalf of unlawful occupiers. Some of these claims have been to the provision of alternative accommodation, with secure tenure, at an appropriate alternative location, with guarantees of dignified living conditions. *Dladla*[12] is the most noteworthy decision in which claims of this type have been recognised. In that case, the Constitutional Court struck down rules, imposed in a shelter provided to people relocated after

---

[7] *Government of the Republic of South Africa v Grootboom* 2000 (1) SA 46 (CC).

[8] *Port Elizabeth Municipality v Various Occupiers* 2005 (1) SA 217 (CC).

[9] *Modder East Squatters v Modderklip Boerdery (Pty) Ltd; President of The Republic of South Africa v Modderklip Boerdery (Pty) Ltd* 2004 (6) SA 40 (SCA).

[10] *City of Johannesburg v Blue Moonlight Properties* 2012 (2) SA 104 (CC).

[11] But even before *Blue Moonlight*, the amendments to eviction law brought about by the Constitution and the PIE Act were being talked of as a "new paradigm". See S Liebenberg *Socio-Economic Rights: Adjudication under a Transformative Constitution* (2010) 268–311.

[12] *Dladla v City of Johannesburg* 2018 (2) SA 327 (CC).

an eviction, that separated families by gender and locked people out of the shelter during daylight hours.

Other claims have involved unlawful occupiers asserting a right to remain on the land from which they stand to be evicted, either by taking advantage of state-sanctioned informal settlement upgrading schemes or the expropriation and development of the land by the state. These claims have attained recognition in the High Court decision in *Fischer*,[13] where the court dismissed an eviction application while at the same time directing the state to take steps to purchase or expropriate the unlawfully occupied land. It was also the end result of the eviction claim considered in *Modderklip*, where initially invaded land ended up as a state-subsidised housing project.[14]

A further set of claims has evolved from organised shack dwellers seeking to resist coercive development practices. The court in *Melani*[15] reviewed and set aside a decision to evict an informal settlement and directed the City of Johannesburg to take steps to upgrade the settlement *in situ*.[16] In *Abahlali 1*[17] the Constitutional Court upheld a challenge by an organised shack-dwellers' movement to a provincial statute which enabled provincial authorities to order the institution of eviction proceedings by municipalities and private landowners. In *Abahlali 2*[18] the High Court set aside an order meant to restrain the unlawful occupation of 1 538 properties within the jurisdiction of the eThekwini Municipality, by authorising the police at the municipality to evict the occupants of the land without further court oversight.

Where the common law of property supported the prompt expulsion of unlawful occupiers, the new eviction law presents opportunities to have the unlawfulness of their occupation addressed in a meaningful manner.[19] Instead of being a quick and easy remedy for the common law owner, eviction now potentially triggers a discursive process in which the patterns of disadvantage to which unlawful occupiers have long been subjected can be addressed through the exploration of the occupiers' needs and vulnerabilities, and welfare-enhancing solutions can be explored. Where the common law destroyed agency, the new constitutional eviction law enhances it.

---

[13] *Fischer v Unlawful Occupiers* 2018 (2) SA 228 (C).

[14] K Tissington "Demolishing Development at the Gabon Informal Settlement: Public Interest Litigation Beyond Modderklip?" (2011) 27 *South African Journal on Human Rights* 192, 200.

[15] *Melani v City of Johannesburg* 2016 (5) SA 67 (GJ).

[16] L Chenwi "Legislative and judicial responses to informal settlements in South Africa: a silver bullet?" (2012) 23 *Stellenbosch Law Review* 540 contrasts vigorous judicial intervention to protect informal settlers' rights with weakly implemented state housing policy.

[17] *Abahlali baseMjondolo v Premier of KwaZulu-Natal* 2010 (2) BCLR 99 (CC).

[18] *MEC for Human Settlements and Public Works of the Province of KwaZulu-Natal v Ethekwini Municipality; In re: Abahlali BaseMjondolo and Others v Ethekwini Municipality* [2015] 4 All SA 190 (KZD).

[19] See M Pieterse "Development, the right to the city and the legal and constitutional responsibilities of local government in South Africa" (2014) 131 *South African Law Journal* 149 for the manifold ways in which the new eviction law might spur on the struggle for a "right to the City" by focusing attention on the constitutional and statutory obligations of local government.

4.1   THE DEVELOPMENT OF A CONSTITUTIONALISED LAW OF EVICTION

4.1.1   Section 26(3) of the Constitution, the PIE Act and the Common Law

At common law, a landowner was entitled to an eviction order if he could prove his ownership of the land, and the fact of occupation of that land by the occupier.[20] Where the owner acknowledged that the occupier was in occupation in terms of a valid lease agreement or some other legal right, the owner bore the onus of proving that the right of occupation had been validly terminated. If the owner did not acknowledge that any such right had ever existed, it was for the occupier to prove the existence of the right, and the fact that it had not been validly terminated. Where the occupier could prove a right to hold against an owner, the owner could not evict, unless and until that right had been terminated. If the existence of a right of occupation could not be proved, then the owner was entitled to evict the occupier, irrespective of the fairness of the eviction, or its wider social impact. This, as André van der Walt put it, embodies a "normality assumption" at the core of the common law of property: "that a landowner is entitled to exclusive possession of his or her property – this is what is considered the 'normal state of affairs' that will most likely be upheld in the absence of good reason for not doing so".[21]

However, the common law "normality assumption" fails to capture the tension between sections 25(1) and 26(3) of the Constitution. On the one hand, section 25(1) provides some security to existing property rights, in that "[n]o one may be deprived of property except in terms of a law of general application, and no law may permit arbitrary deprivation of property". Section 26(3) of the Constitution nonetheless provides that "[n]o one may be evicted from their home, or have their home demolished, without an order of court made after considering all the relevant circumstances. No legislation may permit arbitrary evictions". The problem inherent in reconciling these two rules is to distinguish between arbitrary deprivation of property, on the one hand, and arbitrary eviction on the other. The occupation of land without the permission of the owner is clearly a "deprivation" of property, in the sense that the occupation limits the owner's right to exclusive use and possession of that land. However, when does unlawful occupation itself amount to an *arbitrary* deprivation of property? How far, and to what extent, is an owner required to tolerate unlawful occupation before it becomes "arbitrary deprivation"?

Section 26(3) of the Constitution requires an owner to tolerate the unlawful occupation of their land as the home of another until a court has been able to consider the circumstances relevant to whether an eviction order should be granted and, if it is to be granted, to actually make the order. However, the Constitution does not make explicit what the "relevant circumstances" are, and how these circumstances bear on the grant or refusal of an eviction order. It does not say whether or when an eviction order can be refused. It does not say whether the relevant circumstances can

---

[20] *Graham v Ridley* 1931 TPD 476. This part of the chapter draws upon my article "Breaking the Tie: Evictions from Private Land, Homelessness and a New Normality" (2009) *South African Law Journal* 126. Some phrases and information have been taken verbatim from that article.

[21] A van der Walt *Constitutional Property Law* (2005) 412.

be identified by a court, or whether they must be sourced in common law authority or existing legislation.[22] Section 26(3) of the Constitution's open text is capable of being read restrictively, as having no impact on the common law at all.[23] Equally available, however, is a much broader reading of section 26(3): that "it gives the courts an equitable discretion to refuse to order eviction, even where under the common law the plaintiff would have been entitled to such an order, or a discretion to stay the eviction order".[24]

This ambiguity was initially seized upon to conclude that the Constitution did not really add anything to the common law. All it did was constitutionalise the common law procedural protections that had always been available. The common law remedy of the *mandament van spolie* had always protected a person from the dispossession of land without their consent, a court order or statutory authority.[25] The open text of section 26(3) of the Constitution was taken for vagueness, and courts were quick to draw the conclusion that no significant amendment of the common law was intended. In *Brisley*[26] the Supreme Court of Appeal decided that section 26(3) of the Constitution only entitled a court to consider circumstances that were *"regtens relevant"* (or "legally relevant") to the grant or refusal of an eviction order. The legally relevant circumstances are those set out in legislation or identified by the common law. A court accordingly only had a broad discretion to grant or refuse an eviction order if that discretion was specifically conferred by statute or some other legal authority. It did not in itself confer a general discretion on a court to decide whether an eviction is fair.[27] Accordingly, except when repealed or altered by statute, the common law prevails, together with its associated hierarchies of power, and its tendency toward the dispossession of those without rights.

The decision in *Brisley* is hard to reconcile with the Constitutional Court's characterisation of the impact of section 26(3) on the common law in *Port Elizabeth Municipality*, with which I opened this chapter. The best view is that *Port Elizabeth Municipality* at least impliedly overruled *Brisley*. However, because of the virtually contemporaneous passage of legislation to give effect to section 26(3) of the Constitution, it has never been necessary for a court to expressly address the inconsistency between the two decisions.

The relevant legislation consists of a suite of enactments that deal with a range of situations. The Extension of Security of Tenure Act 62 of 1997 (ESTA) and the Land Reform (Labour Tenants) Act 3 of 1996 (LTA) protect the rights of people who live and work on farms. The Interim Protection of Informal Land Rights Act 31 of 1996 (IPILRA) gives statutory recognition to the customary law rights of occupiers of land under held customary title or administered by traditional leaders,

[22] A van der Walt *Property in the Margins* (2009) 119–120.

[23] T Roux "Continuity and Change in a Transforming Legal Order: the Impact of Section 26(3) of the Constitution on South African Law" (2004) 121 *South African Law Journal* 466, 473.

[24] G Budlender "Justiciability of the Right to Housing: The South African Experience" in S Leckie (ed) *National Perspectives on Housing Rights* (2003) 207, 210–12.

[25] *Nino Bonino v De Lange* 1906 TS 120.

[26] *Brisley v Drotsky* 2002 (4) SA 1 (SCA).

[27] Ibid paras 42–3.

and to long term occupiers of some urban land. The Prevention of Illegal Eviction from, and Unlawful Occupation of Land Act 19 of 1998 (PIE) protects "unlawful occupiers": those who reside on land without any right to do so, and without the consent of the owner or person in charge. This legislation specifies, where necessary, the scope of a court's discretion when exercising its powers under section 26(3) of the Constitution in respect of each class of occupier to which the legislation applies. The Constitution applies indirectly through these enactments. Accordingly, whether or not *Brisley* is correct, the primary resources for a court considering whether to order an eviction are these pieces of legislation, not the Constitution itself.

I will concentrate here on the PIE Act. The other pieces of land reform legislation set out above work by affording statutory recognition to rights that are not known or fully protected in the common law (IPILRA and the LTA) or by deeming an occupier to have had consent or legal rights of occupation in a way that the common law would have precluded (in the case of ESTA). What sets the PIE Act apart is the statutory protection it accords to people without any rights at all. The ESTA, IPILRA and the LTA all implicitly accept the hierarchy implied by the creation and extinction of rights, by granting rights to protected occupiers and then specifying the conditions necessary for their termination. The PIE Act is different because it grants no rights at all. It regulates and limits the power of a common law owner to exercise the right of eviction ordinarily associated with ownership.[28]

A secondary reason for concentrating on the PIE Act is that it is by far the most influential piece of post-apartheid anti-eviction legislation. Although PIE Act protections are much weaker than those contained in the ESTA, the IPILRA and the LTA, PIE Act jurisprudence in the higher courts developed earlier, and tended to influence the major decisions interpreting ESTA, which came later. Constitutional Court decisions in *Scribante* and *Claytile* both rely explicitly on, and apply law developed in, PIE Act decisions that came before them.[29]

The decision to concentrate on the PIE Act also leaves out the fledging constitutional idea of "meaningful engagement".[30] The main reason for this is

---

[28] In limited circumstances, ESTA does this too, but only once the statutory rights it affords have been terminated in accordance with the statutory procedure it sets out.

[29] See *Daniels v Scribante* 2017 (4) SA 341 (CC) paras 53 and 175 to 185. See also *Baron v Claytile* 2017 (5) SA 329 (CC) paras 41 to 44. The cross-pollination between PIE and ESTA has not always had the happiest results. In *Claytile*, the Constitutional Court borrowed heavily from PIE Act jurisprudence which did not obviously apply to the ESTA occupiers before the court in that case. In deploying PIE Act jurisprudence to conclude that those ESTA occupiers were entitled only to the provision of "reasonable" alternative accommodation (para 40), Pretorius AJ all but ignored ESTA's intricate definition of "suitable alternative accommodation". That definition entitles ESTA occupiers to accommodation that reaches far more exacting standards than mere "reasonableness". The result was that the *Claytile* occupiers were evicted to temporary accommodation more than 30 kilometres away from their homes. Had the ESTA definition of "suitable alternative accommodation" been applied, the eviction could not have been justified, and the occupiers would have stayed where they were, or would at least have been given alternative accommodation of a far higher standard.

[30] "Meaningful engagement" is a judge-made pre-litigation step to be taken where an organ of state seeks an eviction order. The first systematic treatment of the idea of meaningful engagement came in *Occupiers of Olivia Road Berea Township and 197 Main Street, Johannesburg v City of Johannesburg* 2008 (3) SA 208 (CC). Although the idea was said first to have been developed in the *Port Elizabeth Municipality v Various Occupiers* 2005 (1) SA 217 (CC) decision (see *Olivia Road* para 12), the phrase does not appear in that decision, which does no more

that the idea of "meaningful engagement" does not, in itself, disrupt or interfere with common law power relationships. Shorn, as it is, of any sense of the power relationships at play between putatively "engaging" parties, "meaningful engagement" brings nothing to an understanding of how agents within a pre-existing common law power relationship will act, if at all, to disrupt that relationship. The idea of "engagement" is normatively empty without an account of the ends to which engagement should reach, and whose interests should receive priority in the process. While meaningful engagement might encourage parties to negotiate a way to reach a pre-defined goal, it cannot generate that goal in the context of clashing legal powers, unequal power relationships and opposed social interests.[31]

A second reason for leaving meaningful engagement beyond the scope of my analysis is that, despite being invited to do so, the Constitutional Court has so far declined to order meaningful engagement between private property owners and unlawful occupiers.[32]

In most eviction proceedings, the valid termination of rights is the end of the line. By contrast, the PIE Act applies to and explicitly protects "unlawful occupiers": those who occupy land "without the express or tacit consent of the owner or person in charge" and "without any other right in law".[33] It requires that eviction proceedings against unlawful occupiers be brought in compliance with strict procedural requirements, and grants a court a wide-ranging discretion to refuse to enforce an owner's right to evict if to do so would not be "just and equitable". The procedural protections involve strong limitations on the circumstances under which urgent eviction proceedings can be brought,[34] and strict requirements that the occupiers concerned be given "written and effective notice" of the eviction proceedings to be brought.[35] Non-compliance with either of these requirements can lead to the refusal of an eviction order.[36]

More suggestive, however, are the substantive provisions of PIE. Owners cannot obtain an eviction order unless a court is satisfied that it is "just and equitable" to grant one, having taken to account all the relevant circumstances, including the

---

than mention, in passing, the desirability of "respectful face-to-face engagement" (see *Port Elizabeth Municipality* para 39).

[31] In exploring "engagement's potential" Brian Ray makes a related point. He suggests that engagement can create space for "legalized accountability" that holds state institutions to programmatic standards that they have set for themselves. It cannot, however, generate those standards, and the Constitutional Court's turn to "engagement" must be read as a deliberate step away from doing so. See B Ray *Engaging with Social Rights: Procedure, Participation, and Democracy in South Africa's Second Wave* (2016) 353–366. S Liebenberg "Remedial Principles and Meaningful Engagement in Education Rights Disputes" 2016 (19) Potchefstroom Electronic Law Journal 2, attempts to help resolve the normative emptiness of meaningful engagement by setting out four remedial principles to guide its implementation. L Chenwi "Democratising the Socio-Economic Rights Enforcement Process" in H Garcia, K Klare and L Williams (eds) *Social and Economic Rights in Theory and Practice: Critical Inquiries* (2015) 178 also seeks to give substantive content to the concept by drawing on the institutional and normative resources provided by notions of participatory democracy.

[32] *Occupiers of Saratoga Avenue v City of Johannesburg* 2012 (9) BCLR 951 (CC) paras 16 to 18.

[33] Section 1 of the PIE Act.

[34] Section 5 of the PIE Act.

[35] Section 4(2) of the PIE Act.

[36] *Cape Killarney Property Investments (Pty) Ltd v Mahamba* [2001] 4 All SA 479 (A) para 18.

manner in which the land was occupied, the duration of occupation, and the needs of the elderly, the disabled, and households headed by women. Where land has been occupied for more than six months, the availability of alternative accommodation must also be taken into account.[37] This explicit conferral of an equitable discretion on courts dealing with eviction proceedings upended the common law hierarchies. It meant that a court could refuse an eviction order if it was not fair to grant one, and could also consider a wide range of social consequences that might follow upon an eviction order.

Nonetheless, the courts received the PIE Act tepidly. In *Ndlovu*,[38] the Supreme Court of Appeal confirmed the PIE Act's broad scope, but sought to downplay its substantive impact. The main issue in *Ndlovu* was whether the PIE Act applied to "holders over": those who had once occupied land lawfully, but whose rights to occupy were terminated, including, for example, tenants or mortgagors whose homes had been sold to recover the mortgage debt. It was argued that the PIE Act was not intended to apply to holders over, but only to those who took occupation of land unlawfully: "squatters" in the true sense. The argument appeared to be that the word "occupies" in section 1 of the PIE Act referred only to the act of taking occupation of property, and not to the state of being in occupation. Accordingly, the PIE Act only applies to occupiers whose presence on the land was unlawful from the outset, not to holders over.

The Supreme Court of Appeal rejected this argument. It held that there was nothing in the legislation that supported such a confined meaning, and that the plain meaning of the word "occupies" clearly applies to both someone whose occupation was unlawful from the outset and someone whose occupation later became unlawful.[39] The Supreme Court of Appeal also accepted that a broader reading of the legislation was preferable to give full effect to section 26(3) of the Constitution.[40]

The court was nonetheless at pains to read down the substantive impact of the PIE Act on common law. In the first place, the court held that the PIE Act did not authorise a court to embark on an investigation into whether an eviction order would be just and equitable. Unless the occupiers turned up to court, and disclosed circumstances that might convince a court to refuse or attenuate an eviction order, a court is bound to grant one.[41] Moreover, the Supreme Court of Appeal held that the effect of the PIE Act is not to expropriate "the landowner and PIE cannot be used to expropriate someone indirectly and the landowner retains the protection of section 25 of the Bill of Rights. What PIE does is delay or suspend the exercise of the landowner's full proprietary rights until a determination has been made whether it is

---

[37] Section 4(6) and (7) of the PIE Act.
[38] *Ndlovu v Ngcobo; Bekker and Another v Jika* 2003 (1) SA 113 (SCA).
[39] Ibid para 11.
[40] Ibid para 16.
[41] Ibid para 19.

just and equitable to evict the unlawful occupier and under what conditions. Simply put, that is what the procedural safeguards provided for" in section 4 envisage.[42]

While this passage accepts, on its face, that a court might theoretically refuse an eviction order, it expresses some doubt about whether this could in practice happen. It appears to assume that a common law owner's rights will always, ultimately, prevail.

That assumption was at the core of how other courts, at least initially, tended to deal with section 26(3) of the Constitution and the justice and equity test under the PIE Act. The decision in *Betta Eiendomme*[43] illustrates not just the courts' early preference for the view that section 26(3) and the PIE Act had not done much to limit common law rights of eviction, but also their often brazen hostility to any suggestion to the contrary. In an intemperate decision on an application to evict a holder-over, Flemming DJP reaffirmed the common law position that it is the owner "only who is entitled to possession except insofar as [the owner's] own acts burden that right".[44] He went on to hold that the object of section 26(3) of the Constitution was to protect only people with rights of ownership, occupation and use against politically motivated evictions such as those that took place under apartheid in District Six in Cape Town and Sophiatown in Johannesburg. The PIE Act, Flemming DJP decided, "does not cover cases of ordinary trespass, whether in the form of squatting or holding over or otherwise".[45] Section 26(3) is in any event "of vertical application" only, and did not apply to eviction applications between private owners and occupiers of their land.[46] Accordingly, Flemming DJP held, section 26(3) of the Constitution had no impact on the right of ownership. Like an "inflatable ball, ownership still reflates to its full content as and when any burden such as the rights created by tenancy falls away".[47]

Read against this remarkably restrictive interpretation of section 26(3) of the Constitution, the PIE Act appeared, so Flemming DJP held, to do little more than create "a servitude of trespass" which was itself constitutionally suspect. To subject the rights of a common law owner to vindicate their property to considerations of justice and equity meant little more than authorising "theft of land" in breach of the right against arbitrary deprivation of property, itself entrenched in section 25(1) of the Constitution.[48] In any event, no sense of justice or equity could, in Flemming DJP's view, lightly displace the owner's right to vacant possession of their property or, as the judge put it, the right not to be "stuck with the family which you found squatting on your erf".[49] After all, it is not easily possible to conceive

---

[42] Ibid para 17.
[43] *Betta Eiendomme (Pty) Ltd v Ekple-Epoh* 2000 (4) SA 468 (W).
[44] Ibid para 6.2.
[45] Ibid para 7.2.
[46] Ibid para 7.3.
[47] Ibid para 10.1.
[48] Ibid para 7.3.
[49] Ibid para 7.4.

"what right" an unlawful occupier or their children could have against a property owner.[50]

Similar sentiments are expressed in other early decisions. In *Groengras Eiendomme*[51] Rabie J quoted liberally and approvingly from the decision in *Betta Eiendomme* before concluding that the PIE Act does no more than provide procedural protection for unlawful occupiers in the process of the granting and execution of an eviction order. It provides no substantive protection at all, and merely serves to ensure that "an eviction should be effected in such a manner that fairness and human dignity prevail".[52] To extend substantive protection to unlawful occupiers, Rabie J suggested, would be to sanction a right to trespass on the property of another, and encourage land invasions. Section 26(3) of the Constitution and the PIE Act cannot, and ought not, Rabie J held, be read in this way.[53]

These decisions, and others like them,[54] are not just a reaffirmation of the common law hierarchy of power between owner and unlawful occupier. They also evince a failure to comprehend, often expressed in the most strident terms, what sort of consideration could possibly limit an owner's unfettered right to their property. The mere passage of reform legislation was accordingly insufficient to spell out the impact of the balancing exercise now required of courts by section 26(3) of the Constitution and the PIE Act. It would require extensive and wide-ranging interventions from the Constitutional Court and the Supreme Court of Appeal to delineate the new relationships between owners and occupiers the Constitution and the PIE Act had set up.

4.1.2 The Construction of Equity in Eviction Proceedings

If section 26(3) of the Constitution and the PIE Act were ever to mean more than token deliberation before invariably authorising an eviction, then the appellate courts were going to have to say so. Inevitably, fierce competition between the interests of capital, and those of millions of urbanising poor people in need of land, gave the courts ample opportunity to delimit an owner's right to eviction. The first, and most important, of the building blocks towards this delimitation was not a case involving whether to order an eviction under the PIE Act, but an acute housing crisis caused by one.

On 18 May 1999, the Sheriff of Wallacedene, in Cape Town, evicted Irene Grootboom and her 900 neighbours from a shack settlement. Ironically, the land had been earmarked for low-cost housing – just not for them.[55] Once evicted, Ms Grootboom and her neighbours rebuilt makeshift shacks with plastic sheeting on the Wallacedene sports field. Within a week, though, the Cape winter had

---

[50] Ibid para 12.4.

[51] *Groengras Eiendomme (Pty) Ltd v Elandsfontein Unlawful Occupants* 2002 (1) SA 125 (T).

[52] Ibid para 26.

[53] Ibid paras 22 to 24.

[54] For example *Joubert v Van Rensburg* 2001 (1) SA 753 (W) and *Emfuleni Local Municipality v Builders Advancement Services* CC 2010 (4) SA 133 (GSJ).

[55] *Grootboom v Government of the Republic of South Africa* 2000 (1) SA 46 (CC) para 4.

virtually destroyed the plastic sheeting, and the Grootboom community was left homeless once again. Grootboom's attorney wrote to the Oostenberg Municipality and demanded that it provide the community with temporary shelter. The Grootboom community claimed that the municipality was obliged to do this in terms of section 26 of the Constitution. The municipality refused to provide the Grootboom community with any shelter. In response, the community launched an urgent application in the Cape High Court to compel the state to provide the shelter to which they said they were entitled. The High Court held that section 26 of the Constitution did not give the Grootboom community the right to shelter on demand, but found that the community's children had a right, under section 28 of the Constitution, to the provision of shelter immediately. The High Court accordingly ordered the state to provide temporary shelter to all of the children in the Grootboom community and to at least one of each of the children's parents.[56]

The state then appealed to the Constitutional Court.[57] That court's approach was markedly different, largely because the immediate needs of the community had been met by a settlement agreement entitling them to the shelter they initially sought. The Constitutional Court was accordingly at large to pronounce on the proper jurisprudential approach to housing rights claims. In doing so, it held that section 26(2) of the Constitution placed a positive obligation on the state to take steps to provide access to adequate housing.[58] The content of that obligation is to act reasonably to further the objective of progressively realising everyone's right of access to adequate housing.[59] The court emphasised that the duty to act reasonably is context-sensitive,[60] but that, to be reasonable, state action would ordinarily have to meet a number of criteria that the judgment set out.[61]

Two of those criteria are of interest here. The first is that a reasonable housing policy must be comprehensive.[62] Steps taken in terms of the policy must generally prioritise, and should, at the very least, not exclude, those most desperately in need of housing.[63] Accordingly, a housing policy that fails to make provision for, and a state that fails to take steps to assist, people with literally "no access to land, no roof over their heads and who were living in intolerable conditions or crisis situations" does not discharge the duty of reasonableness under section 26(2) of the Constitution.

Secondly, the court addressed the appropriate response to land invasions. The courts in *Betta Eiendomme* and *Groengras Eiendomme* had strongly suggested that the only appropriate response to a land invasion was the prompt eviction of

---

[56] Ibid paras 10 and 11.

[57] *Government of the Republic of South African v Grootboom* 2000 (1) SA 46 (CC).

[58] Ibid para 20.

[59] Ibid para 42.

[60] Ibid para 33.

[61] The "*Grootboom* principles" have been helpfully summarised in S Liebenberg "South Africa's Evolving Jurisprudence on Socio-Economic Rights: An effective tool in challenging poverty?" (2002) 6 *Law Democracy and Development* 159, 171.

[62] *Government of the Republic of South African v Grootboom* 2000 (1) SA 46 (CC) para 40.

[63] Ibid para 44.

the occupiers. The Constitutional Court took a more nuanced approach. Implicit in the decision is a distinction between two types of unlawful land occupation. The first, land invasion proper, is an occupation "for the purpose of coercing a State structure into providing housing on a preferential basis to those who participate". In response to this type of occupation, it may well be reasonable to evict the occupiers without providing an alternative.[64] The second type of occupation is undertaken "by the desperate", who are left homeless as a result of a prior eviction or other housing crisis, and "who are left without any form of assistance with no end in sight". The second type of occupation, while undesirable, is simply the result of housing crises not being adequately addressed through policy and state action.[65] The appropriate response to new land occupations is not a knee-jerk eviction but an early stage intervention aimed at resolving "the difficulty on a case-by-case basis after an investigation" of the occupiers' circumstances.[66] Although the Constitutional Court did not expressly say so, the implication is that this second kind of occupation might well require a response that manages the occupation within acceptable limits, or provides alternatives to the occupiers.

The decision in *Grootboom* ought to have placed owners and the state on notice that the common law approach to unlawful land occupation was in the process of being softened. The suggestions that poor people had an immediate entitlement to have their housing crises addressed through reasonable policy and prompt state action, and that land invasions were not always to be met with a prompt coercive response, had potentially far-reaching implications for owners' rights to exclusive possession of their land. *Grootboom* provided the seeds of a clear and direct answer to the question posed by Flemming DJP in *Betta Eiendomme*. The equitable consideration that might balance an owner's common law right to exclusive possession of his property was the plight of desperately poor people who had occupied his land because they had nowhere else to go.

The state's response to the *Grootboom* decision was to draft and promulgate a new Emergency Housing Policy, which it incorporated into the National Housing Code. The National Housing Code has statutory force through section 3(4)(g) of the Housing Act 107 of 1997. The Emergency Housing Policy provided for municipalities to apply for funding from provincial governments to implement rapid response emergency housing programmes. The policy lists a broad range of emergency housing situations, but applies specifically to persons who "are evicted or threatened with imminent eviction from land or from unsafe building or [who live in] situations where proactive steps ought to be taken to forestall such consequences".[67] The Emergency Housing Policy added an additional dimension to the constitutional and statutory rights of unlawful occupiers. Those who had been, or were about to be, made homeless, had a positive right to the provision of shelter

---

[64] Ibid para 92.
[65] Ibid para 65.
[66] Ibid para 87.
[67] South African Government "Emergency Housing Policy" *National Housing Code* (2004) 8. The Code was substantially revised and updated in 2009, but these requirements were left undisturbed.

by the state. Again, however, much was left unsaid about how this right was to be balanced against the rights of the owner of the land from which occupiers stood to be evicted.

The balance finally struck by the Supreme Court of Appeal in *Modderklip*[68] was profound and far-reaching. Modderklip Boerdery (Pty) Ltd owned a farm in the Benoni area. In May 2000, some of the farm was occupied by a few hundred people who had been evicted from the Chris Hani informal settlement at the edge of Daveyton. Originally, the settlement was no more than 50 shacks. By October 2000, the settlement had grown to 4 000 shacks and 18 000 people. By the time Modderklip obtained an eviction order,[69] there were 40 000 people on its land. The cost of executing the eviction order was more than the occupied land was worth. As a result, Modderklip brought an application to the High Court to compel the state to execute the eviction order at its own cost. The High Court granted the order, holding that the state's failure to assist in giving effect to the eviction order breached Modderklip's right against arbitrary deprivation of property under section 25(1) of the Constitution.[70]

The eviction and the enforcement order were then appealed to the Supreme Court of Appeal, and dealt with together. The Supreme Court of Appeal saw the case for what it was: a headlong clash between an owner's right to vindicate his property, and the occupiers' rights to reasonable state action to protect them from homelessness. "Basic to this case", the court held, was Modderklip's section 25 rights on the one hand, and the occupiers' section 26 rights, on the other.[71] The court first noted that the property owner had a right not to be arbitrarily deprived of the exclusive use and possession of its land. Relying on the Constitutional Court's decision in *Grootboom*, the Supreme Court of Appeal then asserted that the occupiers had a right to shelter on eviction. It asked whether the state had discharged its obligation to take steps to provide shelter to the occupiers "who, on all accounts, fall into the category of those in 'desperate need'".[72] The state had clearly not done so.

That being so, and again relying directly on the *Grootboom* decision, the Supreme Court of Appeal held that the occupiers could not be evicted from the property unless and until the state provided some land to relocate them to.[73] The state's failure to provide that land was, the Supreme Court of Appeal held, itself a breach of Modderklip's property right.[74] The only appropriate relief was accordingly to

---

[68] *Modderfontein Squatters, Greater Benoni City Council v Modderklip Boerdery (Pty) Ltd; President of the Republic of South Africa v Modderklip Boerdery* 2004 (6) SA 40 (SCA).

[69] *Modderklip Boerdery (Pty) Ltd v Modder East Squatters* 2001 (4) SA 385 (W).

[70] *Modderklip Boerdery (Edms) Bpk v President van die RSA* 2003 (6) BCLR 638 (T).

[71] *Modderfontein Squatters, Greater Benoni City Council v Modderklip Boerdery (Pty) Ltd; President of the Republic of South Africa v Modderklip Boerdery* 2004 (6) SA 40 (SCA) para 21.

[72] Ibid para 22.

[73] Ibid para 26.

[74] Ibid para 28.

leave the occupiers where they were, but to compensate the owner for the state's breach of its section 25 property rights.[75]

The *Modderklip* decision was a direct rebuke to the notion that section 26(3) of the Constitution and the PIE Act did not affect the ordinary common law hierarchy between ownership and unlawful occupation. Relying on *Grootboom*, the *Modderklip* decision explicitly linked the right to vindicate land to the sufficiency of the state's efforts to provide emergency housing to the evicted occupiers in need of it. Harms JA, who wrote the *Modderklip* judgment, was later to parse the effect of *Grootboom* in even clearer terms: "[e]viction ... triggers an obligation resting on the [state] to provide emergency and basic shelter" to any affected occupier.[76] Once an owner's right to vindicate his property was linked to the ability of the state to provide alternative accommodation, the "justice and equity" of an eviction under the PIE was bound to come down, in most cases, to whether the eviction would lead to homelessness.

The Supreme Court of Appeal's decision in *Modderklip* was appealed to the Constitutional Court. The Constitutional Court left the Supreme Court of Appeal's remedy intact, but decided the case on a different footing. It located the breach of Modderklip's right in section 34 of the Constitution, the right of access to court, in that the state's failure to provide land meant that Modderklip was unable to execute the eviction order.[77] This did little to alter the basic structure of the Supreme Court of Appeal's decision: an owner's right to vindicate their land was inextricably linked to the social consequences of doing so.

André van der Walt characterised the link as a call for "patience and empathy" in "enforcing property rights to make sure that other, weaker or more marginalised members of society are not treated unfairly in the process".[78] But *Modderklip* went further than that. It demonstrated that the interests protected by the right of access to adequate housing may well, in appropriate circumstances, limit the right of an owner to exclusive possession of his property. This is clearest from the remedy granted in *Modderklip*. It was declared "that the residents are entitled to occupy the land until alternative land has been made available to them by the State or the provincial or local authority".[79] In place of its right to exclusive possession of its property, Modderklip was given compensation.[80] This diminishes the common law principle that an owner is entitled to claim their property anywhere, at any time, from anyone, and replaces it with a personal right to payment of money. This was something much further-reaching than the exercise of patience or empathy. Housing rights were limiting ownership rights. If more evidence of this were needed from

---

[75] Ibid paras 43 and 44.

[76] *City of Johannesburg v Rand Properties* 2007 (6) SA 417 (SCA) para 47.

[77] *President of the Republic of South Africa v Modderklip Boerdery (Pty) Ltd* 2005 (5) SA 3 (CC) para 43.

[78] A van der Walt "The state's duty to protect property owners v the state's duty to provide housing: Thoughts on the *Modderklip* case" (2005) 21 *South African Journal on Human Rights* 144, 159.

[79] *President of the Republic of South Africa v Modderklip Boerdery (Pty) Ltd* 2005 (5) SA 3 (CC) para 68(3)(c).

[80] Ibid para 68(3)(b).

beyond the decision itself, it is that the *Modderklip* occupiers are still present on the land, benefiting from a state-subsidised housing project.[81]

Just before it heard the *Modderklip* case, the Constitutional Court had already confirmed the reach of housing rights in limiting common law ownership rights. It did this through a detailed excursus of the concept of "justice and equity" under the PIE Act. In *Port Elizabeth Municipality*, the court linked the nature and extent of the state's performance of its housing rights obligations with an owner's right to vindicate their property. It also articulated the general rule latent in the *Grootboom* and *Modderklip* decisions: "a court should be reluctant to grant an eviction against relatively settled occupiers unless it is satisfied that a reasonable alternative is available".[82]

Although this did not imply an unqualified constitutional duty on the state to provide alternative accommodation to everyone evicted from their home, it did imply that the general rule is that evictions should not lead to homelessness. Section 26(3) of the Constitution and the PIE Act require a court to decide "case-by-case"[83] what equitable remedy would reconcile the competing interests of owners and occupiers in a way that did not lead to homelessness. Such a remedy would, in practice, involve searching questions about the reasonableness of the steps the state had taken, in terms of section 26(2) of the Constitution, to progressively realise the rights of unlawful occupiers to adequate housing. It would not be enough for the state "to show that it has in place a programme that is designed to house the maximum number of homeless people over the shortest period of time in the most effective way". Such a programme, while going some way to fulfil the state's section 26(2) obligations would not be "determinative of whether and under what conditions an actual [eviction] order should be made in a particular case".[84] The strong implication of this is that an eviction order under PIE is only justified if the state can show that it has the capacity to house any unlawful occupiers who would otherwise be rendered homeless immediately on eviction. If this could not be shown, an eviction order may well be refused.[85]

Nor were "land invaders" to be excluded from judicial protection against homelessness. The decision in *Port Elizabeth Municipality* developed and made explicit the distinction first drawn in *Grootboom* between a land invasion undertaken in a bad faith attempt to secure preferential allocation of permanent housing, and an occupation undertaken by homeless people in emergency circumstances with nowhere else to go. "The term land invasion", the court warned, "must be used with caution", and eviction should not necessarily follow on a land invasion. The court again drew distinctions between different types of unlawful land occupation,

---

[81] K Tissington "Demolishing Development at the Gabon Informal Settlement: Public Interest Litigation Beyond Modderklip?" (2011) 27 *South African Journal on Human Rights* 192, 200.

[82] *Port Elizabeth Municipality v Various Occupiers* 2005 (1) SA 217 (CC) para 28.

[83] Ibid para 31.

[84] Ibid para 29 fn 29.

[85] See, for example, *All Builders and Cleaning Services CC v Matlaila* (42349/13) [2015] ZAGPJHC 2 (16 January 2015), in which an eviction order was refused because of the absence of alternative accommodation.

and suggested that even where there had "been a deliberate and premeditated act culminating in the unlawful invasion and occupation of a large tract of land", there may still be circumstances that justify making an eviction conditional upon the provision of alternative accommodation.[86]

Just how far the inquiry into the reasonableness of the state's housing policies could go is illustrated by the Constitutional Court's decision in *Blue Moonlight*.[87] In that case, a property speculator, Blue Moonlight Properties, purchased a set of garages and industrial workshops behind a block of flats in Berea, Johannesburg. For several years before the purchase, the property had been informally let as residential accommodation to around 100 very poor people, and the property speculator wanted them out so that it could redevelop the property. The occupiers resisted the subsequent eviction application on the basis that an eviction would render them homeless, so no eviction order could equitably be made. They brought an application to join the City of Johannesburg, to stay the eviction proceedings, and to direct the City of Johannesburg to provide them with alternative accommodation in the event that they were evicted from the property.

The City responded to the occupiers' application by saying that it would not provide accommodation to the occupiers because its emergency housing policy (adopted in terms of the *Grootboom* decision) was to only give accommodation to people evicted from dangerous buildings, and not people who faced eviction by an owner who sought no more than to vindicate his property.[88] The occupiers then brought a further application to declare that policy unconstitutional, because it drew an unreasonable distinction between occupiers evicted from dangerous buildings, and those evicted on the basis of a private owner's right to vindicate his property.

The Constitutional Court's decision was the most explicit account yet of the way in which section 26(3) of the Constitution and the PIE Act had limited common law ownership rights. The court placed that limitation on a clear constitutional and statutory footing. It explained that the clashing rights of owners, not to be arbitrarily deprived of their property, and occupiers, not to be arbitrarily evicted, were mediated through section 26(3) of the Constitution and the PIE Act. The court acknowledged that the PIE Act's limitation on an owner's right to vindicate his property was a "deprivation" of property for the purposes of section 25(1) of the Constitution. However, that deprivation was non-arbitrary, because it only limited the right of eviction insofar as a court had determined it was just and equitable to do so.[89] A court-determined, case-by-case limitation on eviction could not be arbitrary. Accordingly, what Flemming DJP and Rabie J criticised as "servitude of trespass" in *Betta Eiendomme* and *Groengras Eiendomme*, the Constitutional Court explained as a non-arbitrary deprivation of property. Property owners simply did

---

[86] *Port Elizabeth Municipality v Various Occupiers* 2005 (1) SA 217 (CC) para 20 fn 22. Read with *Port Elizabeth Municipality v Peoples Dialogue on Land and Shelter* 2000 (2) 1074 (SE).

[87] *City of Johannesburg v Blue Moonlight Properties* 2012 (2) SA 104 (CC).

[88] Ibid paras 79 and 80.

[89] Ibid para 37.

not have the right to vindicate their property anymore, unless it would be "just and equitable" under the PIE Act to do so.

What "justice and equity" require is likely to boil down, in most cases, to whether the unlawful occupiers would be left homeless by eviction.[90] Since unlawful occupiers generally have a right, based on section 26(2) of the Constitution and *Grootboom*, to the provision of emergency shelter, the question of whether the eviction would lead to homelessness is inseparable from the question of whether the state has discharged its obligation to provide emergency shelter. The state is accordingly a necessary party to all eviction proceedings that might lead to homelessness.[91] The state's duty, once joined, is to provide a report setting out what steps it will take to provide alternative accommodation to occupiers whose eviction might lead to homelessness. In assessing that report, a court may interrogate the reasonableness of the position adopted, and require the state to remove unreasonable exclusions or distinctions drawn in it.[92] Ultimately, a court can order the state to provide alternative accommodation whether or not the report says the state can or will do so. The property owner must wait out the period that the state needs to provide the accommodation. The owner must also be, as the court put it, "somewhat patient" in the process.[93] In *Blue Moonlight*, the court ordered an eviction, but made it conditional upon the provision of alternative accommodation. It also declared the City's emergency housing policy unconstitutional to the extent that it excluded people evicted by private landowners from its ambit.[94]

Read together, the *Grootboom*, *Modderklip*, *Port Elizabeth Municipality* and *Blue Moonlight* decisions provide a comprehensive account of the equitable considerations to which an owner's right to exclusive possession of his land is now subject. The right to vindicate land is subject to strong procedural and substantive protections against homelessness for the occupiers. While not amounting to a "servitude of trespass", they do amount to a right not to be made homeless on eviction, an inquiry into the availability of alternative accommodation, and the ability to hold the state to account for its duty to provide emergency housing. If no alternative accommodation is available, an eviction order may be refused, and the owner's right to vindication may be substituted for a right to compensation. If there

---

[90] Ibid para 39. See also *The Occupiers, Shulana Court, 11 Hendon Road, Yeoville, Johannesburg v Steele* [2010] 4 All SA 54 (SCA) para 16 and *Occupiers, Berea v De Wet NO* 2017 (5) SA 346 (CC) para 76.

[91] Ibid para 45.

[92] Ibid para 92.

[93] Ibid para 40.

[94] Ibid para 104. The outcome in *Blue Moonlight* has provoked a variety of critical responses. M Kruger "Arbitrary deprivation of property: an argument for the payment of compensation by the state in certain cases of unlawful occupation" (2014) 131 *South African Law Journal* 328 argues that the *Blue Moonlight* decision fails to strike a proper balance between the rights of owners and unlawful occupiers, in its omission to provide for compensation to be paid for landowners who have to endure a "commercially unbearable" delay while the state provides occupiers with alternative accommodation. D Davis "The Scope of the Judicial Role in the Enforcement of Socio-Economic Rights" in H Alviar Garcia, K Klare and L Williams (eds) *Social and Economic Rights in Theory and Practice: Critical Inquiries* (2015) 197, 202 argues exactly the opposite. He criticises the court for effectively subsidising private property speculators as they knowingly buy up occupied properties expecting the state to pick up the cost of re-accommodating the occupiers.

is alternative accommodation, the owner's right to vindication will be suspended, usually without compensation, until the occupiers can be relocated.

These are substantial inroads into ownership rights. They create spaces in which unlawful occupiers can act to resist, and at the very least delay, the implementation of an owner's rights to exclusive possession of his property. They also create important spaces in which unlawful occupiers can hold the state to account for the performance of its obligations to give effect to their housing rights. What was once an uncomplicated site of repression and exclusion for poor and vulnerable people, has become a site of agency and opportunity.

This site soon became a space for even more ambitious experimentation and success in enhancing the rights of poor people to access urban land and housing. The construction of equity in eviction proceedings created the space for a wide variety of sophisticated housing rights struggles. Not now concerned exclusively with staving off eviction, unlawful occupiers began to demand the right to remain on the land on terms that they would shape for themselves. These new housing rights struggles were the fruits of the spaces the law now provided to unlawful occupiers.

4.2   NEW HOUSING RIGHTS STRUGGLES

These spaces created for poor people by the structured equity inquiry in eviction proceedings were soon exploited to raise new claims to give effect to housing rights more extensive than the right against arbitrary eviction. Even small limitations on an owner's right to evict – a delay in eviction proceedings or the need to obtain an order under the PIE Act before removing a land invader – can create important spaces in which communities can reflect, plan and act to give effect to their needs and aspirations. If communities of the poor are doing more than fighting off constant threats to their occupation, or trying to find another place to live, their ability to make meaningful choices about their development and well-being is enhanced. Where these choices involve the use of the law and engagement with lawyers, the stability of a respite from eviction can enable them to formulate legal and other strategies, and to interact with their legal representatives on terms that are not limited to managing an immediate crisis situation. This often includes deliberation about how to shape the terms and conditions of relocation, and the nature and quality of the alternative accommodation to be provided; how, if at all, it might be possible to strengthen their claims to the land they currently occupy; and how to resist coercive development practices.

Five major decisions illustrate these possibilities. In *Dladla*, a community provided with alternative accommodation after an eviction challenged repressive rules and practices imposed on them in the shelter provided. In *Fischer*, a recently formed informal settlement community resisted an eviction by seeking to engage provisions of the Housing Act 107 of 1997, which empower the state to expropriate unlawfully occupied land. In *Melani* an organised informal settlement community reviewed and set aside a policy decision to relocate it to a greenfield housing project, and compelled the state to develop and implement an informal settlement upgrading project that would allow the community to stay where it was. In *Abahlali 1* and *Abahlali 2*, a shackdwellers' movement resisted repeated attempts by the KwaZulu-Natal provincial government to programme and manage mass evictions of informal settlements across its jurisdiction.

4.2.1 Managing Relocations

Unlawful occupiers have been able to use the spaces provided by structured equity in eviction proceedings to shape the terms of their participation in temporary shelter programmes developed by the state in response to the *Grootboom* decision. In the aftermath of *Blue Moonlight*, the City of Johannesburg had to redesign its emergency housing policy to cater for those evicted by land owners, as well as those it sought to remove from unsafe buildings. This implied a substantial expansion of emergency housing capacity, but the City was unwilling or unable to significantly expand the stock of properties it would make available to house very poor people. Instead, it sought to provide a limited number of places in temporary shelters for people evicted from their homes, and to do so only for a limited period. The plan was that poor people would rotate through emergency housing shelters. A person evicted from their home would be given six months in a shelter to enable them to "transition" from "a state of homelessness to a state of independence". After the end of the six month period, the evicted person would be expected to find their own accommodation and leave the shelter. This transitional model would allow a reduced number of places in emergency accommodation to be provided, because one bed in a temporary shelter would be used by a different person every six months. [95]

The success of this model hinged on the willingness of the occupier concerned to move on after their six-month stay in the shelter came to an end. In reality, however, there was little chance of a person who had been too poor to rehouse themselves on eviction being able to enter the housing market after six months in shelter accommodation. Structural imbalances in the urban housing market that exclude the poor were the very reason that shelter accommodation was required in the first place. These imbalances would not evaporate simply because an evicted person was given six months' respite in a shelter.[96] If, as was overwhelmingly likely, the occupier concerned was still unable to house themselves after six months, then they would either have to be evicted, or be allowed to stay. Eviction proceedings against the occupier would not be successful, because the City would not be able to show that the occupier had alternative accommodation available to them.

Another way would have to be found to encourage shelter occupiers to move on. The City found this in the imposition of a shelter regime designed to compel the shelter occupiers to move on as soon as possible. It split families up into gender-differentiated dormitories, and locked all shelter occupants out during

---

[95] City of Johannesburg, Heads of Argument submitted in *Dladla v City of Johannesburg* 2018 (2) SA 327 (CC) paras 8 and 13.

[96] Nomsa Dladla, Heads of Argument submitted in *Dladla v City of Johannesburg* 2018 (2) SA 327 (CC) para 60.

daylight hours.[97] The purpose and effect of these rules were to coerce shelter occupants to leave as soon as possible, often for accommodation that was just as unsafe and left them just as vulnerable to eviction as the accommodation from which they had been moved to the shelter.[98] Although the stated purpose of the shelter was to provide an agency-enhancing space in which poor people could exercise meaningful choice about access to jobs and other economic opportunities,[99] it was actually experienced as a deeply humiliating space that stifled any attempt by its occupants to choose how to live their lives.[100]

Those of the shelter residents who did not simply move out of the shelter back into an abandoned building or a shack, accordingly decided to challenge the rules as unconstitutional. Ultimately, the Constitutional Court upheld that challenge. It found that the rules imposed by the City were a breach of the constitutional rights to privacy[101] and dignity.[102] The right to privacy, the majority held, entails "a place [the occupants] can call their own to which they can retreat at any time".[103] The right to dignity entitles shelter occupants to the "associative privileges that inhere in and form the basis of a family".[104] The shelter regime fairly obviously extinguished each of these incidents of both rights and were unconstitutional as a result. The City and its service provider that operated the homeless shelter programme on its behalf, were interdicted from applying the regime in future.[105]

The Constitutional Court's decision is an important example of the way in which the new eviction law can affirm the agency of the poor, and facilitate action to enable poor people to craft policies and programmes appropriate to their needs. Apart from affirming the dignity and privacy rights of people in occupation of state-run shelters for the poor, the court's decision also meant that the City would inevitably have to expand the stock of shelter places available to it. The City could not just rotate poor people through a limited number of shelter beds every six months. It had to accept the likelihood that it would have to house poor people evicted from their homes for an indefinite period, at least until it could be demonstrated that they were capable of finding accommodation unassisted.

It is interesting to contrast the Constitutional Court's decision with the Supreme Court of Appeal decision it overturned. The Supreme Court of Appeal appeared to see the shelter regime as an inevitable consequence of the City's service provider's property rights over the shelter. The Supreme Court of Appeal criticised the shelter

---

[97] *Dladla v City of Johannesburg* 2018 (2) SA 327 (CC) para 3.

[98] Nomsa Dladla, Heads of Argument submitted in *Dladla v City of Johannesburg* 2018 (2) SA 327 (CC) para 57.

[99] City of Johannesburg, Heads of Argument submitted in *Dladla v City of Johannesburg* 2018 (2) SA 327 (CC) para 13.

[100] Nomsa Dladla, Heads of Argument submitted in *Dladla v City of Johannesburg* 2018 (2) SA 327 (CC) para 52. See also S Wilson "Curing the Poor: State Housing Policy in Johannesburg after Blue Moonlight" (2014) 5 *Constitutional Court Review* 279, 291.

[101] Section 14 of the Constitution.

[102] Section 10 of the Constitution.

[103] *Dladla v City of Johannesburg* 2018 (2) SA 327 (CC) para 50.

[104] Ibid para 49.

[105] Ibid para 54.

occupants for seeking to impugn these property rights.[106] The Constitutional Court, on the other hand, affirmed that, whatever the arrangements between the City and its service provider were, the associated property rights had to yield to the shelter occupants' rights to housing, dignity and privacy.[107]

4.2.2 Taking Back the Land

Even putative land invaders have been able to turn structured equity to their advantage, by contextualising their unlawful occupation of land within the broader picture of the state's inability or refusal to accommodate poor people through its formal housing programme. The pace of formal housing delivery in South Africa has never been able to remotely match the demand for it, at least for the poorest. In order to register for a state-subsidised house, an applicant must demonstrate that they are a South African citizen or permanent resident, earning less than R3 500 per month, with at least one dependent. In Cape Town, the municipality has registered 350 000 people as being in need of state-subsidised housing within its area of jurisdiction. This registered need is increasing at a rate of approximately 18 000 people per year. The municipality plans to resolve this by delivering formal housing units at a rate of 6 100 per year. Clearly, the housing backlog will never be resolved at this pace of delivery.[108]

The inevitable consequence of failing to meet the demand for housing among poor people in urban areas is widespread unlawful occupation of land. When demand for housing outstrips supply, the cost of housing increases, and those who cannot afford to pay the increased price must leave the housing market and occupy land unlawfully.

It was this process that led one of the largest urban land occupations in recent South African history. Between April 2013 and June 2014, approximately 60 000 people unlawfully occupied vacant land in Philippi, Cape Town. They formed what became known as the "Marikana informal settlement". The land occupation began when a small number of people were evicted from backyard shacks in Lower Crossroads, a neighbouring suburb, and built shacks on the edge of an existing informal settlement that abutted the Marikana land. The Cape Town municipality sought to repel the occupation by repeatedly demolishing the occupiers' shacks, but this did little more than advertise the occupation to an ever-larger number of people in need of somewhere to build a rudimentary home. The municipality soon abandoned any attempt to control the occupation.[109] The owners of the land brought an application to evict the occupiers, but recognised that a court bound by the structured equity principles set out above was unlikely to order the eviction

---

[106] *City of Johannesburg v Dladla* 2016 (6) SA 377 (SCA) paras 23, 24 and 68.
[107] *Dladla v City of Johannesburg* 2018 (2) SA 327 (CC) para 52.
[108] Unlawful Occupiers' Heads of Argument in *Fischer v Unlawful Occupiers* 2018 (2) SA 228 (WCC) para 4.
[109] Ibid paras 10–15.

of 60 000 people. The owners accordingly sought an order in the alternative compelling the state to buy the land at a price calculated as if the land were unoccupied.[110]

The problem was that the kind of buy-out sought by the owners was legally incompetent. The Supreme Court of Appeal ruled in *Dada NO*[111] that it was not permissible for a court to direct an organ of state to purchase property to secure the tenure of unlawful occupiers. The principal reason for this was that there was no enabling statutory or other legal framework authorising such relief.[112]

Realising this, the occupiers in *Fischer* took a different approach. They counter-applied for and were granted relief directing the municipality to exercise its statutory powers to expropriate the occupied land, or explain why it would not do so.[113] The owners adopted this relief in the alternative to their main claim for a buy-out.

The court in *Fischer* upheld the occupiers' argument. It recognised that at the core of the *Fischer* case lies "a historical, social and economic situation that cannot be ignored". The court held that "the occupiers moved to these properties after being evicted from various areas where they lived under desperate conditions. Unlike many other people in Cape Town, these occupiers did not, at the time, and at present, have the luxury of choosing where to settle with their families. They settled on these properties out of desperation".[114] Relying on *Grootboom*, the court held that the occupiers were entitled to a "reasonable" response to their plight. However, the state, and in particular the municipality, had failed to respond reasonably to the occupation from the outset, allowing it to grow rapidly, and quickly to become unmanageable. The result was that the only reasonable response by the time the matter got to court, was for the municipality to acquire the land using its statutory powers under section 9(3) of the Housing Act 107 of 1997.[115]

Section 9(3) of the Housing Act permits a municipality to negotiate to purchase or, if no agreement can be reached, expropriate land required to implement any national housing policy. The emergency housing programme, which is part of the National Housing Code, and which was adopted to comply with the Constitutional Court's decision in *Grootboom*, is such a policy. The court in *Fischer* accordingly ordered the relatively modest remedy of directing the City to exercise its statutory powers, because that was the only reasonable course of action available on the facts of that case. The result for the occupiers, however, was anything but modest, because it had the effect of enabling them to go from putative "land invaders" to having secure tenure, and a place in the national housing programme, in just a few years. Such was the power of structured equity in eviction proceedings.[116]

---

[110] Notice of Motion, dated 27 May 2018, in *Fischer v Unlawful Occupiers* 2018 (2) SA 228 (WCC).

[111] *Ekurhuleni Metropolitan Municipality v Dada NO* 2009 (4) SA 463 (SCA).

[112] Ibid para 14.

[113] *Fischer v Unlawful Occupiers* 2018 (2) SA 228 (WCC) para 196.

[114] Ibid para 161.

[115] Ibid paras 167, 168 and 196. The High Court's decision is currently subject to appeal.

[116] The *Fischer* case was eventually settled on appeal. The City of Cape Town agreed to buy the Marikana land, at a price to be determined through arbitration.

4.2.3   We Won't Move

Making the eviction of unlawful occupiers more difficult has opened up spaces in which occupiers can resist the coercive implementation of state development plans. The Slovo Park informal settlement houses 10 000 people in 3 700 households. It was established in 1995.[117] For many years, multiple representatives and agencies of the state had promised the residents of Slovo Park that the settlement would be upgraded *in situ*, but nothing was ultimately done to give effect to these undertakings.[118] In the end, the City of Johannesburg reneged on all of the promises it and other state organs had made, and announced that the residents of Slovo Park would instead be relocated to a greenfield housing development called Unaville, some 11 kilometres from Slovo Park.[119] The residents of Slovo Park applied to the High Court to review and set aside this decision, and to compel the City of Johannesburg to give effect to the previous undertakings to upgrade the settlement *in situ*. They argued that the failure to honour the promise to upgrade was in breach of the National Housing Code, which made upgrading informal settlements compulsory where it was practically possible.[120]

Relying on the standard of reasonableness established in *Grootboom*, the High Court held that deciding "to relocate the residents without appropriate attention to the requirement as clearly set out in the Housing Code, that relocation is to be considered as a matter of last resort" was unreasonable and therefore unlawful.[121] It held that national policy enabling the upgrading of informal settlements is compulsory where it is reasonable to apply it.[122] The City had given no acceptable reason why it could not apply national policy requiring upgrading, and so was directed to do so.

Abahlali 1 concerned the constitutional validity of the KwaZulu-Natal Elimination and Prevention of Re-Emergence of Slums Act 6 of 2007 ("the Slums Act"). Section 16 of the Slums Act authorised the Member of the Executive Council for Human Settlements to issue a notice requiring any municipality or private land owner to institute eviction proceedings in respect of any informal settlement within its area of jurisdiction. This provision essentially authorised the provincial government to trigger the eviction of unlawful occupiers – potentially every unlawful occupier in the province at once – by administrative fiat.

The Slums Act was marketed as a piece of development-oriented legislation intended to eradicate informal settlements and replace them with newer, safer formal accommodation for their inhabitants. The Act was, however, laden with provisions dealing with eviction and the prevention of unlawful land occupation, and was curiously light on any concrete rights for informal settlers to be upgraded and given housing. Seeing the Slums Act for what it was – a recipe for widespread

---

[117] *Melani v City of Johannesburg* 2016 (5) SA 67 (GJ) para 3.
[118] Ibid para 4.
[119] Ibid para 7.
[120] Ibid para 32.
[121] Ibid para 48.
[122] Ibid paras 32 and 43.

eviction and social exclusion – an organised group of shack-dwellers, *Abahlali baseMjondolo*, challenged the constitutional validity of section 16 of the Act. The essence of the challenge was that the Act was not a reasonable measure to give effect to the right of access to adequate housing, because it was incompatible with the case-by-case approach that structured equity requires.

The Constitutional Court agreed. It accepted that the scheme for compelling eviction set up by the Slums Act was incompatible with what it called the "dignified framework" of structured equity developed for eviction proceedings by the courts over a number of decisions.[123] In particular, the Act violated the principle that evictions should generally be the option of last resort in the implementation of housing development projects. Consensual solutions as to the timing and manner of relocations should ideally be explored and agreed upon through meaningful engagement. The coercive character of section 16 of the Slums Act was at odds with this requirement.[124]

A second attempt to implement a programme of mass evictions was defeated in *Abahlali 2*. In that case, the High Court had to consider the validity of a court order, obtained by the KwaZulu-Natal Provincial Government against the eThekwini Municipality and the Minister of Police, which obliged them to "prevent" unlawful land occupations by "demolishing" any "structures" found on one of 1 538 parcels of land in the Durban area and "removing" the material from which the "structures" were constructed.[125] The organs of state cited in the order argued that the order did not authorise the eviction of people from their homes, but rather the prevention of the occupation of the various parcels of land to which it applied. The Constitutional Court had previously held that the order was, in essence, an eviction order, and the use of words such as "removing material" from land in the order was a mere fig leaf meant to authorise eviction.[126] The High Court held that the order could not stand for that reason, and set it aside. The court also held that the order should be set aside because none of the occupants of the properties to which it applied had been joined to the proceedings in which it was granted.[127]

The effect of each of these cases has been to protect poor people in occupation of the settlements and communities that they have formed for themselves, often preserving fragile but important networks of economic support and social solidarity. Plans to move them, or interfere with their tenure, must be reasonable, consistent with national policy, formulated and implemented in engagement with the communities concerned, and subject to court oversight. These cases have accordingly created a secure space in which communities can continue to deliberate about and act to

---

[123] *Abahlali baseMjondolo v Premier of KwaZulu-Natal* 2010 (2) BCLR 99 (CC) para 122.
[124] Ibid para 113.
[125] *MEC for Human Settlements & Public Works of the Province of Kwazulu-Natal v Ethekwini Municipality and Others; Abahlali baseMjondolo and Others v Ethekwini Municipality* [2015] 4 All SA 190 (KZD) para 13.
[126] *Zulu v eThekwini Municipality* 2014 (4) SA 590 (CC).
[127] Ibid paras 23 to 27.

further their own development interests, rather than having what is thought to be good for them being imposed by the state from the outside.[128]

4.3   CHANGED SPACES

Under the common law, the expulsion of poor people from their homes was assumed to be a natural and appropriate consequence of the enforcement of property rights. The only way that poor people could resist this was by acquiring such rights themselves. However, almost by definition, poor people are unable to bargain for property rights on the open market, and the state has, as yet, proven unequal to the task of redistributing such rights to the poor. The common law therefore has little to offer them.

The realignment of property relationships through structured equity has, however, opened up wide spaces in which unlawful occupiers are able to deliberate, reflect and make a broad range of claims for more dignified accommodation, stronger tenure rights and less coercive development policies. It has done so by opening property law itself up, by making it much more sensitive to the range of social needs it has to meet, by providing the space in which those needs can be deliberated over, and by constructing new principles of law that balance the rights of property owners against the justified claims of those without common law rights.

It is the creation of this space that has led to widespread social change for thousands, perhaps millions, of unlawful occupiers in South Africa. Where before the common law defined their fate with dreadful certainty, structured equity allows the imagination of new alternatives and the recognition of new rights to give effect to them.[129]

---

[128] It is, perhaps, in this sort of space, where the ends of development are clearly defined, and the right of the occupiers to remain has been secured, that meaningful engagement may have some potential to foster emancipatory development processes.

[129] In M Langford "Housing Rights Litigation" in M Langford, B Cousins, J Dugard and T Madlingozi (eds) *Socio-Economic Rights In South Africa: Symbols or Substance?* (2014) 187, 222 Malcolm Langford affirms that housing rights litigation has opened a "state-centric housing model to the voices and demands from the bottom". I would argue that this has been achieved by making it virtually impossible to remove a community of poor people from land lawfully without revising housing delivery plans to accommodate them elsewhere. Structured equity has forced the state to accommodate the poor in its planning processes. This is one example of the way in which the law has reshaped the spaces in which agency has exercised. Arguably, at the same time as it has enhanced the agency of the poor, structured equity has placed increased demands on the state's planning processes.

CHAPTER FIVE

JUST LETTING

The Constitution and the PIE Act brought unlawful occupiers some legal recognition, where the common law supplied them with none. But the interaction between sections 25 and 26 of the Constitution also subjected pre-existing common law relationships to constitutional control.

In the case of landlord and tenant relationships, before the advent of the Constitution, "the only clogs inhibiting a lessor's common law power" were those "expressly legislated". Nonetheless, "the Constitution has fundamentally changed the setting within which the rights of lessors and lessees stand to be evaluated. Constitutionalism has wrought significant changes to [these] private law relationships".[1] It has done this in two ways. First, it has influenced the way in which common law contractual remedies between landlord and tenant are developed and applied.[2] Secondly, it has authorised the passage of legislation to comprehensively balance and regulate the interests of landlords and tenants in residential settings.[3]

In the same way that the PIE Act applies to and regulates relationships between property owners and unlawful occupiers, the Rental Housing Act 50 of 1999 has transformed the field of residential letting, by accounting for and regulating a wider range of interests than were recognised by pre-constitutional statutory interventions. At the same time, it has tended to recognise and give effect to tenants' interests in a way that the common law did not. The landlord and tenant relationship, especially in residential settings, is inherently unequal, at least so long as the demand for property to let exceeds the supply of it.[4] The terms of this inequality are hardwired into common law principles that regulate the actions of either party to give effect to their interests.

At the core of the landlord–tenant relationship in residential settings are three sets of tenants' interests. First, there is the interest of tenants in organising and associating with each other to correct the economic power imbalance between tenant and landlord. In the same way that employees form unions, tenants form tenants' associations. Secondly, there is the interest tenants have in being able to withhold rent to compel a landlord to perform their obligations. Withholding may involve, for example, reducing rental payments when the landlord has failed to supply services to a dwelling, or failed to perform necessary maintenance. Thirdly, there is the tenant's interest in curbing excessive rent increases, where a landlord's

---

[1] *Maphango v Aengus Lifestyle Properties* 2012 (2) SA 531 (CC) para 31.
[2] *Mpange v Sithole* 2007 (6) SA 578 (W).
[3] Through the passage of the Rental Housing Act 50 of 1999.
[4] "Tenant Protection" WA Joubert (ed) *The Law of South Africa* (1986) volume 26 para 373.

expectations of financial returns on his property exceed the returns the tenant can reasonably supply with increased rental payments.

In each of these areas, the common law either does not recognise or account for the tenant's interests, or is structured in a manner that makes it difficult for a tenant to give effect to them. First, the common law offers no specific protection for a tenant's right to organise. Such protection that might be available from the common law depends on being able to convince a court that the exercise of a landlord's contractual rights in a way that seeks to stifle tenant organisation (by for example terminating the lease of a tenant leader)[5] is contrary to public policy. Secondly, the right to remit rent can easily be contracted out of.[6] Where it is not, there is some confusion about whether the common law requires the tenant to be able to liquidate the amount remitted, or pay the full rent in advance, and claim a remission in separate proceedings. The approach taken in *Pilco*[7] was that a tenant is only entitled to remit rent when the amount to be remitted is capable of "prompt ascertainment". The approach in *Thompson*,[8] however, was that a tenant could remit rent and then raise the *exceptio non adempleti contractus* as a defence to any claim for specific performance. Clearly, the value of being able to remit rent to a residential tenant lies in its tendency to encourage a landlord to fulfil their maintenance obligations. This purpose is blunted if a tenant has to pay in full and claim a remission of rent later in separate proceedings, particularly if a tenant cannot afford to institute the proceedings necessary to do so. Thirdly, the common law has no way of ascertaining a fair and reasonable rent. The rent payable is whatever the landlord can bargain for on the open market. Where market conditions favour the landlord (as they almost always do), what the tenant can reasonably afford tends to play little to no role in rent determination.

The dominant position of the landlord in residential settings has long been recognised. Some form of tenant protection legislation has been enacted in South Africa since the First World War.[9] Historically, it has tended to focus on controlling rent increases, and limiting the range of circumstances under which a lease can be brought to an end.[10] The advent of the Constitution, however, saw the end of rent control legislation. In its place was substituted the Rental Housing Act 50 of 1999, a supple and wide-ranging piece of legislation that did much more than regulate the rent payable and conditions of termination of a lease. The Act substituted the strict and narrow limitations on landlords' powers under rent control with a broad

---

[5] As was attempted, unsuccessfully, in *Fernflat Share Block (Pty) Ltd v Willemse* [2019] ZAGPJHC 345 (3 October 2019).

[6] *Tudor Hotel Brasserie & Bar (Pty) Ltd v Hencetrade 15 (Pty) Ltd* (793/2016) [2017] ZASCA 111 (20 September 2017) para 22.

[7] *eThekwini Metropolitan Unicity Municipality v Pilco Investments CC* (320/06) [2007] ZASCA 62 (29 May 2007). This and the previous cited case concern the letting of commercial property, but the common law draws no general distinction between commercial and residential leases.

[8] *Thompson v Scholtz* 1999 (1) SA 232 (SCA).

[9] The Tenants Protection (Temporary) Act 7 of 1920 extended First World War measures that controlled the price of rental housing.

[10] Rent Control Act 80 of 1976.

set of regulations which sought to set out the overall scheme of landlords' and tenants' rights and interests, and provide an adjudicative apparatus within which those rights could be reconciled case by case. This apparatus appears in the form of nine provincial Rental Housing Tribunals that, within the broad limits set by the Rental Housing Act itself, exercise an equitable jurisdiction to resolve individual landlord and tenant disputes.

In this chapter, I argue that the Tribunals have constituted important spaces in which poor and vulnerable tenants have been able to reshape the landlord and tenant relationship, by resisting unfair or excessive rent increases or attempts to profiteer through the imposition of "service charges", by preventing landlords' efforts to stifle tenant organisation, and by asserting the right to remit rent in response to a landlord's failure to deliver a dwelling fit for occupation. Freed of the strict conceptualism of the common law, the Tribunals have become important resources for tenants, although they have not always delivered unambiguously pro-tenant outcomes.

First, I deal with the legislative scheme set up by the Rental Housing Act, and the Unfair Practice Regulations made in terms of it. In particular, I examine the statutory rights afforded to landlords and tenants by the Act, the manner in which the Act regulates the Tribunals' dispute resolution and remedial process, and the way in which the Act was initially received and interpreted by the courts. Secondly, I consider a range of Rental Housing Tribunal decisions in which tenants have been able to assert important rights not to be subjected to unfair practices by landlords. Finally, I argue that, although the Rental Housing Tribunals have had important agency-enhancing effects for tenants, they have yet to establish a coherent, equitable jurisprudence. New courts and tribunals, such as the Rental Housing Tribunal, tend to experiment with their new jurisdiction, and take time to develop a structured re-balancing of the relationships they are supposed to regulate. Even basic heuristics in decision-making can take time to develop. In the meantime, courts and tribunals tend to use the normative resources most conveniently to hand to determine matters that come before them, without developing a substantive account of the purpose of the jurisdiction they exercise. This places limits on their capacity to bring about a sustainable rebalancing in landlord and tenant relationships.

5.1   THE RENTAL HOUSING ACT AND REGULATIONS

5.1.1   *The Rent Control Act*
Until the Rental Housing Act 50 of 1999 repealed it, the Rent Control Act 80 of 1976 governed landlord and tenant relationships in respect of "controlled premises". Controlled premises constituted a much wider range of property than rental housing, and included "any dwelling, garage, parking space or business premises".[11] The two primary objectives of the Rent Control Act were to limit rent increases, and to narrow the range of circumstances under which a landlord was permitted to terminate a lease.

---

[11] Section 1 of the Rent Control Act 80 of 1976.

Both of these objectives served the fundamental purpose of staving off gentrification, and ensuring a stable supply of low-cost rental housing, at least for white people. Rents were fixed at the rate charged on or before 1 April 1949,[12] but higher rents could be charged with the consent of a Rent Board,[13] or if they constituted recovery of a cost which fell into the Rent Control Act's definition of a "reasonable rental". A reasonable rental was a rental sufficient to provide a landlord with an 8.5% annual return "on the value of the buildings and the land", and to defray a range of other costs associated with the letting of property, including, for example, costs associated with maintenance, the employment of staff and the payment of rates and taxes.[14] Rent Boards could investigate and adjudicate complaints about unreasonable rentals,[15] or consider and grant applications for rent increases in a manner consistent with the Rent Control Act's definition of a "reasonable rental".[16]

The Rent Control Act also limited the lessor's right to terminate the lease and evict a tenant from rental housing. Grounds for terminating a lease were limited to non-payment of rent, material damage to the rented property caused by the lessee, the lessee causing a nuisance, the property being required for use by a local authority, the property being required for the lessor's personal occupation, the lessee being an employee of the lessor, whose employment has come to an end, or the renovation or reconstruction of the property. The lease could not otherwise be terminated, unless the lessor could convince a court that there was some other good reason to do so.[17]

Not surprisingly, the Rent Control Act contained few provisions protecting tenants against discrimination.[18] Nor did it protect the right to associate, or deal in any systematic way with unfair lease provisions. It did not provide specific remedies for tenants whose landlords had failed to effect maintenance. It was a narrow and idiosyncratic piece of legislation that failed to capture the full range of landlord and tenant interests that required regulation. Much was left to the common law, and the inherent inequality that the common law permitted.

5.1.2   The Rental Housing Act

Rent control fell out of vogue in the 1980s and 1990s. Riding the wave of market-led social policy implemented across the world in those decades, landlords argued that rent control diminished the supply of rental housing property, and that fixing the price of rental housing stifled competitive practices that would increase the quality and availability of such housing.[19] At the same time, section 26(2) of the Constitution required the state to take legislative measures to promote access to adequate housing. Stimulating the supply of rental housing, for those who could

---

[12] Section 6.

[13] Section 1, definition of "reasonable rental".

[14] Section 8.

[15] Section 13.

[16] Section 14.

[17] Section 28.

[18] Section 45 did make it unlawful for a lessor to refuse to let a dwelling to someone with children.

[19] For a comparative review of rent control legislation see S Maas "Rent Control: A Comparative Analysis" (2012) 15 *Potchefstroom Electronic Law Journal* 41.

afford it, would assist the state in meeting housing demand, and allow it to devote resources to subsidised housing for those not able to afford rent.

In the context of rapid urbanisation at the end of apartheid, it was particularly important that something be done to widen the availability of rental housing. It was equally important to ensure that rental housing was made available without discrimination on an equitable basis. A sound conflict management mechanism was also necessary, both to deal with complaints of discrimination, and to deal with disputes about rent increases, which frequently led to rent boycotts under apartheid.

The Rental Housing Act 50 of 1999 was the state's effort to meet all of these needs. The Act places the state under an obligation to take defined steps to promote rental housing by adopting a national policy framework with the objective of doing so.[20] It also empowers the Minister of Human Settlements to introduce a rental housing subsidy programme.[21] Section 4 of the Act enshrines a tenant's right not to be discriminated against in letting practices[22] and a right to privacy during the period of the lease.[23] Section 4 also sets out a series of landlords' rights, including the right to rental payments; the right to recover rent from the tenant; and the right to claim compensation for damage to rental housing property.[24] Section 5 of the Act creates a right to a written lease for a tenant, and a series of standard terms that a lease is deemed to include whether or not it is reduced to writing.

The linchpin of the Rental Housing Act is the concept of an "unfair practice". Section 1 defines the concept as "any act or omission by a landlord or a tenant in contravention of this Act", or somewhat circuitously, as "any practice prescribed as a practice unreasonably prejudicing the rights or interests of a landlord or tenant". Unfair practices other than contraventions of the Act, are prescribed by regulations made by the MEC for Human Settlements in each Province.[25] The landlord's right to terminate a lease is only effective if it does not constitute an unfair practice.[26] The allegation that an unfair practice has been committed is the jurisdictional trigger for a complaint to one of the provincial Rental Housing Tribunals.[27] Sections 6 to 12 of the Act deal with the establishment, composition, membership, staffing and functioning of the Tribunals.

Section 13 of the Act deals with complaints to the Tribunals, and by doing so, it effectively delineates their jurisdiction. Complaints must be founded on an allegation of an unfair practice, but section 13(2) and (3) of the Act endows the Rental Housing Tribunal with wide-ranging investigative and mediatory powers to find facts, and to ripen a dispute to the point at which the nature of an alleged unfair

---

[20] Section 2.

[21] Section 3.

[22] Section 4(1).

[23] Section 4(2) and (3).

[24] Section 4(5).

[25] See, in particular, the definition of the word "prescribed" in section 1, and the Gauteng Unfair Practice Regulations, *Provincial Gazette Extraordinary* 124 Notice 4004 of 2001, 4 July 2001 (Gauteng Unfair Practices Regulations, 2001).

[26] Section 4(5)(c). See also *Kendall Property Investments v Rutgers* [2005] 4 All SA 61 (C).

[27] Section 13(1).

practice can be defined and adjudicated upon. The Tribunal may take evidence about the nature and existence of an unfair practice,[28] and appoint inspectors to find facts and give evidence in relation to them. Sections 13(3) and 14 of the Act also envisage that the Tribunal will be supported by a Rental Housing Information Office in performing its fact-finding and adjudicative functions.

The Tribunal's remedial powers may be exercised if it is "of the view" that an unfair practice has been committed.[29] Once that view has been formed, the Tribunals may direct that the Act be complied with, refer an unfair practice for investigation to another body having jurisdiction, or "make any other ruling that is just and fair to terminate any unfair practice" including a ruling to "discontinue overcrowding, unacceptable living conditions, exploitative rentals or lack of maintenance".[30] The Tribunals may also interfere with the rent agreed between the parties, and determine a different rent if they so choose. In doing so, the Tribunals must consider the norms, standards, incentives and other measures introduced by the Minister in his rental housing policy framework, prevailing economic conditions of supply and demand and the need for a "realistic return" for investors in rental housing.[31] Tribunals may also make costs orders, issue spoliation orders, attach property and grant interdicts.[32] Tribunals may not make eviction orders.[33]

The Tribunal's jurisdiction to make rent determinations is hobbled by the Minister's failure to adopt a rental housing policy framework to which it can have regard.[34] The scope of the Tribunals' powers are, however, significantly enhanced by provincial government regulations that define an extensive array of "unfair practices". The Gauteng Unfair Practice Regulations, 2001, for example, deal with a wide range of matters of mutual interest between landlord and tenant, including provisions of leases. The Regulations specifically outlaw most exclusion clauses, meaning that neither landlord nor tenant can contract out of rights of action, or specific common law remedies, such as the right to remit rental.[35] They guarantee the right to form and participate in a tenants' association.[36] The Regulations also deal with duties of maintenance and repair,[37] rental payments,[38] processes for managing

---

[28] Section 13(2) and (3).
[29] Section 13(4).
[30] Section 13(4).
[31] Section 13(5).
[32] Section 13(12).
[33] Section 13(14).
[34] The policy framework required by section 2(3) of the Act has not been promulgated.
[35] Regulation 3(3)(b) and (c).
[36] Regulation 3(3)(d).
[37] Regulation 6.
[38] Regulation 7.

tenants' rights during renovations,[39] protections against unlawful eviction,[40] house rules[41] and charges for municipal services.[42]

Perhaps most far reaching are the "general" provisions.[43] These contain general protections against unfair discrimination (in every aspect of the landlord and tenant relationship, not just in letting decisions).[44] They prohibit "oppressive or unreasonable conduct" by either party.[45] They import a duty of good faith in dealings between landlords and tenants.[46]

The unfair practice regime is accordingly comprehensive, far-reaching and supple. It superimposes itself over the contract that parties enter into,[47] and substantially pushes that contract into the background. It provides a framework within which to infuse landlord and tenant relationships with equity and fairness. It constitutes a significant departure from either the common law or the rent control regime. The Rental Control Act concerned itself with setting rents and limiting evictions, and very little else. The common law depends on the parties to make rules for themselves. Often, because of inherent inequalities of bargaining power, that boils down to the imposition of the will of the landlord through a standard form contract. The Rental Housing Act and Unfair Practice Regulations, however, create substantial space for tenants to assert rights, to protect themselves against unfair or unlawful reprisal for doing so, and to level the playing field with the landlord, no matter what the contract says.

5.1.3   The Rental Housing Act in Court

The courts did not initially greet this substantial revision of the common law position with much enthusiasm. In *Mpange*[48] the Rental Housing Act and Regulations were ignored altogether in favour of the indirect application of the Constitution through the common law. In that case, 113 people lived in a disused warehouse in Jeppestown.[49] The warehouse had been subdivided with bricks to create "a warren of boarded-up rooms"[50] for residential accommodation. All 113 tenants had to share two toilets, meaning that parts of public areas of the building had been used as places to urinate. Refuse was not collected. The tenants had to share a single water tap. There was exposed electrical wiring throughout the building.[51] The tenants paid between R450 and R900 to fund the construction of each of their

---

[39] Regulation 8.
[40] Regulation 9.
[41] Regulation 11
[42] Regulation 13.
[43] Regulation 14.
[44] Regulation 14(1)(a).
[45] Regulation 14(1)(d).
[46] Regulation 14(3).
[47] *Maphango v Aengus Lifestyle Properties* 2012 (3) SA 531 (CC) para 51.
[48] *Mpange v Sithole* 2007 (6) SA 578 (W).
[49] Ibid para 5.
[50] Ibid para 31.
[51] Ibid para 29.

brick rooms[52] and R420 per month per room for rent. The lease had apparently not been reduced to writing. The tenants paid rent in cash directly into the landlord's bank account and then presented their deposit slips to the building caretaker as proof of payment.[53] The tenants approached the court in person, making a number of complaints about the building, which centred upon the fact that they paid rent to live in these substandard conditions, but their landlord, the putative purchaser of the property, was not paying municipal rates and taxes necessary to supply the property with water and electricity, [54] and could not prove that he actually owned the property.[55] The facts underlying these complaints were not seriously disputed by the landlord.[56]

This was a classic case of slumlording. The landlord had clearly committed several unfair practices in breach of the Rental Housing Act and the Gauteng Unfair Practice Regulations, 2001. However, the judgment in *Mpange* does not engage the provisions of the Act or the Regulations at all. Instead, the case was construed as a claim for specific performance of a landlord's contractual obligations to maintain the property, coupled with a claim for remission of rent.[57] The court reviewed various common law authorities that debated whether an order of specific performance on a claim to maintain rental property could be granted[58] and whether a tenant was entitled to claim a remission of rent while in occupation of the rented property, and how that remission should be calculated.[59] In the end, despite expressing the strong *prima facie* view that the Constitution required the common law authorities to be read to permit a court to order a landlord to effect maintenance, the court ultimately decided that it would be "inappropriate" for it "to be overly interventionist" by ordering specific performance, because there was insufficient particularity on the evidence before it about what form of maintenance and repair was required.[60] The court instead ordered a reduction in rent, and directed the landlord to carry on providing the same services as he did at the point the case against him was instituted.[61]

The court in *Mpange* was clearly animated by a desire to provide some relief to the residents. It is apparent from its decision that the court felt hobbled by the common law's tendency to limit relief that might be advantageous to a tenant, such as an order to perform maintenance and a reduction in rental. The problem is that it defaulted to the common law without considering the constitutionally authorised legislation that actually applied to the dispute. It is hard to resist the conclusion that the court would have felt less constrained in its approach had it considered the

---

[52] Ibid para 6.
[53] Ibid para 5.
[54] Ibid para 7.
[55] Ibid para 11.
[56] Ibid para 30.
[57] Ibid para 35.
[58] Ibid paras 36 to 47.
[59] Ibid paras 64 to 74.
[60] Ibid paras 81 and 82.
[61] Ibid para 89.

content and application of the Rental Housing Act and Gauteng Unfair Practice Regulations, in terms of which the case, and the remedy, was an easy one. The nature of the maintenance required could have been ascertained by a rental housing inspector, and compliance with an order to effect maintenance could have been supervised by a Rental Housing Information Office. A rent determination, in terms of section 13(5), could have been made. The common law's controversies and potential deficiencies need not have been considered at all. The complaint might have been resolved through mediation. Just as the courts in early PIE Act cases appeared to lack the imaginative resources to see beyond the common law hierarchies of power between owners and unlawful occupiers, the court in *Mpange* found it difficult to see the dispute before it in anything other than ordinary common law terms, even though it was obviously keen to break free of the constraints that implied.

Even where the Rental Housing Act was placed before them and specifically relied upon, the courts' reception of it could be chilly. In *Maphango*[62] the Supreme Court of Appeal had to consider the effect of the Act on a lessor's entitlement to terminate a lease for the sole purpose of tripling the rent. The appellants were 18 lessees of a block of flats called Louwliebenhof in Braamfontein, Johannesburg. The block was originally one of seven buildings included in a pilot project of the Gauteng Department of Housing to provide subsidised flats in the inner city of Johannesburg to people who would not ordinarily be able to afford them. The project was a mixed-income development. Some of the lessees were to be provided with subsidised accommodation, and enhanced security of tenure, such that their leases could not be terminated without their consent so long as they continued to pay a low rent, that could not be escalated beyond a small increment every year.[63] Others, though not subsidised, and not given the contractual tenure protections afforded to the subsidised tenants, were also part of the scheme. They were provided with housing at a rent that was higher than the subsidised tenants, but which was still more affordable than the rent they would have to pay for similar accommodation on the open market.[64]

The scheme eventually came to an end and Louwliebenhof was sold on to Aengus Lifestyle Properties. Aengus wanted to run the building on purely commercial terms. Aengus gave the appellants a choice: agree to rent increases of at least double, or leave the property. When the appellants refused to do either, but continued paying their rent in terms of their lease agreements, Aengus terminated their leases on notice and sued for their eviction. The High Court evicted all of the appellants, save for the two whose leases were at the will of tenant.[65] The appellants appealed. One of the arguments raised on appeal was that the rent increases Aengus sought to impose were so exploitative that they constituted unfair practices within the meaning of section 1 of the Act. Because section 4(5)(c) of the Act only permitted

---

[62] *Maphango v Aengus Lifestyle Properties (Pty) Ltd* 2011 (5) SA 19 (SCA).
[63] Ibid para 35.
[64] Ibid para 6.
[65] Ibid para 2.

Aengus to terminate the appellants' leases "on grounds that do not constitute an unfair practice",[66] the termination was ineffective, and the eviction order was wrongly granted.

The way in which the Supreme Court of Appeal dealt with that argument appeared to presume that the Rental Housing Act did little to affect common law rights. It held, firstly, that the termination of a lease could never constitute an "unfair practice" in terms of the Act, because the word "practice" in the Act did not mean "unacceptable conduct by the landlord on an isolated occasion" such as the termination of a lease, but "incessant and systemic conduct by the landlord which is oppressive or unfair". Termination of a lease "could not therefore qualify as a practice".[67] In any event, the termination of the leases could not, so the Supreme Court of Appeal held, be "unfair" because a landlord "is not a charitable organisation" and was perfectly within its rights to evict a tenant to be able to extract a higher rental.[68]

Had this decision been upheld, the capacity of the Rental Housing Act to effectively regulate landlord and tenant relationships in the interests of fairness would have been substantially diminished. If the termination of a lease could never amount to an unfair practice, then the application of the unfair practice regime could be avoided simply by evicting any tenant that complained about unfair treatment. It is hard to conclude that the Supreme Court of Appeal could have intended that result, but such was the consequence of the interpretation of the Act it adopted. In addition, the Supreme Court of Appeal appeared to accept, more or less as a natural consequence of ownership,[69] the right of a landlord to terminate a lease in order to extract from incoming tenants whatever rent the market would bear. This, too, was at odds with the text and the purpose of the Act, which provides for a multi-factor test to be applied to determine rents on a case-by-case basis. Market conditions and the right to a return on investments in rental housing property are part of the determination, but they are not the only considerations to be taken into account.

Ultimately, the Supreme Court of Appeal's decision was overturned. When the *Maphango* case reached the Constitutional Court, the majority of the judges were prompt to ascertain the application of the Rental Housing Act and the extent to which it had altered common law relationships.[70] The unfair practice regime set up by the Act is "superordinate".[71] The "statutory scheme it sets up does not stop at contractually agreed provisions, and conduct in reliance on them. It goes beyond them".[72] In defining an unfair practice as something that unreasonably interferes with landlords' and tenants' rights and "interests", the Act means to apply itself to "all factors bearing upon the well-being of tenants and landlords. It encompasses the benefits, advantages and security accruing to them".[73] For these reasons, any

---

[66] Section 4(5)(c).
[67] *Maphango v Aengus Lifestyle Properties (Pty) Ltd* 2011 (5) SA 19 (SCA) para 34.
[68] Ibid para 25.
[69] Ibid para 30.
[70] *Maphango v Aengus Lifestyle Properties* 2012 (3) SA 531 (CC).
[71] Ibid para 51.
[72] Ibid para 53.
[73] Ibid para 52.

conduct touching on a matter of mutual interest to a landlord and a tenant in the context of the landlord and tenant relationship could be an unfair practice, provided that it met the definitional requirements specified in the Act or Regulations. This included a single act on an isolated occasion, including action to terminate a lease.[74]

The Constitutional Court did not ultimately decide whether the particular termination in the *Maphango* case constituted an unfair practice.[75] It held that the statutory scheme set up by the Rental Housing Act assigned that function to the Gauteng Rental Housing Tribunal. So long as a complaint about an unfair practice is not predated by other proceedings in a court, the Tribunal must determine the complaint, even if a landlord subsequently institutes eviction proceedings.[76] The Constitutional Court accordingly stayed the eviction and referred the matter back to the Gauteng Rental Housing Tribunal.[77] The complaint was eventually settled. The landlord decided not to enforce the rent increase, and the eviction application against the tenants who appealed to the Constitutional Court was withdrawn.

The Constitutional Court's decision in *Maphango* finally established, some 13 years after it was passed, that the Rental Housing Act had subsumed common law landlord and tenant relationships into a broad field of equity and fairness, at least insofar as these relationships involved rental housing property. In doing so, the Act opened up spaces, opportunities and resources to tenants that neither rent control legislation nor the common law could realistically offer. In the Rental Housing Tribunals, it also established an accessible institutional apparatus through which the unfair practice regime could be enforced, and placed considerable breaks on a landlord's recourse to litigation if the regime was engaged by a tenant. It was in the arenas set up by the Tribunals that tenants could begin to act.

5.2   THE TRIBUNALS IN ACTION

To appreciate the scope and current limits of the Rental Housing Tribunals as spaces in which tenants can act to assert and give effect to their rights and interests, I now consider a series of cases in which the Tribunals have exercised their powers in ways that would be inconceivable under a common law regime. I begin with two cases involving rent determinations, where the Tribunals have interfered with the core term of any rental housing agreement: the rent agreed upon. I then consider the case of one community's multiple interactions with the Gauteng Rental Housing Tribunal over a number of years in matters that were not primarily concerned with the determination of rent. These cases demonstrate the spaces opened up to poor people by the unfair practice regime the Tribunals administer, and the ability of the poor to act in these spaces to resist gentrification. However, they also demonstrate

---

[74] Ibid paras 56 and 57.

[75] Brian Ray locates this decision in what he calls the Constitutional Court's habit of "deep proceduralisation" of socio-economic rights. By referring the case to the Tribunal, the court avoided engaging with how, substantively, the Act might balance interests between landlords and tenants. See B Ray *Engaging with Social Rights: Procedure, Participation and Democracy in South Africa's Second Wave* (2016) 164.

[76] *Maphango v Aengus Lifestyle Properties* 2012 (3) SA 531 (CC) paras 63 and 64.

[77] Ibid para 70.

the limits of the Tribunals' administrative capacities, and the tendency of Tribunal members to fall back on common law principles that do not bind them, or, worse, to substitute unexamined moral judgements for reasoned conclusions about fairness.

5.2.1   Rent Determinations

Assigning statutory tribunals with broad discretions to decide what is fair on a given set of facts does not mean that the outcomes determined by those tribunals will in fact be fair. The Rental Housing Act successfully disrupts the authority structure between landlord and tenant set up by the common law of property, but it does not provide a precise blueprint for working out who is to prevail in landlord and tenant disputes. This is a problem common to all attempts to reform common law regimes with open-text legislation that requires courts and tribunals to determine "just", "fair", "equitable" or "reasonable" outcomes case by case. The administration of justice, fairness and equity requires tribunals to make social and moral judgements which they are often ill-equipped to make. That does not mean that those judgements should not be made, but it does mean that courts and tribunals administering equitable jurisdictions need to develop a structured sense of what equity and fairness require in a particular kind of legally regulated social relationship. There is nothing in the jurisprudence of the Rental Housing Tribunals that yet suggests any coherent sense of the principles that guide them in their administration of the unfair practice regime.

In the *Fairview Tenants Case*,[78] the Gauteng Rental Housing Tribunal considered a complaint from tenants residing in four houses in Fairview near the Johannesburg inner city. The tenants had lived in the houses for periods of between nine and 24 years.[79] During 2009, the houses were purchased by "Afcon" a property management company owned and controlled by Arnoldus and Trudie Vosloo. The Vosloos apparently intended to redevelop the properties, but lacked the capital to do so at time of the purchase. Instead, they decided to let the tenants stay in the properties, but demanded a rent increase of over 200%, from R800 to R3 000 per month. Having successfully extracted this increase, the Vosloos refused to undertake any maintenance or repairs on any of the houses. By their lights, the tenants were being allowed to stay pending the redevelopment of the properties. The rent was their rightful return on owning it. Maintenance of the properties pending the renovation was a waste of time.

The tenants were unhappy with absorbing a large rent increase while at the same time having to repair and maintain the properties on their own. The houses needed roof repairs, rewiring, new bathroom fittings and new pipes. The tenants were people of few means, and much of the required work was beyond their financial capacity. Nor did it fall within the scope of their duties under the Gauteng Unfair Practice Regulations, 2001. Regulation 7(1)(g) and (h) of the Gauteng Unfair Practices

---

[78] *Tenants of ERF 69, 70, 71, 72 Fairview v AJ and T Vosloo* Gauteng Rental Housing Tribunal Case No 1560/17 (26 November 2018).

[79] Founding Affidavit of Angeline Khoza in *Khoza v Mohlala-Mulaudzi NO*, Gauteng Local Division of the High Court, Case No 15119/19.

Regulations, 2001 required the Vosloos to maintain and repair the exterior of the houses, and to ensure that electrical, plumbing, heating and sanitation systems were maintained "in good order and repair". Over time, the houses deteriorated. Holes appeared in the roofs, fittings in the kitchens and the bathrooms of each house deteriorated in condition, and eventually became unusable.[80]

The tenants asked the Vosloos to lower their rent. The Vosloos refused.[81] The tenants then complained to the Gauteng Rental Housing Tribunal. For reasons that are not clear from the record, the Tribunal failed or refused to process the complaint. The tenants remitted half of their rent anyway.[82] The Vosloos responded by seeking the tenants' eviction, ostensibly on the grounds of breach of lease. There followed a substantial procedural delay. The Vosloos' application to evict the tenants was referred to the Gauteng Local Division's notoriously clogged trial court roll, and languished there for several years, with the trial being repeatedly postponed to enable the tenants to obtain legal representation. Eventually, the court appointed a judge to case-manage the trial and a legal representative to act for the tenants without charge.[83] Throughout this time, the tenants paid, and the Vosloos accepted, R1 500 per month in (reduced) rent.

In 2017, the judge appointed to manage the trial referred the matter back to the Gauteng Rental Housing Tribunal, and directed it to determine the complaint that had been filed with it six years earlier. The tenants complained that the Vosloos had failed to maintain the properties. They asked for a ruling reducing their rent to R1 500 per month from the date on which they began to remit it, to the date on which the Vosloos performed the necessary maintenance and repairs.

The Tribunal finally issued its Ruling in November 2018. The Tribunal found that the Vosloos had committed an unfair practice in that they had failed to maintain the tenants' houses.[84] But then the exercise of its discretion went awry. Relying on common law authority that landlords and tenants have reciprocal obligations (the landlord to maintain and repair the property, the tenant to pay rent), the Tribunal decided that the tenants had placed the Vosloos "in a difficult position" because they had failed to pay rent the Vosloos needed to maintain the properties.[85] The Tribunal then criticised the tenants for failing to maintain the property themselves with the money they saved from remitting their rent, characterising this failure as an "act of dishonesty"[86] apparently evident from the tenants' failure to demonstrate that every Rand they remitted had been expended on maintenance.[87] Suffice it to say, the tenants were denied the rental reduction they sought.[88] The Tribunal decided that,

---

[80] Ibid para 24.
[81] Ibid para 26.
[82] Ibid para 27.
[83] Ibid para 31.
[84] *Tenants of ERF 69, 70, 71, 72 Fairview v AJ and T Vosloo* Gauteng Rental Housing Tribunal Case No 1560/17 (26 November 2018) para 15.2.
[85] Ibid para 15.2.
[86] Ibid para 17(a).
[87] Ibid para 15.4.
[88] Ibid para 17(c).

whoever was ultimately to blame for the deterioration of the properties, three out of four of them were "dilapidated ... [un]inhabitable and hazardous". It ruled that three out of four of "the houses have to be immediately locked".[89] The implication of this ruling is that the tenants were not only disentitled to compel the Vosloos to maintain and repair the houses, but that they were also liable to be evicted because the houses were in such a bad state.

The Tribunal's reasoning is clearly perverse. Its ruling cannot be justified. The High Court later reviewed it and set it aside. The application for judicial review of the ruling was unopposed. In other words, not even the Vosloos or the Tribunal itself found themselves able to defend the ruling on its merits.

However, the point here is not to criticise the outcome of the complaint. The importance of the *Fairview Houses* case is rather to illustrate the opportunities and constraints placed on tenants in attempting to use the spaces opened up for them by the Rental Housing Act. The Vosloos had purchased occupied properties for purely speculative purposes. They sought to extract as much rent out of the properties as they could while at the same time refusing to maintain or repair them in a state fit for occupation. They did this with the objective of accumulating the capital necessary to redevelop the properties, which would, in any event, have seen the tenants evicted in the end. The predatory nature of this scheme should be obvious.

On the one hand, the Act and the Tribunal created the apparatus within which the Vosloos' attempt to evict the tenants could be redirected into an argument about the fairness of the Vosloos' predatory conduct. The process itself ensured that the tenants could remain in occupation of the houses for several years, staving off what would have been a fairly prompt eviction otherwise. On the other hand, the normative confusion evident in the Tribunal's ruling makes that space an uncertain one to navigate. Because the Tribunal had not supplemented the unfair practice regime with a clear sense of structured equity, it had little to go on other than what appear to be its unexamined, instinctive responses to the facts put up by the Vosloos and the tenants. Seizing on the concept of "reciprocity" in landlord–tenant relationships, the Tribunal adopted the attitude that "both parties have been prejudicing each other's interest unreasonably".[90] This had the unfortunate consequence that at least three of the houses had deteriorated to the point where they had become uninhabitable and had to be vacated. The Tribunal's response to the challenge of the value-based, context-sensitive reasoning required by the Rental Housing Act's injunction that it reach a "just and fair outcome", was to apportion the blame equally between the parties. But the net effect of doing so was that the weaker parties came out worse off, because they had more to lose.

In other cases, the Rental Housing Tribunals have found the value-based reasoning required by the Rental Housing Act more straightforward. In *Salie*[91] the

[89] Ibid para 17(e).
[90] Ibid 15.2.
[91] *Faieza Salie v Ebrahim Kaskar* Western Cape Rental Housing Tribunal Case Nos. 21/3/1/21654/S47 & S48 (5 November 2018).

Western Cape Rental Housing Tribunal had to deal with a complaint from Faiza and Omar Salie, an elderly couple who had lived in a house in Salt River, Cape Town for 36 years. Salt River is a rapidly gentrifying suburb between Woodstock and Observatory at the edge of Cape Town's central business district. Salt River was home to a large population of Cape Coloured people throughout apartheid, and still is. However, gentrification is now doing some of what apartheid could not, in that poor, and usually elderly, people on fixed incomes are being pushed out by sales of, and rent increases in, newly valuable properties.

The Salies are a case in point. Between November 2015 and January 2018, their rent more than doubled from R3 600 per month to R7 500 per month. This was substantially beyond what the Salies could afford.[92] While the rent went up, the landlord's maintenance work on the property ceased.[93] After absorbing three rent increases – the first from R3 600 to R4 500; the second from R4 500 to R5 000; and the third from R5 000 to R5 500 – the Salies baulked at the fourth increase from R5 500 to R7 500. The landlord met their protests with a notice to vacate their home.[94]

This was a classic case of gentrification. Rent increases are prompted by a property owner's desire to capitalise on the enhancement in property values caused by gentrification. Rents go up. The current occupants cannot pay. They are evicted and replaced by tenants of a higher social class, who can afford the rent.

The Salies complained to the Rental Housing Tribunal about the rent increase from R5 500 to R7 500. They argued that the large number of increases over such a short period was "exploitative"[95] within the meaning of section 13(4) of the Rental Housing Act. They also argued that the rent demanded was well beyond the range of rents currently reported for the Salt River area, which was between R5 000 and R6 160.[96] Relying on the Constitutional Court's decision in *Maphango*, the Tribunal reasoned that it had to weigh the interests of the landlord in an increased rent against the tenants' ability to absorb it.[97] Although it did not expressly set out the steps it took in this balancing exercise, the Tribunal came to the conclusion that an increase beyond the market maximum for the area was "exorbitant and unfair".[98] The Salies' rent was reduced to R5 500 per month, meaning that the landlord ultimately received only half of the rent increase that he sought to impose.[99] The notice to vacate was also set aside.[100]

The Tribunal's ruling is open to criticism on the basis that it appeared to use a market-based measure for the determination of a just and fair rental. However, the basic logic of the ruling, that a context-sensitive balancing of interests had to be undertaken, encompassing the affordability of the increase, placed downward

---

[92] Ibid para 6.4.
[93] Ibid para 6.8.
[94] Ibid para 6.9.
[95] Ibid para 14.
[96] Ibid para 6.7.
[97] Ibid para 11.
[98] Ibid para 14.
[99] Ibid para 3.
[100] Ibid para 4.

pressure on the rent determination that was ultimately made. The Tribunal was apparently as yet unable to find a counter-weight to the market in rent determination. However, disentitling the landlord to his full increase disrupted the gentrification process to which the Salies had been subject.

5.2.2   The Plettenberg Cases

The *Plettenberg* Cases[101] illuminate the nature and limits of the Rental Housing Tribunals' capacity to provide a resource to poor tenants seeking to resist the exploitative practices of a landlord in the context of gentrification. Plettenberg is a multi-storey tenement in Hillbrow, Johannesburg, containing about 80 flats.[102] Until 2018, most tenants had lived in Plettenberg for very long periods of time – some for as long as 25 years.[103] The tenants had, perhaps as a consequence of their tenure in the building, a strong tenants' association that conducted negotiations with the owner of the property, Young Min Shan.

One matter of ongoing concern to the tenants was a service charge of R385 per month per tenant that was levied against each of the tenants' electricity accounts. The tenants believed that the charge was unfair, in that it did not reflect any service of value that the owner actually provided. They approached the Gauteng Rental Housing Tribunal to complain about it. The tenants relied on regulation 13 of the Gauteng Unfair Practice Regulations, 2001, which requires a landlord to "charge a tenant the exact amount for service consumed in the tenant's dwelling if such dwelling is separately metered" and "in a multi-tenanted dwelling not recover collectively from the tenants" amounts "in excess of the amounts totally charged by the utility service provider and the landlord". They said that the effect of these two regulations was that the landlord was not entitled to turn a profit on the electricity supplied to the tenants. The landlord could only charge the tenants what it cost to supply electricity to them, and nothing more.

The landlord disagreed. It argued that the words "and the landlord" in regulation 13 permitted it to charge for the supply of electricity to the tenant through the electrical installations it owned in the building. The landlord argued that it was re-selling electricity delivered to the building to the tenants, and that regulation 13 expressly authorises this resale. The service charge levied is reasonable in the circumstances, and pays for the maintenance of the water and electricity reticulation systems at the property.[104]

The Tribunal decided that the service charge was unlawful. Regulation 13 of the Gauteng Unfair Practice Regulations, 2001, precluded it. The landlord's argument

---

[101] *Jele v Young Min Shan CC* Gauteng Rental Housing Tribunal Case No 909/12 (31 May 2013); *Young Ming Shan CC v Chagan NO* 2015 (3) SA 227 (GJ); *Young Min Shan v Jele* Gauteng Local Division of the High Court Case No 2013/40258; *Tenants of Plettenberg v Urban Task Force* Gauteng Rental Housing Tribunal Case Nos 91/2017 and 182/2017; *Lewray Investments v Mtunzi* (2018/15129) [2018] ZAGPJHC 432 (23 May 2018).

[102] Founding Affidavit in *Jele v Young Min Shan CC* Gauteng Rental Housing Tribunal Case No 909/12 (31 May 2013) para 9.

[103] Answering Affidavit in *Lewray Investments v Mtunzi* [2018] ZAGPJHC 432 (23 May 2018) para 23.

[104] Complainants' Heads of Argument in *Jele v Young Min Shan CC* Gauteng Rental Housing Tribunal Case No 909/12 (31 May 2013) para 6.

that the proceeds from the service charge were being used to maintain the property was no justification either, because the landlord's duty to maintain the property was a service the tenants paid for with their rent. The landlord was not entitled to unbundle the various aspects of its performance as a landlord and charge separately for each one, unless this was specifically agreed.[105]

A review of the Tribunal's decision to the High Court failed. The High Court's judgment was significant in that it confirmed that the decisions of the Rental Housing Tribunal are subject to the Promotion of Administrative Justice Act 2 of 2000 (PAJA). The basic approach of the High Court was to consider whether, taken as a whole, the Tribunal's decision was reasonable, within the meaning of PAJA. After analysing the Tribunal's decision in some detail, the High Court ruled that the Tribunal's conclusions were reasonable in the circumstances. This allows the Tribunals significant latitude in deciding cases before them, and widens the space in which they can act to assist tenants. The question on review will never be whether the Tribunal is "right or wrong, but whether its decision was so unreasonable that no reasonable person or, more specifically, rental tribunal could have come to that conclusion in the circumstances".[106]

The service charge was accordingly discontinued. However, the landlord was not content to leave matters there. It soon brought an application to evict thirteen of the tenants, most of whom had been active in the tenants' association's complaint to the Tribunal. The basis for the eviction application was that the tenants had not paid their rent. But whether rent had in fact been paid was in dispute between the parties.[107] The real reason for the eviction application appeared to be retaliation against the tenants association for their successful complaint about the electricity service charge.[108]

This kind of retaliation itself constitutes an unfair practice. In *Kendall*[109] the Western Cape High Court refused an eviction order against a tenant who faced eviction because she had complained to the Western Cape Rental Housing Tribunal about what she thought was an unfair rent increase. In that case, the court found that section 4(5)(c) of the Rental Housing Act places an additional onus on a landlord in eviction proceedings. As well as proving that a tenant's lease has been terminated, a landlord must also allege and prove that the grounds of termination do not constitute an unfair practice.[110] Since the landlord had failed to disclose the circumstances of the termination and failed to allege that the termination did not have a retaliatory effect, the eviction application was refused.[111]

---

[105] *Jele v Young Min Shan CC* Gauteng Rental Housing Tribunal Case No 909/12 (31 May 2013) para 78.

[106] *Young Ming Shan CC v Chagan NO* 2015 (3) SA 227 (GJ) para 65.

[107] Answering Affidavit in *Young Min Shan v Jele* Gauteng Local Division of the High Court Case No 2013/40258 paras 32 and 33.

[108] Ibid para 9.

[109] *Kendall Property Investments v Rutgers* [2005] 4 All SA 61 (C).

[110] Ibid 70.

[111] Ibid 71.

The eviction application in Plettenberg never got that far, because it was not persisted with once the tenants filed their answering affidavit. Had the case come to a hearing, however, it appears that the application could not have succeeded, given the retaliatory purpose of the eviction application. The protection afforded by the Rental Housing Act to tenants who make complaints to Tribunal nurtures and protects tenants' rights to use the Tribunals as a resource.

Four years after the eviction application was abandoned, Plettenberg's owner sold the building on to a property company known as Lewray Investments. Lewray's business model is to purchase large tenements, and subdivide them to create a larger number of smaller flats. This increases the rental yield at the property without attracting complaints of substantial or unreasonable rent increases, both because the rent per flat in the renovated property is seldom significantly in excess of the rent per flat before the renovation (there are just more, smaller flats), and because the apparent basis for evicting the current occupiers of the purchased properties is not the intention to impose a substantial rent increase, but to renovate the property. Even under the Rent Control Act 80 of 1976, a landlord could suspend leasehold rights if he wished to renovate the property.[112]

This was the model Lewray implemented at Plettenberg, through its agent, Urban Task Force. On 1 January 2018, Urban Task Force issued a "notice to vacate". The notice alleged that the property was in need of renovation, and that the tenants would have to move out to allow the renovation to take place. Urban Task Force offered to provide accommodation at the same rent and quality in other buildings owned by Lewray in the vicinity of Plettenberg.[113] Suspecting that Lewray and Urban Task Force wanted to subdivide their flats, the tenants construed this notice as an eviction threat, and referred it to the Rental Housing Tribunal.

The Tribunal drew the parties' attention to regulation 8 of the Gauteng Unfair Practice Regulations, 2001, which comprehensively regulates the steps to be taken when a landlord wishes to renovate a property. Regulation 8(1) first draws a distinction between rental housing property that has become completely uninhabitable, and property that is simply in need of renovation. A landlord may cancel a lease in respect of property that has become uninhabitable. But if a property is simply in need of renovation or repair that cannot be done while the property is occupied, then the lease continues. A landlord may simply "request" a tenant to vacate. If the tenant fails to vacate, then the landlord is absolved, in terms of regulation 8(4), from liability for any loss or damage caused to the tenant as a result of the renovation. In the event that the tenant does vacate, regulation 8(2) requires the landlord to remit the tenant's rent for the period of the renovations, to complete the renovations in

---

[112] Section 28(d)(iv).
[113] Answering Affidavit in *Lewray Investments v Mtunzi* [2018] ZAGPJHC 432 (23 May 2018) para 25.

a reasonable time, and to ensure that the tenant is able to return to the dwelling as soon as possible after the completion of any renovation.

The Tribunal interpreted the notice to vacate as a request under regulation 8, and not an eviction threat.[114] It found that the renovations that Lewray and Urban Task Force wanted to carry out could not be done while the tenants were in occupation, but ordered them to comply with the provisions of regulation 8(2), and to provide the tenants with alternative accommodation as promised.[115] In making this ruling, the Tribunal arguably went too far. Regulation 8 appears, on its face, to preserve a tenant's election to remain in a property during a renovation. In directing Lewray and Urban Task Force to provide the tenants with alternative accommodation, the Tribunal made that decision for the tenants.

This notwithstanding, the tenants then began to approach Lewray and Urban Task Force for alternative accommodation. In order to obtain alternative accommodation, the tenants were required to sign new leases, and accept flats that were significantly smaller than the flats they had at Plettenberg. Some of the tenants were refused accommodation altogether.[116] In the meantime, Lewray and Urban Task Force began renovating the property, before the tenants had vacated. The lifts at the property were disconnected, and the water and electricity supply were cut off. An urgent application to the High Court restored these services temporarily.[117]

Lewray and Urban Task Force then brought an application to evict the tenants in terms of the PIE Act. The tenants defended the application on the basis that they were still lawful tenants of the property, and not unlawful occupiers. During that course of that litigation, Lewray and Urban Task Force made an undertaking to provide alternative accommodation to all of the tenants, including those who it had refused to accommodate previously. The High Court granted the application to evict the tenants, on condition that they were all given alternative accommodation, and that they were able to return to Plettenberg once the renovations were complete.[118] However, the flats to which the tenants would be returning would be subdivided. The High Court appeared somewhat taken aback by the suggestion that the tenants did not want their homes to be subdivided. The court held that it is "inconceivable that the owner of a property can be prevented from effecting changes to its property as it deems necessary because its present tenants who occupy the premises in terms of monthly tenancies say so". [119] In light of this conclusion, the court's ultimate order that the tenants ought to be allowed to return to "their units" after the renovation rings particularly hollow.[120]

The Plettenberg community's interaction with the Rental Housing Tribunal reveals an ambiguous picture. The community's use of the Tribunal enabled it

---

[114] *Tenants of Plettenberg v Urban Task Force* Gauteng Rental Housing Tribunal Case Nos 91/2017 and 182/2017 para 9.

[115] Ibid paras 20–22.

[116] Answering Affidavit in *Lewray Investments v Mtunzi* [2018] ZAGPJHC 432 (23 May 2018) paras 34–7.

[117] Ibid paras 60 and 63.

[118] *Lewray Investments v Mtunzi* [2018] ZAGPJHC 432 (23 May 2018) para 30.

[119] Ibid para 24.

[120] Ibid para 30.2.2.6.

to secure important benefits on each occasion. Young Min Shan's overcharging for electricity was brought to an end. A retaliatory eviction attempt was stifled. Lewray and Urban Task Force were held to their undertaking to provide alternative accommodation. The Tribunal's ruling that the tenants were to be allowed back to Plettenberg was enshrined in the High Court's ultimate order. The immiseration of the tenants through the subdivision of their flats was not, however, avoided. The Tribunal and the unfair practice regime was unequal to Lewray's and Urban Task Force's scheme, which ultimately saw the tenants paying the same rent for significantly less space.

5.3   AN UNRELIABLE RESOURCE?

The principal advantage of the rent control regime was that, by regulating rent increases, it redressed the balance of power between landlord and tenant. It did so not just by insulating individual tenants from unaffordable rent increases, but also by fixing the market conditions within which a landlord and tenant contract. If rent is controlled, a landlord has fewer incentives to evict tenants to obtain higher rentals from others. Nor can a landlord use the threat or implementation of a rent increase as a way of removing an unwanted tenant. More broadly, rent control prevents gentrification. The cycle of increasing rents, high tenant turnover, and renovations intended to extract higher rental yields by slicing a building into smaller and smaller apartments, can neither begin nor be sustained under rent control.[121]

The abolition of rent control exposed South African tenants to gentrification. There is little in the unfair practice regime, or in the cases of its application set out above, that suggests that the Rental Housing Act has been wholly successful in protecting tenants from all of gentrification's negative effects. The unfair practice regime has, though, opened up a space in which tenants can organise and engage with Rental Housing Tribunals to moderate gentrification's worst effects. Under rent control, there were few restrictions on a landlord's right to discriminate in letting decisions, and there was no protection against retaliatory eviction for tenants who organised or who attempted to exercise their legal rights.[122] The Rental Housing Act, on the other hand, specifically recognises a tenant's right to organise. The courts have been prompt to protect tenants who do organise against retaliatory action, by requiring landlords to show that the cancellation of a lease is not unfair in the circumstances.

Within the spaces created by the unfair practice regime, some tenants have held gentrification to a score-draw. The *Maphango* tenants fought off the rent increase sought to be imposed on them. The *Fairview* tenants were able to withhold rent and stave off eviction for several years, in response to the brazenly exploitative conduct of the property speculator who bought their homes. The *Salies* were able to moderate the excessive rent increases that gentrification generally triggers.

---

[121] Although rent control may reduce private sector investment in rental housing, it need not reduce overall supply if the state is willing to build and supply rental housing where the private sector does not.

[122] There was arguably little need for such protection, because lease cancellations and rent increases were so heavily regulated anyway.

The *Plettenberg* tenants were able to engage the unfair practice regime over a period of several years, first to prevent their landlord from profiteering on their electricity supply, secondly to fight off a retaliatory eviction, and thirdly to prevent a renovation from making them completely homeless, even though they will not be able to return to the homes they left.

These initiatives are important, but it is hard to discern from them what the unfair practice regime adds up to. Under the PIE Act, the law has been developed to prevent evictions from leading to homelessness. The rent control regime prevented gentrification, and equalised bargaining power between landlords and tenants by setting rents, clamping down heavily on a landlord's common law right to terminate a lease, and by doing very little else. The unfair practice regime, coupled with the Tribunals' structure, appears, at least at this stage, to have created value-based adjudication without a clear purpose. Tribunal members, and sometimes judges, have located this purpose in confused and arbitrary judgements about the propriety of individual conduct, as the Rental Housing Tribunal in the *Fairview* case did, or in fairly unreconstructed ideas about common law ownership powers, as the judge in the *Plettenberg* case did.[123]

Much of the lack of purpose in the unfair practice regime might be attributable to the Minister's failure to establish the norms and standards required in terms of section 2 of the Rental Housing Act. Tribunals may have been left to wonder what fair policy balance they are supposed to strike in what is a fundamentally social relationship between landlords and tenants. However, despite the Tribunals' failure to attribute a clear underlying purpose to the unfair practice regime, tenants have, with the albeit unreliable assistance of the Tribunals themselves, done much to shape the unfair practice regime to suit their needs. They have moderated rent increases, resisted homelessness, prevented landlord profiteering on utility charges, and successfully defended their rights to associate. The suppleness of the unfair practice regime itself clearly offers multiple future opportunities for tenant action.

---

[123] The administration of reform legislation by specialised tribunals has an uneven history. See T Roux "Pro-Poor Court, Anti-Poor Outcomes: Explaining the Performance of the Land Claims Court" (2004) 20 *South African Journal on Human Rights* 511 for an excoriating critique of the Land Claims Court's inability to free itself of the doctrinal force of the common law and the conservative influence of legal culture. Roux's analysis supports the view that legal reasoning and legal culture exercise a powerful drag on legally based social transformation projects. See G Carpenter "Constitutional interpretation by the existing judiciary in South Africa – can new wine be successfully decanted into old bottles?" (1995) 28 *Comparative and International Law Journal of Southern Africa* 322.

CHAPTER SIX

LOOSENING THE BONDS

6.1 DEBTORS, CREDITORS AND POWER

Elsie Gundwana lives in Thembalethu township, just outside George in the Western Cape. In the late 1990s, she acquired ownership of her township home through the conversion of her previous, apartheid-era, title to full ownership. This was part of a process initiated by the late apartheid government to transfer state-owned housing stock to its occupants.[1] Once she took transfer of her home, Ms Gundwana found herself an owner of immoveable property for the first time in her life. She also found herself with access to a valuable asset, but without a job or a reliable income. So she decided to leverage the asset into an income. She borrowed R52 000 from Nedbank, one of South Africa's four largest commercial banks. The loan was secured against her newly acquired ownership right by means of a mortgage bond. Ms Gundwana used this money to expand her home into the first black-owned bed and breakfast establishment in the George area.[2]

Ms Gundwana's business had its ups and downs. Sometimes she was able to make her bond repayments; sometimes not. She was generally able to keep broadly to her repayment obligations – just not strictly to the instalment schedule specified in her loan agreement. In 2003, her defaults became more serious. She fell further behind with her repayments. In response, the bank called up her bond, obtained default judgment against her, and was given permission, by the Registrar of the Western Cape High Court, to sell her home to recover the capital and interest outstanding on the mortgage bond. For a period of four years thereafter, the bank continued to accept payments from Ms Gundwana, but it did not sell her house. Occasionally, it threatened to act on the authority to do so that it had received from the Registrar, in order to induce Ms Gundwana to bring her payments up-to-date. It invariably cancelled scheduled sales of the property when Ms Gundwana did so. However, finally, in 2007, the bank lost patience and followed through on its threat to sell the property.

The bank's conduct in Ms Gundwana's case will strike many as unfair. They will see a large financial institution playing cat-and-mouse with a small business owner from a historically oppressed group. There was no suggestion that she was a recalcitrant debtor. Ms Gundwana was making an effort to meet her obligations to

---

[1] Conversion of Certain Rights into Leasehold or Ownership Act 81 of 1988. See also *Nzimande v Nzimande* 2005 (1) SA 83 (W) paras 5 to 13.

[2] Founding Affidavit in the Application for Leave to Appeal to the Constitutional Court in *Gundwana v Steko Development CC* 2011 (3) SA 608 (CC). See also S Wilson, J Dugard and Michael Clark "Conflict Management in an era of Urbanisation: Twenty Years of Housing Rights in the Constitutional Court" (2015) 31 *South African Journal on Human Rights* 472, 495. The opening paragraphs of the *Gundwana* judgment appear to be at variance with what its recorded in the Founding Affidavit. I rely here on the Founding Affidavit.

the bank, but was sometimes unable to do so. She was doing her best, in what we can assume were very difficult financial circumstances, to run a successful business, to improve her circumstances and those of her family through self-reliance, and to invest in her property and her community by providing what was, at least then, a rare thing: bed and breakfast accommodation in an African township in the Western Cape. The bank should have supported her in any way it could. Its conduct was instead threatening and capricious. There could have been no serious suggestion that Ms Gundwana's loan was a particularly important investment for the bank. The bank could, if it chose, simply have forgiven Ms Gundwana's debt, with absolutely no impact on its balance sheet or profitability. The power game it played with her was cruel and unnecessary.

Others will see things differently. Ms Gundwana was a business woman who took a calculated risk. Nobody forced her to put her home up as collateral. She wanted a successful business. That is not given for the asking. In addition to hard work and determination – which Ms Gundwana had in spades – it also requires luck, of which Ms Gundwana had rather less. It is in the nature of banks to fund calculated risk-taking of this nature. When the risk pays off, so much the better. The bank gets its investment back with interest, and Ms Gundwana gets an enhanced capital asset and a successful business. But if the risk does not pay off, then the bank is entitled to mitigate its losses by selling the asset that Ms Gundwana freely put up as security for the loan advanced to her. In this case, more than most, the bank exercised patience and empathy. It tolerated several acts of default. That tolerance kept Ms Gundwana going through lean times. Even when it took steps to execute against Ms Gundwana's home, the bank did so slowly and hesitantly, giving Ms Gundwana every chance to get back on track and meet the obligations she had freely assumed. In the end, though, the bank was entitled to call time on these efforts, which is exactly what it did.

My purpose here is not to suggest that either of these analyses is the correct one. It is to call attention to the structure of authority that is sustained by the underlying legal relationship between Ms Gundwana, as the owner of her home, and the bank, as the owner of the security taken out against it. The authority structure set up by the common law of property creates a hierarchy between these two types of ownership right. It creates hierarchies between owners of securities (such as mortgage bonds) and owners of other types of property, whose assets become collateral for their debts.

Debtor and creditor relationships have been an important site of social power relations since at least the advent of urban society. The history of the debtor and creditor relationship has often been assumed to revolve around the imposition and cancellation of debt, of historical instances of debt peonage and jubilee.[3] But debtor and creditor relationships are far more complex than mere states of indebtedness and redemption. They are ongoing and pervasive, and have social and legal terms that are dynamic and mutable. The precise terms on which debts

---

[3] D Graeber *Debt: the First 5000 Years* (2011) 82.

are incurred, executed and redeemed matter for the distribution of power in which the debtor and creditor relationship is formed and sustained. Harsh terms, that admit of no requirement on the creditor to act with restraint or circumspection, and provide no opportunity for the debtor to negotiate the terms of repayment or stave off execution against a valuable asset, are the sign of an unjust society that limits people's agency and subjects them to the exercise of arbitrary power and no small degree of immiseration. Harsh credit terms also assume a moral dimension. Execution or bankruptcy is a humiliating subjugation. The easier it is for a creditor to resort to them, the more society as a whole is encouraged to think of debtors as the authors of their own misfortune, as bad people, as open to criticism on moral grounds.

That is the hierarchy of morality and power that the bank exploited when it took and sold Ms Gundwana's home. At common law, an owner who falls into debt that they cannot reasonably repay risks losing the things they own. This is so whether or not the debtor puts up their property as security for repayment of a debt. But if a debtor agrees to secure the debt against a particular asset, as Ms Gundwana did, the creditor's common law position is enhanced. In that event, the common law creates a series of mechanisms that provide the creditor with "real" security. That sort of security has two distinct advantages. First, it generally entitles the creditor to cause the specific asset against which the debt is secured (in this case Ms Gundwana's house) to be sold to recover the debt.[4] Secondly, the creditor is entitled to do so even if the debtor is no longer the owner of the asset against which the debt is secured, so long as the real security right has been registered against the asset.[5] In other words, even if Ms Gundwana had sold her house and bed and breakfast business on, the bank would still have been able to extract its mortgage security from the purchaser of the property.

The ability of a creditor to take and sell an asset subject to a real security right is often justified on the basis that the real security right is almost always created with the consent of the owner of the asset.[6] Ms Gundwana voluntarily placed her home at risk, and so made her ownership rights conditional upon the repayment of a debt.[7] However, this justification fails to account for at least two things. First, the owner's successors-in-title, who are also subject to the creditor's real security rights over the asset, clearly did not choose to place the asset at the disposal of the creditor, and it is far from clear why they should be bound by the original owner's decision to encumber the asset. Secondly, an owner's "choice" to place an asset at risk of execution is almost never "free". It will nearly always be constrained by the social conditions under which it is made – conditions that have led to the decision to borrow in the first place. Ms Gundwana needed to leverage her asset into an income. Had another source of income been available to her, such as wage labour, she might have chosen that and kept ownership of her home risk-free. But wage

---

[4] *Gerber v Stolze* 1951 (2) SA 166, 172 E-G.
[5] *Standard Bank v Saunderson* 2006 (2) SA 264 (SCA) para 2.
[6] The landlord's tacit hypothec may be a partial exception, but that need not concern us here.
[7] Ibid. See also *Gundwana v Steko Development CC* 2011 (3) SA 608 (CC) paras 42 and 44.

labour, much less secure wage labour, is scarce in South Africa, especially for black women who live in townships.

The law of real security, then, does far more than recognise the logical and natural consequences of one owner's freely made choice to put an asset up as collateral. It is rather the result of a legal policy choice to strengthen the enforcement of creditors' rights, where those rights are backed up by real security. That choice has consequences for the distribution of social power. Creditors lend money, or buy debt, because they have the excess capital necessary to invest in making or buying the loan. In other words, they are likely already to be at the upper end of the property distribution. By providing creditors' rights to realise their collateral with enhanced legal protection, the law of real security strengthens the social position of an already dominant class. Accordingly, anything that weakens those rights, or tempers their enforcement, will affect the balance of social power between debtors and creditors, and lead to social change.

The power relationships between debtors and creditors assume even more importance where they concern assets with a particularly high social value, such as a home. Here, Ms Gundwana was exceptional. She took transfer of her home from the state as part of a time-limited scheme to transfer state assets into private hands. Most homeowners, though, purchase or expand their homes with capital advanced by large financial institutions in return for a promise to repay that capital with interest, and an agreement to put the home up as security for the repayment of the debt. Mortgage bonds accordingly do more than support commercial risk-taking. They fund the purchase of an essential social good. For this reason, the rules that govern the terms on which a home can be sold to defray a debt have profound social consequences. If those rules enhance a lender's power, by placing few restrictions on the circumstances under which they can sell a debtor's home, the spaces in which the debtor can act to protect their home, negotiate with the lender, and hold the lender to account for the fairness of its conduct, will be constricted. If, however, the process of selling a debtor's home in execution of the debt is closely regulated to ensure that the sale is, in all the circumstances, fair, the position of the debtor will be enhanced. They will have multiple opportunities to negotiate their relationship with the lender, to hold the lender to account for unfair conduct, and, perhaps, to retain ownership of their home, notwithstanding their failure to meet repayment obligations to the lender.

In this chapter, I set out how the Constitution has brought about changes in the enforcement of mortgage bonds over residential property. I argue that, in subjecting the enforcement of mortgagees' rights to call up debts secured on a debtor's home to the requirements of proportionality, section 26 of the Constitution has triggered a significant rebalancing in power relationships between debtors and creditors. It has done so by creating spaces within which debtors can negotiate their relationships with creditors, and challenge, restrict or temper the enforcement of creditors' rights. These spaces, created first by a particular interpretation of the text of section 26 of the Constitution itself, and then by the passage of subordinate legislation in the form of the National Credit Act 34 of 2005, rule 46A of the Uniform Rules of

Court, and by High Court practice directions introduced to facilitate the application of these provisions, have placed significant breaks on the enforcement of creditors' rights that might lead to the loss of the debtor's home.

In the first part of the chapter, I deal with the importation of the concept of proportionality into the legal enquiry undertaken when considering whether to permit a bank to enforce the terms of a mortgage bond by selling the mortgagor's home in execution to the debt secured on it. At common law, the question was simple. A mortgagee could execute against mortgaged property whenever they could prove that the mortgagor was in default of the repayment terms of the loan the bond secured. Unless the terms of the loan provided otherwise, even late payments or relatively small defaults triggered the mortgagee's right to accelerate the loan and demand immediate repayment of the full capital amount secured. After the mortgagor's almost inevitable failure to pay that sum on demand, the process of taking and selling the mortgagor's home was simple and straightforward. It was long characterised by courts as almost entirely administrative, and was eventually taken beyond the purview of judges altogether.[8]

But the advent of proportionality meant that mere default on the loan was no longer enough. The proportionality inquiry meant that a value judgement had to be made, which required the lender's interest in debt recovery to be weighed against the debtor's interest in maintaining access to their home. The question became whether the sale of the home was a step proportionate to the need to recover the debt in all the circumstances. That complex value judgment could only be made by a court, which meant that judges were brought back to the centre of the mortgage bond enforcement process.

I then show how this refocusing of the inquiry resonated with, and helped trigger, a range of other protections, all of which can fairly be justified as intended to ensure that the sale of a home is reasonable and proportionate in all the circumstances. These protections are: the refusal of the right to execute when either the outstanding arrears are too low to justify it, or when the capital amount owing on the bond is not sufficient to justify the sale of a house that is worth substantially more than the amount secured; the rights, in terms of the National Credit Act 34 of 2005 to notice of alternatives to execution and to reinstate a loan agreement at any point prior to execution; and the qualified right to the setting of a reserve price in the event that execution is ordered. These protections have opened up significant spaces in which debtors have been able to act to prevent the sale of their homes, secure their tenure, and hold large financial institutions to account for the exercise of the power the common law gives them to take and sell an asset to defray a debt.

6.2   PROPORTIONALITY IN THE DEBT EXECUTION PROCESS

Christina van Rooyen lived in Prince Albert in the Western Cape. She was poor and unemployed. In 1995, Ms van Rooyen purchased R190 worth of vegetables on credit from a local store. Because she was unable to repay this debt, her creditor

---

[8] *Gundwana v Steko Development* 2011 (3) SA 608 (CC) para 53.

approached a local attorney, who took out default judgment for the amount owing plus interests and costs. On the strength of that judgment, Ms van Rooyen's creditor arranged for her home to be sold to satisfy Ms van Rooyen's debt. Ms van Rooyen's home was eventually sold at public auction for R1 000 in August 2001. On the same day, Maggie Jaftha's home was also sold. Ms Jaftha had taken a loan for R250 in 1998. Through practices that seem, on their face, nothing short of usurious, the debt ballooned with the addition of interest and costs, to R7 000. To help satisfy this debt, Ms Jaftha's home was sold for R5 000.[9]

Neither Ms van Rooyen's nor Ms Jaftha's debts were secured against their homes. Their creditors instead engaged section 66(1)(a) of the Magistrates' Courts Act 32 of 1944. Section 66(1)(a) codified the basic common law rule that a creditor owed money on an ordinary debt could obtain judgment for the debt, and, if the judgment was left unpaid, sell the debtor's moveable property to satisfy the judgment. Section 67 of the Act protected some classes of essential goods from execution in this way, such as bedding, food, a debtor's tools of trade and so on. But the rest of a debtor's property was up for grabs. If, however, the debtor had insufficient moveable property to satisfy the judgment, a creditor could then proceed against a debtor's immoveable property, including the debtor's home. The process of executing a judgment debt was entirely administrative, and overseen, for the most part, by a clerk of the Magistrates' Court and the local sheriff.[10]

Clearly, what happened to Ms van Rooyen and Ms Jaftha was grossly unfair. No reasonable account of a just law of property would countenance the sale of a person's home for the unpaid debt incurred through the purchase of a few vegetables for the family pot. Yet, the common law hierarchy set up between owners of debt and owners of other forms of property enabled just that.

When it was faced with the facts underlying the sale of Ms van Rooyen and Ms Jaftha's homes, the Constitutional Court decided to significantly complicate the debtor and creditor relationship. In *Jaftha*[11] the Constitutional Court held that the process of executing a debt against a person's home always constitutes a limitation of the right of access to adequate housing, entrenched in section 26(1) of the Constitution, because it significantly weakens the home owner's tenure.[12] Accordingly, where property is occupied for residential purposes by its owner, the question is not whether executing a debt against it infringes the right to housing. It clearly does. The real question is whether the infringement is justified.[13] Section 36 of the Constitution sets out the test for determining whether an infringement of rights is justified. Although potentially complex and multi-staged, the test in execution proceedings boils down to a "balancing exercise" that takes into account whether "the creditor's advantage in execution outweighs the harm to the debtor".[14]

---

[9] *Jaftha v Schoeman; Van Rooyen v Stoltz* 2005 (2) SA 140 (CC) paras 4 and 5.
[10] Ibid paras 15 and 16.
[11] Ibid.
[12] Ibid paras 25 to 30.
[13] Ibid para 34.
[14] Ibid para 42.

This opens up a much broader range of questions than would ordinarily be relevant at common law. In addition to whether the debt had actually been validly incurred and remained unpaid at the time of execution, the balancing exercise must take into account "[t]he circumstances in which the debt was incurred; any attempts made by the debtor to pay off the debt; the financial situation of the parties; the amount of the debt; whether the debtor is employed or has a source of income to pay off the debt and any other factor relevant to the particular facts of the case before the court".[15]

This significant reworking of the debt execution process affected both procedure and substance. Because the question of execution against a home was now an open-ended context-sensitive enquiry, it could not be left in the hands of a court clerk. Execution against a home now had to be subject to judicial oversight.[16] Only a judicial officer is equipped to consider all the relevant circumstances of a case to determine whether there is good cause to order execution. Judicial oversight is necessary even where judgment for the outstanding debt is taken by default, in order to protect "people who, because of their lack of knowledge of the legal process, are ill-equipped to avail themselves" of legal remedies that might be open to them.[17] For this reason, the Constitutional Court declared section 66(1)(a) of the Magistrates' Courts Act unconstitutional, because it did not provide for judicial oversight over the process of executing a debt against a person's home. To remedy the defect found in section 66(1)(a), the court inserted the requirement that only "a court, after considering all the relevant circumstances, may order execution" against immoveable property.[18] In each case, it was now for the courts to decide whether executing a debt against a person's home was fair, notwithstanding the debtor's default.

The consequences of this decision were not lost on more conservative parts of the judiciary. Just as some judges had sought to limit the impact of the PIE Act on owners' rights, there was, at least initially, a rear-guard action fought against the obvious consequences of the *Jaftha* decision for the mortgage bond market. If execution of a grocer's account against a home was legitimately the subject of a judicial inquiry into the proportionality of selling a debtor's home, then it seemed clear that it was only a matter of time before mortgage bond execution was subjected to the same stringent process.

In *Mortinson*[19] a Full Bench of the Johannesburg High Court had to consider the impact of *Jaftha* on the mortgage bond execution process. It was already faced with a decision of the Cape Town High Court,[20] which had held that a judge, and not a Registrar, had to consider the proportionality of executing a mortgage bond against a home, taking into account the factors enumerated in *Jaftha*. However, the court in *Mortinson* sought to distinguish the mortgage bond execution process from the

---

[15] Ibid para 60.
[16] Ibid paras 54 and 55.
[17] Ibid para 55.
[18] Ibid para 67.
[19] *Nedbank v Mortinson* 2005 (6) SA 462 (W).
[20] *Standard Bank of SA Ltd v Snyders and Eight Similar Cases* 2005 (5) SA 610 (C).

execution of ordinary debts. The court emphasised that, in the case of a mortgage bond "the debtor has participated in a commercial transaction and has willingly utilised his or her immoveable property as security and thus put it at risk".[21] This, the court held, distinguished mortgage bond executions from the execution process considered in *Jaftha*. Neither Ms Jaftha nor Ms van Rooyen had agreed in advance that their homes could be sold if they did not repay their debts. But mortgagors always did.

The court also emphasised what the Constitutional Court had itself said in *Jaftha*: that "if the judgment debtor willingly put his or her house up in some or other manner as security for the debt, a sale in execution should ordinarily be permitted where there has not been an abuse of court procedure. The need to ensure that homes may be used by people to raise capital is an important aspect of the value of a home which courts must be careful to acknowledge".[22] This, so it was held in *Mortinson*, meant that routine judicial oversight is in fact unnecessary, because "[i]n the overwhelming majority of cases, the application for default judgment and the application for the immoveable property to be declared executable would be a formality and would not require judicial oversight".[23]

Here, the court in *Mortinson* was clearly mistaken. The remarks of the Constitutional Court in *Jaftha* were made in the context of setting out what a judicial officer must consider when deciding whether to order execution against immoveable property. The Constitutional Court intended to signal that the choice to put up a property as security for a debt was relevant to considering whether to order execution, and that judges should consider the impact of their decisions on the integrity of the mortgage bond market itself, which serves the important social function of allowing people to raise money against their property. Placing too great a burden on mortgagees seeking execution might affect the cost and accessibility of credit. But this is just one, albeit important, factor for judges to bear in mind. It was clearly not intended to licence a blanket exemption for mortgagees from the proportionality inquiry that *Jaftha* required.

In addition, the nature and extent of the "choice" made in putting up a home as security for a debt is itself properly the subject of the proportionality inquiry. It is not simply something to be assumed. The Constitutional Court adverted to this when it specified that "the circumstances in which the debt was incurred"[24] must be considered as part of the proportionality inquiry. Clearly, a mortgage bond for R15 million to purchase a luxury property in Sandton is on a different footing to a mortgage bond for R52 000 to extend a township house in George. Both are "choices" to put up a home as security for a debt, but they are made in radically

---

[21] *Nedbank v Mortinson* 2005 (6) SA 462 (W) para 25.
[22] *Jaftha v Schoeman; Van Rooyen v Stoltz* 2005 (2) SA 140 (CC) para 58.
[23] *Nedbank v Mortinson* 2005 (6) SA 462 (W) para 25.
[24] *Jaftha v Schoeman; Van Rooyen v Stoltz* 2005 (2) SA 140 (CC) para 60.

different circumstances. Proportionality requires that the court consider and attach the appropriate weight to these different "choices".

Nonetheless, the courts were, at least initially, unwilling to see things that way. In *Saunderson*[25] the Supreme Court of Appeal decided that the procedure and substance of the proportionality inquiry required by *Jaftha* did not extend to mortgaged property. The Supreme Court of Appeal first pointed out that not all mortgaged property is "adequate housing" that attracts constitutional protection. Section 26(1) of the Constitution, and accordingly the *Jaftha* decision, could only apply to mortgaged property that is occupied as the primary residence of the mortgagee. Section 26(1) did not apply to "a luxury home" or a holiday home, because, presumably, these are not examples of "adequate housing", but of luxurious or superordinate housing.[26] *Jaftha*, the Supreme Court of Appeal suggested, could only apply to people who faced a real risk of homelessness – a loss of "access to adequate housing" – if their home was sold.[27]

Following *Mortinson*, the court emphasised the "choice" made by a mortgagor to put his home up a security for the debt secured. This "choice", so the court held, "fuse[s] the debt into the title of the property itself".[28] In light of this, it is, the court held, "particularly hard to conceive of instances where a mortgagee's right to reclaim the debt from the property will be denied altogether".[29] The most that *Jaftha* might encompass, the court suggested, was "a court delaying execution where there is a real prospect that the debt may yet be paid".[30] None of this, however, meant that a mortgagee had to allege and prove in advance the circumstances that rendered the sale of a home proportionate to the need to collect on the debt secured in all the circumstances of a particular case. The burden rests on the mortgagor to prove the opposite.[31] For this reason, a registrar, and not a court, may in the first instance grant permission to sell a home in the execution of a debt secured by a mortgage bond, unless the mortgagor discloses circumstances that might dissuade a court from authorising the sale of their home.[32]

The effect of *Saunderson* was, albeit temporarily, to insulate mortgagees from the burden that *Jaftha* had attached to all other creditors: that of having to justify the execution of debts secured by mortgages against homes. The decision was no doubt motivated by concerns about how extending *Jaftha* to mortgage bond execution would affect the cost of credit and the housing market generally.[33] But, despite the Supreme Court of Appeal's attempts to distinguish *Saunderson* from *Jaftha*, the underlying policy motivations that animated the *Saunderson* decision clashed

---

[25] *Standard Bank v Saunderson* 2006 (2) SA 264 (SCA).
[26] Ibid para 17.
[27] Ibid para 16.
[28] Ibid para 18.
[29] Ibid para 19.
[30] Ibid para 20.
[31] Ibid paras 20 and 21.
[32] Ibid paras 23 and 24.
[33] Ibid paras 1–3.

head-on with the principles set out in *Jaftha*.[34] The Supreme Court of Appeal's arguments about the "choice" to obtain a mortgage bond suffer from the same flaws as the similar arguments advanced in *Mortinson*. The decision to take out a mortgage on one's home is a factor to be taken into account in the proportionality inquiry. It does not render that inquiry unnecessary.

The Supreme Court of Appeal could not imagine circumstances under which the right to execute against a home would be "denied altogether".[35] But this misses the point. The proportionality inquiry is not about denying a mortgagee the right to sell the mortgaged property forever. It is concerned with whether execution is justified "in the circumstances of the case"[36] initiated by the particular act of default on which the mortgagee chooses to litigate. There are plenty of examples available of when execution will be denied in these circumstances: where the default on the mortgage bond is itself trifling,[37] where a sale takes place for an unreasonably low price[38] or where a sale takes place on amounts owing to the bank that are extraneous to the judgment debt.[39]

The circumstances in which execution of mortgaged property might not be justified illustrate why the Supreme Court of Appeal was mistaken in placing the burden on a mortgagor to disclose facts that might lead to the refusal of execution. Characterising the enquiry as one of onus misconceives the nature of the decision. In *Jaftha* the Constitutional Court held that the burden of deciding whether execution is justified rests on the court, even where an application for permission to execute against a home is undefended.[40] Accordingly, the question is not really one of onus, but of whether, on all the facts available to it, the court will allow its machinery to be used to forcibly sell a person's home. Answering that question entails a value judgement, not merely the calculation of the incidence of the onus and a consideration of whether the onus has been discharged. That sort of value judgment must be made by a court – not a clerk or a registrar. The Supreme Court of Appeal in *Saunderson* failed to capture the true nature and extent of the decision in *Jaftha*. Had it appreciated the consequences of the *Jaftha* decision fully, it would

---

[34] S Liebenberg *Socio-Economic Rights: Adjudication under a transformative Constitution* (2010) 351–358 deals particularly well with the deep doctrinal inconsistency between the *Jaftha* and *Saunderson* decisions.

[35] Ibid para 19.

[36] *Jaftha v Schoeman; Van Rooyen v Stoltz* 2005 (2) SA 140 (CC) para 56.

[37] *Absa Bank v Ntsane* 2007 (3) SA 554 (T).

[38] *Nxazonke v ABSA Bank Ltd* [2012] ZAWCHC 184 (4 October 2012). See also R Brits "Sale in execution of property at unreasonably low price indicates abuse of process: *Nxazonke v ABSA Bank Ltd* [2012] ZAWCHC 184 (4 October 2012)" (2013) 76 *Tydskrif vir Hedendaagse Romeins-Hollandse Reg* 451.

[39] *Thwala and Another v First National Bank Limited and Others* (2015/19201) [2013] ZAGPPHC 514 (11 December 2013).

[40] *Jaftha v Schoeman; Van Rooyen v Stoltz* 2005 (2) SA 140 (CC) para 55.

have been driven to the conclusion that mortgagees, too, were obliged to yield to the standard of proportionality.

After some hesitation,[41] the Constitutional Court confirmed this in *Gundwana*.[42] In that case, Ms Gundwana challenged the sale of her home by Nedbank on the ground that the sale was impermissibly authorised by a High Court registrar, and not by a judge, after considering all the relevant circumstances. In opposing Ms Gundwana's application, Nedbank rehearsed two arguments developed in *Saunderson*. The first of these was that not all mortgaged property could be assumed to be "adequate housing" protected by section 26(1) of the Constitution. Holiday or luxury homes, so the bank argued, do not fall within the scope of the *Jaftha* proportionality inquiry. The second argument was that the mortgagor's "choice" to place mortgaged property at risk took mortgaged homes beyond the scope of the protection afforded to debtors in *Jaftha*.[43]

Now confident of the implications of its decision in *Jaftha*, the Constitutional Court made short work of both arguments. The court confirmed that execution of all debts, including mortgage debts, can only follow on the judgment of a court,[44] and that, where a mortgagor was at risk of losing his home, a court had to consider whether execution was proportionate in all the circumstances. While the fact that a mortgagor put his home up as security for a debt is relevant to the inquiry, that fact does not dispense with the need for the inquiry altogether.[45]

In relation to the argument that not all mortgaged property is "adequate housing" within the scope of section 26(1) of the Constitution, the Constitutional Court pointed out that, while this is obviously true, it reinforces rather than dispenses with the need for judicial oversight: "[s]ome preceding enquiry is necessary to determine whether the facts of a particular matter are of the *Jaftha* kind. An enquiry of that sort requires an evaluation that goes beyond merely checking the summons to determine whether it discloses a proper cause of action," which is the limit of a registrar's competence.[46]

The Constitutional Court went on to hold that the "choice" to place the mortgaged property at risk was not a decision to consent to execution in all circumstances.

---

[41] *Campus Law Clinic (University of KwaZulu-Natal Durban) v Standard Bank of South Africa Ltd* 2006 (6) SA 103 (CC). The Constitutional Court refused leave to appeal against the Supreme Court of Appeal's decision in *Saunderson* on procedural grounds.

[42] *Gundwana v Steko Development* 2011 (3) SA 608 (CC).

[43] Ibid para 42.

[44] This assertion of the judicial role in all debt enforcement proceedings emphasises that it remains an open question whether the proportionality inquiry will only ever be relevant to execution against a person's home. The Constitutional Court's decision in *Governing Body of the Juma Musjid Primary School v Ahmed Asruff Essay NO* 2011 (8) BCLR 761 (CC) makes clear that constitutional limits on the exercise of common law powers are not restricted to protecting the right to housing. In principle, any constitutionally protected interest might, in the right circumstances, outweigh the exercise of a common law proprietary power. There is no bar, in principle, to a court asserting a proportionality jurisdiction over a creditor's right to execute against any property that is sufficiently closely linked to the exercise of a constitutional right. It is at least possible that a court might find the attachment of, say, a nebuliser of a chronically ill person to be a disproportionate interference with the right to health.

[45] *Gundwana* paras 41 and 49.

[46] Ibid para 43.

Judicial oversight was necessary to ensure that execution is not being levied disproportionately or in bad faith.[47] The court accordingly overturned the decisions in *Saunderson* and *Mortinson*,[48] and ruled that a Registrar may not summarily permit the execution of a debt against a person's home.[49]

The court summed up the *Jaftha* and *Gundwana* decisions as requiring no more than a proportionality "between the means used in the execution process to exact payment of the judgment debt, compared to other available means to attain the same purpose".[50] But this was no small innovation. The common law had always prioritised the quick and easy realisation of well-defined rights of security against moveable and immoveable property. It is central to the debtor and creditor relationship that the creditor will be able to act against the debtor with ease in the event that the debt is left unpaid.

By interposing, between the creditor and their security, the complex question of whether the creditor's move to execute against a debtor's home was "proportionate" in all the circumstances, and on insisting on a "balancing" of interests by reference to a multi-factor test, the Constitutional Court had significantly changed the relationship between debtors and creditors. It created the space in which mortgagors could deploy a range of sophisticated legal strategies, and draw on a wide variety of new legal arguments, to resist execution against their homes. The construction of "proportionality" in mortgage bond execution proceedings created the space to make arguments that could – and often did – stave off execution.

6.3   RESISTING EXECUTION

Shortly before the decision in *Gundwana*, the Uniform Rules of Court had been amended to make execution against a person's primary residence subject to court oversight. Rule 46(1)(a)(ii) of the Rules was changed to require that where property sought to be executed against "is the primary residence of the judgment debtor" execution would not be authorised unless "the court, having considered all the relevant circumstances, orders execution against such property".[51] The rule change effectively neutered the Supreme Court of Appeal's decision in *Saunderson*, which

---

[47] Ibid paras 44 to 49.

[48] Ibid para 52.

[49] Ibid para 65. The academic response to *Gundwana* has not been entirely positive. See L Juma "Mortgage bonds and the right of access to adequate housing in South Africa: Gundwana v Stoke [sic] Development and Others 2011 (3) SA 608 (CC) (2012) 37 *Journal for Juridical Science* 1, for a critique of the decision. The critique boils down to the proposition that the Constitutional Court failed to strike the right balance between the need to respect what the author suggests is a "freely" entered into mortgage bond agreement and the need to protect vulnerable debtors. However, the author does little to set out what that balance is and how we would know if it had been appropriately struck. It is a signal feature of much of the academic literature on judge-made amendments to constitutional property law that a particular decision is criticised either for failing to protect the vulnerable or for prejudicing settled commercial expectations. Neither criticism is coherent without a pre-existing theory of how the balance between these two values ought to be struck. My purpose in this book, of course, is not to say where the balance is, but to point out that tipping it one way or another has real social consequences.

[50] Ibid para 54.

[51] The rule was amended by Government Notice R981 of 19 November 2010, and took effect from 24 December 2010.

had sought to insulate most mortgage bond executions from judicial oversight and the proportionality inquiry. The *Gundwana* decision came hard on the heels of the rule change. The combined effect of the decision and the amended Rule was that a judge now had to scrutinise every application to sell a home in execution of a mortgage debt, by considering whether execution was proportionate in all the circumstances of each case.

The Constitutional Court's decision in *Jaftha* had suggested a fairly narrow inquiry in mortgage bond execution cases: whether there had been an abuse of court process. Absent such an abuse, execution should be permitted.[52] But what did this mean? In *Folscher*,[53] a Full Bench of the Pretoria High Court was constituted to consider how the rule change and the decision in *Gundwana* affected the substantive inquiry judges now had to undertake. In answering this question, the court in *Folscher* defined "abuse of process" extremely wide, and delineated an open-ended set of considerations to be taken account of in deciding whether to execute a mortgage bond against a person's home.

An abuse of process, the court held, is not simply "wilfully dishonest or vexatious conduct", but any conduct that engages the Rules of Court to pursue "a purpose extraneous" to seeking the truth. Accordingly, a creditor seeking execution of a bond may commit an abuse of process even though they act in good faith if the consequences are such that a debtor "will lose his home, while alternative modes of satisfying the creditor's demands might exist, that would not cause any significant prejudice to the creditor".[54] In other words, a mortgagee commits an abuse of process every time they seek execution against a person's home in circumstances where execution would be disproportionate. The attempt to put mortgage bond executions in a different category to the execution of ordinary debts against a home was well and truly dead.

The court acknowledged that it is impossible to anticipate every potentially relevant consideration in deciding whether to order execution against a home, but it gave a very long list. The list included: whether the mortgaged property is the debtor's primary residence; the circumstances under which the debt arose; the arrears outstanding when the bond was called up; the arrears outstanding at the time default judgment is sought; the total amount secured by the mortgage bond; the debtor's payment history; the relative financial strengths of the debtor and the creditor; whether it would be possible to clear the arrears owing on the mortgage loan agreement without recourse to execution; the prejudice to the debtor if execution is ordered; the prejudice to the creditor if execution is not ordered; whether the creditor has sent a notice in terms of section 129 of the National Credit Act 34 of 2005 to the debtor; the debtor's reaction to the notice; the period of time between sending the notice and the institution of the application to execute against the debtor's home; whether the debtor's home was acquired with a state subsidy;

---

[52] *Jaftha v Schoeman; Van Rooyen v Stoltz* 2005 (2) SA 140 (CC) para 58.
[53] *Firstrand Bank v Folscher* 2011 (4) SA 314 (GNP).
[54] Ibid para 40, citing *Hudson v Hudson* 1927 AD 259 and *Beinash v Wigley* 1997 (3) SA 721 (SCA) 734F.

whether execution might render the debtor homeless; whether the application to execute has been instituted with an ulterior motive; and the position of the debtor's dependents, if they live in the property sought to be executed against.[55] This is a broad list of considerations by any standard. It implies a wide judicial discretion to decide whether execution is fair in all the circumstances of a particular case.

It also had one further, critical, consequence. The enquiry mandated in *Folscher* encompassed the extent of the parties' performance of their obligations under the loan agreement secured by the mortgage bond, rather than just the consequences of execution for the debtor. This implicated not only the right of the mortgagee to execute, but the right to accelerate the debt and demand the full amount secured by the bond. In *Fraser*,[56] it was held that the proportionality enquiry did not authorise a court to frustrate the creditor's right to accelerate the debt on non-payment of one or more of the instalments, and claim the full capital amount secured by the bond.[57] But this position is hard to sustain if the parties' conduct under the loan agreement itself is relevant to the proportionality inquiry. If that conduct militates against execution, it should also prevent the creditor from demanding the full amount secured by the bond. It is hardly worth considering the parties' conduct under the agreement if the debt has already been accelerated and the loan agreement is effectively being wound up. In addition, there is a clear tension between refusing to allow execution while at the same time allowing the creditor to demand immediate payment of the full amount secured by the mortgage bond rather than just the instalments that have fallen due but not been paid. In *Mokebe*[58] a Full Bench of the Johannesburg High Court confirmed that, save in exceptional circumstances, the right to accelerate and the right to execute had to be determined simultaneously. In other words, it was not generally permissible to grant leave to accelerate a mortgage debt, but not to execute against the mortgaged property. A court should order both or neither.[59]

Ultimately, then, *Jaftha* led to both the mortgagee's right to execute against a home and the right to demand repayment of the loan secured by the mortgage being subject to judicial control. This control must be exercised in a manner that ensures that acceleration and execution are proportionate in all the circumstances of the case. The breadth and application of the proportionality principle accordingly provide a series of opportunities for the debtor to resist execution against their home, and the immiserating acceleration of their debt. Although the enquiry is very broad, there have generally been three classes of cases in which the rights to accelerate and execute against a home have been denied or attenuated. These are: when either the outstanding arrears are too low to justify it, or when the capital amount owing on the bond is not sufficient to justify the sale of a house that is worth substantially more than the amount secured; where, in terms of the National Credit Act 34 of 2005 the debtor has not been given notice of alternatives to execution or

---

[55] Ibid para 41.
[56] *Nedbank v Fraser* 2011 (4) SA 363 (GSJ).
[57] Ibid para 35.
[58] *ABSA v Mokebe* 2018 (6) SA 492 (GJ).
[59] Ibid para 31.

has reinstated a loan agreement at any point prior to execution; and where a reserve price has been set that cannot be achieved at the sale itself.

6.3.1   The Arrear Amount or Overall Debt Claimed is Disproportionately Low

Section 10.7 of the Practice Manual of the Gauteng Local Division of the High Court is in many respects remarkable. It is intended to provide a set of guidelines to assist judges in giving effect to the *Jaftha* proportionality principle, in cases where a mortgagor seeks to execute against mortgaged property used as a home. It sets out, in some detail, a series of drastic limitations on what, at common law, is a mortgagee's unconditional right to accelerate the loan and execute against the mortgaged property to recover the debt. Section 10.7 first requires personal service of the application for leave to execute against a home. If personal service is not possible, then the court itself must issue service directions reasonably capable of bringing the application to the mortgagor's attention.[60] The personal service requirement is an attempt to ensure that a mortgagor has every opportunity to involve themselves in the bond execution proceedings.

The need for participation of the mortgagor is made clear by paragraph 10.17.3 of the Practice Manual, which records a court's discretion to refuse to order execution against the mortgagor's home if "arrears are low, and/or the period of non-payment is a few weeks/months". In that event, the mortgagee may not re-enrol the application to execute for a further six months. Nor may a court grant judgment for the total accelerated debt "as this will defeat the object of postponing the matter i.e. to allow the [mortgagor] to take advice and seek to make arrangements to bring the arrears up to date or purge the default".[61]

All of this amounts to the proposition that the court will refuse leave to execute against a mortgaged home when the arrears run up by missed payments are relatively low. The application of this principle is illustrated in *Zwane*.[62] In that case, the court set out and defended its discretion to postpone applications to execute against mortgaged homes. The purpose of the discretion was to enable a mortgagor who had not fallen particularly far behind with his repayments to be afforded a reasonable opportunity to bring his repayments up to date.[63] The court confirmed that this meant that the bank's contractual right to accelerate the debt was also subject to "a discretion in an appropriate case to defer immediate enforcement of contractual entitlements flowing from" non-payment.[64] The court then declined to enforce either the right to accelerate or the right to execute against the mortgaged property in two of the three cases before it, because the mortgagors were only

---

[60] Paragraph 10.17.1 of the Practice Manual. The requirement of personal service in the first instance was resented by the major banks, which procured the assembly of a Full Bench to consider its lawfulness. The Full Bench confirmed the requirement. See *ABSA v Lekuku* [2014] ZAGPJHC 244 (14 October 2014).

[61] This aspect of the Practice Manual was also contested by the major banks – again, to no avail. See *ABSA v Mokebe* 2018 (6) SA 492 (GJ).

[62] *Firstrand Bank v Zwane* 2016 (6) SA 400 (GJ).

[63] Ibid para 12.

[64] Ibid para 19.

three months behind with their repayments, and could still conceivably bring their accounts up to date.[65]

A similar approach has sometimes been taken when considering the relationship between the value of the property, the amount achieved at a sale-in-execution, and the overall amount secured by the bond. In *Nxazonke*,[66] the Western Cape High Court was confronted with the sale of a property worth R81 000, to recover a debt of just under R28 000. The sale had gone through – for just R10 – and the court was asked to interdict further sales pending an application to challenge the validity of the first one. The home was occupied by an elderly retired couple who had taken transfer of the property from the apartheid state and had lived in it for 28 years. Those facts, taken together with the facts that the debt owing at the time of the sale was far less than the value of the property; that the amount achieved at the sale was negligible (probably because of irregularities in the sale itself); and the fact that no alternatives to execution had been considered at the time of the initial application to sell the property, induced the court to grant the interdict sought.

It is clear, then, that courts will fairly readily grant mortgagors substantial breathing space to try to find ways of reducing or eliminating their indebtedness while at the same time staving off the attachment and sale of their homes. These breathing spaces are important. In addition to allowing mortgagors to consider ways of bringing their payments up to date, they provide important opportunities for mortgagors to acquire knowledge of more substantive rights that may assist them in the long run.[67]

6.3.2   Non-compliance with the National Credit Act 34 of 2005

The National Credit Act 34 of 2005 encodes the relationship between debtor and creditor in public law. It seeks to strike an equitable balance between the "rights and responsibilities" of creditors and debtors by subjecting the common law to statutory control.[68] The Act is a substantial piece of legislation that has attracted a great deal of commentary.[69] The Act's capacity to provide substantive or permanent resolutions to mortgage bond execution cases has also seen the interpretation and application of its provisions become an important part of mortgage bond execution proceedings.[70] In particular, section 129 of the Act has often become central to the question of whether it is proportionate for a court to execute against a debtor's home.

---

[65]   Ibid paras 26 to 31.

[66]   *Nxazonke and Another v ABSA Bank Ltd and Others* (18100/2012) [2012] ZAWCHC 184 (4 October 2012).

[67]   B Hugo and E du Plessis "Sales in Execution of Immovable Property, the Rules of Court and the Consumer Protection Act Regulations: Back to the Drawing Board" (2014) 25 *Stellenbosch Law Review* 55 also draws attention to the linkages between the bond execution process and the Consumer Protection Act 68 of 2008.

[68]   Section 3 of the National Credit Act 34 of 2005.

[69]   See, as just a few examples, JW Scholtz *Guide to the National Credit Act* (2008); J Otto *The National Credit Act Explained* (2016); R Brits "Constitutional property law, Mortgage, National Credit Act, Reckless credit and Remedies" (2018) 21 *Potchefstroom Electronic Law Journal* 1.

[70]   R Brits and A van der Walt "Application of the housing clause during mortgage foreclosure: a subsidiarity approach to the National Credit Act" (2014) 2 and 3 *Tydskrif vir die Suid Afrikaanse Reg* 228 and 508.

Section 129 sets out two important rights for "consumers" of credit, which is the terminology adopted in the Act for debtors.[71] Section 129(1) of the Act requires that before instituting proceedings to enforce a credit agreement, a creditor must draw "the default to the notice of the consumer in writing and propose that the consumer refer the credit agreement to a debt counsellor, alternative dispute resolution agent, consumer court or ombud with jurisdiction, with the intent that the parties resolve any dispute under the agreement or develop and agree on a plan to bring the payments under the agreement up to date". Section 129(3) permits a debtor "at any time before the credit provider has cancelled the agreement, to remedy a default in such credit agreement by paying to the credit provider all amounts that are overdue, together with the credit provider's prescribed default administration charges and reasonable costs of enforcing the agreement up to the time the default was remedied".

Both provisions constitute substantial inroads into a creditor's common law rights. Section 129(1) permits a consumer to stave off enforcement proceedings by unilaterally referring a loan agreement to one of a range of alternative avenues, including a debt counsellor, who could, in theory, trigger the restructuring of the debt altogether.[72] The purpose of section 129(3) of the Act is clearly to permit mortgagors to avoid the consequences of the acceleration of the mortgage debt by making good on their arrears.[73] Precisely because of the substantial revisions of the common law they embrace, the precise meaning and application of both provisions has engaged the jurisdiction of the Constitutional Court.

In *Sebola*[74] the Constitutional Court had to decide exactly what section 129(1) meant when it required that a credit provider (a creditor) draw the default and the availability of alternative dispute resolution methods "to the attention" of the debtor. The High Courts had split fairly evenly between two interpretations. The first interpretation required the creditor to show simply that a notice in terms of section 129 had been sent to the debtor's address using one of the modes of delivery approved by section 65 of the National Credit Act itself, and selected by the debtor in the loan agreement. In other words, it did not matter that the notice had not been received. It was enough that it had been sent.[75] Other decisions had emphasised that section 129 itself provided a higher standard. The contents of the notice required by section 129 had to be drawn to the consumer's attention. In other words, they had to meet the mind of the consumer.[76]

The Supreme Court of Appeal eventually weighed in with an interpretation of section 129 that placed substantial emphasis on the "choice" exercised by the consumer when they selected a mode of delivery under section 65 of the Act. With that choice, so the Supreme Court of Appeal held, came the responsibility of accepting

---

[71] Section 1.
[72] *Sebola v Standard Bank of South Africa Ltd* 2012 (5) SA 142 (CC) para 46.
[73] *Nkata v Firstrand Bank Limited* 2016 (4) SA 257 (CC) paras 59 and 60.
[74] *Sebola v Standard Bank of South Africa Ltd* 2012 (5) SA 142 (CC).
[75] See, for example, *Munien v BMW Financial Services (SA) (Pty) Ltd* 2010 (1) SA 549 (KZD) para 22.
[76] See *Firstrand Bank Limited v Dhlamini* 2010 (4) SA 531 (GNP) para 55.

the consequence that the chosen mode of delivery might be unsuccessful.[77] While the High Courts had proceeded substantially on an interpretation of the words in the Act, the Supreme Court of Appeal put a moral spin on the question. "With every choice" the court held "lies a responsibility" and "it is after all within a consumer's sole knowledge which means of communication will reasonably ensure delivery to him". The court held that "it is entirely fair in the circumstances to conclude from the legislature's express language in section 65(2) that it considered dispatch of a notice in the manner chosen by the appellants in this matter sufficient for purposes of section 129(1)(a) and that actual receipt is the consumer's responsibility".[78]

The Supreme Court of Appeal's decision was particularly odd. It is straightforwardly wrong to conclude that the mode of communication that is most likely to succeed is within a debtor's "sole knowledge", especially if the mode of communication being selected is to be used over the course of an agreement that may last several years. Decisions about how to communicate are almost entirely contextual. The question is what form of communication is likely to succeed in a given set of circumstances. A consumer can hardly be expected to assume the moral responsibility to receive a notice by registered post if, between selecting the mode of delivery and the dispatch of the notice, the consumer goes blind and cannot read the notice, or is admitted to hospital and so does not receive it. The attachment of a moral dimension to the choice of a mode of delivery indicates that the Supreme Court of Appeal had already decided that debtors in default are in a state of moral turpitude, and are likely to try to avoid the consequences of their arrears. This unfortunate reasoning is more about social shaming than it is about the interpretation of the law.

The *Sebola* case provides another example of why it makes no sense to hold a debtor "responsible" for their selected mode of delivery. In *Sebola*, a notice in terms of section 129 had been sent by registered post, but had gone astray. It had been delivered to the wrong post office, and the Sebolas never had any indication that it had been sent to them.[79] In these circumstances, the Sebolas clearly could not be held "responsible" for their choice. A majority of the Constitutional Court agreed. The court held that the purpose of section 129(1) of the Act read in context, was to ensure that the notice dispatched in its terms actually reached the debtor. The onus is on the creditor to establish, on a balance of probabilities, that this had happened.[80] That did not mean that the creditor had to demonstrate conclusively that the debtor had received, read and understood the notice, merely that the notice had come into debtor's possession.[81]

The consequence of the *Sebola* decision was that where a mortgagee sought to execute against a mortgagor's home, execution could not be granted if it appeared that a notice in terms of section 129 of the National Credit Act had not come into

---

[77] *Rossouw v Firstrand Bank Ltd* 2010 (6) SA 439 (SCA).
[78] Ibid para 31.
[79] *Sebola v Standard Bank of South Africa Ltd* 2012 (5) SA 142 (CC) para 5.
[80] Ibid para 74.
[81] *Absa Bank v Mkhize* 2014 (5) SA 16 (SCA) paras 45–9.

the mortgagor's possession. But the matter did not end there. The effect of the decision would have been a substantial increase in the number of mortgagors becoming aware of alternatives to execution, and in the number of mortgagors actually exercising these alternatives. This radically shifted the balance of power between mortgagors and mortgagees. The prospect of a large number of debtors seeking to avoid execution through debt counselling or other alternatives alarmed the major mortgage providers, and efforts to roll *Sebola* back were engaged almost as soon as the decision was handed down. In *Mkhize* the decision was attacked as "extraordinary and absurd"[82] because it allowed debtors to avoid the enforcement of credit agreements by evading the delivery of a section 129 notice.

There was, in truth, never much substance to this. The "evasion" argument depended on the assumption that most creditors know the importance and effect of non-delivery of a section 129 notice. But the notice requirement is itself based on the assumption that consumers have limited knowledge of their rights. It makes no sense to suppose that an uninformed consumer will use the machinery of the Act in bad faith to evade enforcement if they do not know what the machinery really is. In any event, a strategy of evasion would also require a debtor to turn up to court and actually complain that the notice had not been delivered, in order to avoid enforcement. Of course, at that point, the debtor could simply be handed the notice, and the requirements of section 129 would have been fulfilled. Any "evasion" encouraged by the decision on *Sebola* would have been ineffectual, short-lived, and far outweighed by the benefits to non-evading consumers of a strong delivery requirement.

Nonetheless, the Constitutional Court appeared moved by the banks' criticism, and soon found an opportunity to revise its position. In *Kubyana*[83] a debtor, Mr Kubyana, had not received a section 129 notice because he did not collect it from the post office. There was no indication of whether Mr Kubyana had ever known that there was a notice waiting for him, or of the nature and importance of it.[84] When Standard Bank sought to execute a debt against his car, now advised by an attorney, Mr Kubyana raised the defence that he had never been given the benefit of the notice, and that, if he had, he would have exercised his rights in terms of it. The High Court ruled against Mr Kubyana, on the basis that he "had a duty to explain why the notice did not reach him".[85] On the Constitutional Court's decision in *Sebola*, of course, Mr Kubyana had no such duty. It was for the bank to show, on a balance of probabilities, that the notice had reached him. Assuming that Mr Kubyana was not trying to deliberately evade delivery of the notice, there was also nothing Mr Kubyana could reasonably say to explain why it did not reach him.

The Constitutional Court approached the matter on the footing that Mr Kubyana was indeed trying to evade delivery of the notice. There was no evidence of this, but that did not appear to matter. What the court appeared anxious to do was revisit the

[82] Ibid.
[83] *Kubyana v Standard Bank of South Africa Ltd* 2014 (3) SA 56 (CC).
[84] Ibid para 5.
[85] Ibid para 8.

Sebola decision in light of the criticism levelled at it by the major banks. In doing so, the court adopted the unfortunately moral tone that had led the Supreme Court of Appeal into error in *Rossouw*. In strident language, the court warned that the National Credit Act should not be read as "relentlessly one-sided" and "concerned with nothing more than devolving rights and benefits on consumers without any regard for the interests of credit providers".[86] The court warned that "the noble pursuits of that statute should not be open to abuse by individuals who seek to exercise those protections unreasonably or in bad faith".[87]

What followed was essentially a re-tooling of the *Sebola* decision. In place of *Sebola's* burden of proving that the notice, on a balance of probabilities, actually reached the consumer, the court adopted a vaguer standard. The creditor was still under an obligation to ensure that the notice was sent to the consumer at the proper address and in the correct mode of delivery. However, in the event of non-delivery, the consumer had to demonstrate that the reason that they did not receive the notice was not attributable to their own fault. In other words, "even if there is evidence indicating that the section 129 notice did not reach the consumer's attention, that will not amount to an indication disproving delivery if the reason for non-receipt is the consumer's unreasonable behaviour".[88]

The net effect of this was that, indications of non-delivery of the notice would not in themselves frustrate the enforcement of the credit agreement without an explanation from the debtor of why delivery did not take place. This strange requirement – can anyone explain why they did not receive a notice they did not know was coming and the importance of which they were likely unaware? – is attributable to a kind of moral panic on the part of courts faced with debtors who, often, are painted by creditors as not entirely trustworthy. This panic is itself related to the insidious way in which common law categories can be endowed with moral power. It has long been a feature of debtor and creditor law that a simple contractual status as a person who owes money, becomes endowed with moral content. That moral content grounds social characteristics that are assigned to the members of the class. Borrowers have to contend with social stereotypes that they are untrustworthy and will attempt to evade their obligations, unless subject to harsh penalties for doing so.[89] In *Kubyana*, the Constitutional Court found itself unable to break completely from seeing the debtor and creditor relationship in these stereotypical terms.

Nonetheless, the requirement finally settled on by the Constitutional Court – that section 129 notices are sent out in such a manner that they come to the attention of a reasonable consumer – creates an important opportunity for debtors to negotiate and restructure their debts, and to stave off execution against their homes. It is, perhaps, in this context, that a constitutionally inspired requirement of "meaningful

---

[86] Ibid para 20.

[87] Ibid para 46.

[88] Ibid para 53.

[89] In *Debt: The First 5000 Years* David Graeber draws out the historical links between debtor and creditor relationships on the one hand, and moral obligations, honour and degradation on the other. See D Graeber (note 3 above) 73–126 and 329–30.

engagement" might appropriately be imported. Because of the existence of the standard of proportionality and the statutory requirements imposed by the National Credit Act, much of the normative space left blank by meaningful engagement can be filled in. An explicit requirement that mortgagor and mortgagee meet with each other to discuss the alternatives to execution against the mortgagor's home set out in the legislation, and any other expedient that might be appropriate, would further integrate constitutional values with the bond execution process. However, given the extent to which *Kubyana* demonstrated that the Constitutional Court appears to have bought in to official suspicion of the debtor class, a meaningful engagement requirement in bond execution matters seems unlikely.

In any event, the revised bond execution process as it currently stands is still a far cry from the straightjacket in which the common law placed non-paying mortgagors. Even after *Kubyana*, a debtor who, through no fault of their own, did not have the benefit of the notice, will always be able to raise non-receipt of a section 129 notice as a defence to enforcement of the debt.

Section 129(3) of the National Credit Act has met with less obvious controversy, perhaps because it is necessarily triggered by a "responsible" debtor trying to meet their obligations. The meaning and application of the provision were considered in *Nkata*.[90] Section 129(3) permits a debtor to "reinstate" a loan agreement after they have defaulted through non-payment, so long as the creditor has not cancelled the agreement, and the debtor brings their instalments up to date and pays the creditor reasonable costs of taking steps to enforce the agreement in response to the debtor's default. In mortgage bond cases, the loan agreement is never cancelled, because the creditor will instead always opt for specific performance, in the form of the attachment and sale of the mortgaged property.

Two questions then arise. The first is whether there are any formalities required to reinstate an agreement. The second is when, other than cancellation, a mortgagor's right to reinstate an agreement expires. In *Nkata*, the mortgagee bank argued that it was incumbent on the debtor to formally communicate her intention to reinstate the agreement and ask the bank to identify the costs of doing so. It also argued that reinstatement should be impossible after the bank has taken any steps at all to execute against the mortgaged property. Had the bank's arguments been accepted, mortgagors would have been afforded significantly less space and opportunity to reinstate a mortgage loan agreement.

A majority of the Constitutional Court rejected both of the bank's arguments, however. It first held that reinstatement is a unilateral act that requires no notice, and which occurs by operation of law.[91] The debtor simply pays the instalments outstanding. It is then up to the creditor to liquidate and demand its enforcement costs.[92] Secondly, the majority held that the mortgagor could prevent execution at any time before the bonded property was sold in execution of the debt, and the

90 *Nkata v Firstrand Bank Limited* 2016 (4) SA 257 (CC).
91 Ibid para 105.
92 Ibid para 124.

auction price has been paid.[93] This expansive interpretation of the Act was clearly intended to provide the maximum space possible for a debtor faced with execution against their property.

A great many mortgage bond execution cases now revolve around whether there has been compliance with the notice requirements of section 129(1) of the National Credit Act, and whether it is possible for the mortgagor to reinstate the loan agreement in terms of section 129(3).[94] That these questions have now been hardwired into the proportionality inquiry in execution proceedings signals just how radical a departure from the common law the proportionality inquiry in *Jaftha* permitted.

6.3.3   The Qualified Right to a Reserve Price

In *Folscher*, the court observed that a mortgaged home constitutes "the most important investment of their lives, to build up a nest egg, and to eventually enjoy the fruits of capital growth, quite apart from acquiring an asset that may provide security for further access to capital".[95] Much of the courts' hesitancy in ordering execution against a mortgaged home can be attributed to the very real danger that forced sales tend to substantially undervalue the property sold, and can be catastrophic for the investment a mortgaged home represents for the mortgagor.

That preoccupation has only very recently found expression in rule 46A(9) of the Rules of Court, which was adopted in 2018. The rule requires a court to consider setting a reserve price when it orders execution against a mortgaged home. The point of a reserve price is to prevent a home from being sold for substantially less than it is worth, and to ensure some protection for the mortgagor's investment in the property. In *Mokebe* the court held that a reserve price should generally be set unless "the debt is so hopelessly in excess of the value of the property that the reserve price would be irrelevant compared to the value of the property".[96]

It is not yet clear what practice the courts will adopt in setting, or refusing to set a reserve price, but the function of a reserve price in protecting the value of the mortgagor's investment is obvious. The additional importance of setting a reserve price to the mortgagor is that it can delay the final act of execution, giving the mortgagor more space in which to act to protect their home. This vital time and space acts as further amelioration to the common law position: viz. that the house is sold to whoever will bid for it, at whatever price. It remains to be seen how this new space forms, and what opportunities it affords to distressed mortgagors.

6.4   DEBTORS, CREDITORS AND SOCIAL CHANGE

The South African courts have not entirely been able to separate the fact of indebtedness from the attribution of moral blame. However, I have argued that, by introducing the concept of proportionality into the debtor and creditor

---

[93] Ibid paras 129–35.
[94] See, for example, *ABSA v Mokebe* 2018 (6) SA 492 (GJ) paras 35–43.
[95] *Firstrand Bank v Folscher* 2011 (4) SA 314 (GP) para 39.
[96] *ABSA Bank v Mokebe* 2018 (6) SA 492 (GJ) para 62.

relationship, the Constitution has triggered a profound rebalancing of the common law relationship between debtor and creditor. It has changed debt enforcement from the occasion for the naked assertion of the common law's authority structure between owner of debt and owners of property on which debt is secured, into a more reasoned arena for engagement and negotiation of the least socially destructive terms on which a debt can be settled.

This constitutes a profound adjustment of social power relationships, and has triggered no small degree of social change. Because debt enforcement procedures take place case by case, in the daily grind of the opposed and unopposed motion courts across South Africa's High Court divisions and Magisterial Districts, it is hard to accurately quantify what difference has been made, to the population as a whole, by the fairer and more equitable arrangements for mortgage bond executions that have taken place. Nor is it possible to say, with any precision, what alternations to the debt enforcement regime have been most effective. That must await another research project. But it is possible to say that the trigger for the readjustment of debt enforcement was, in all probability, the decision in *Jaftha*, which subjected the common law to the constitutional requirement of proportionality. The developments that have taken place would not have occurred at all, or in the way that they did, unless it was possible to ask whether, in all the circumstances, execution of a debt is fair, reasonable and proportionate.

The answer to that question was of critical importance to Elsie Gundwana, who still lives in her home in Thembalethu. The Constitutional Court set aside the sale of her home. It also ordered Nedbank to pay her lawyers' legal fees. Ms Gundwana's lawyers had taken the case on the basis that they would not be paid unless the court ordered the bank to pay Ms Gundwana's legal costs. Nedbank offered to waive its claim over Ms Gundwana's home, and pay the costs of transferring into her name, so long as it did not have to pay Ms Gundwana's legal fees. That this condition was imposed at all speaks volumes of the social difference the bank thought had been made by debtor litigation in the higher courts.

CHAPTER SEVEN

WHAT'S PROPERTY LAW GOT TO DO WITH IT?

Isiah Mahlobo sits on the edge of his three-quarter mattress and base set in his room on the third floor of "MBV Phase 1". The MBV building is an old military veterans hospital, renovated into a new transitional housing facility, provided by the City of Johannesburg in response to the decision of the Constitutional Court in *Olivia Road*.[1] Isiah and his 600 or so neighbours fought for several years against the City of Johannesburg's plan to evict them from their flats in San Jose, which are just over a kilometre and a half away from where Isiah now sits.

As we saw at the start of this book, San Jose was what the City referred to as a "bad" building": a rundown, abandoned tenement occupied by poor and homeless people who were shut out of the private residential housing market, and for whom the state had provided no realistic alternative.[2] Conditions at San Jose were harsh. There was no running water and no electricity. The drains were backed up, meaning that a great deal of sewage had accumulated in the building's parking garages.

Isiah and his neighbours had no trouble with moving out of San Jose, if the City would only give them somewhere else to go. However, the City's prescription for San Jose was limited to the eviction of its residents.

Having won his case in court, Isiah has now forced the City to provide him with somewhere else to go. After six years of exhausting effort: organising the San Jose community, coping with repetitive police raids meant to drive the community out of the building, administering cleaning rotas which structure the residents' communally agreed obligations to clean the common areas of the building; unblocking sewage pipes; carrying water up the stairs to elderly and infirm residents; and all the time working with lawyers to resist eviction and compel the City to provide the residents a better place to live, Isiah sits in his new room. That room is supplied with running water and electricity; it is secure and clean; and perhaps most importantly, the state-subsidised rent (including services) is capped at 25% of Isiah's means-tested income.

Isiah now, for the first time, thinks about the long-term future, not just the next community meeting, police raid or court date. He is free to plan and act to give effect to his aspirations. The boundaries of his agency have shifted dramatically. He has more space to forge a path through life. He thinks about having a child with his partner, approaching the City for skills training or a bursary to register

---

[1] *Occupiers of 51 Olivia Road and 197 Main Street, Johannesburg v City of Johannesburg* 2008 (3) SA 208 (CC).

[2] S Wilson "Planning for Inclusion in South Africa: The State's Duty to Prevent Homelessness and the Potential of 'Meaningful Engagement'" (2011) 22 *Urban Forum* 265, 275.

for a qualification, or setting up a small business. He has not thought about these possibilities for a long time. Their reappearance is sensuous and exciting.[3]

This opening up of space to think and act, I have argued throughout this book, is an important mechanism of action through which law brings about social change. Law is more than just reflective of the balance of economic and political forces. It is more than an instrument with which to trigger and influence the course of institutional policy and behaviour. It is a fundamentally social phenomenon, that structures the spaces within which ordinary men and women conceive of and pursue their goals. The forms and content of law both constrain and enable agency, and shape the spaces in which people are free to act.

For this reason, the forms and content of law matter at a much more fine-grained level than the law and social change literature has previously acknowledged. Law and social change scholarship tends to concentrate on elite struggles to achieve high-level public policy goals, such as a desegregation of schools,[4] gendered pay equity,[5] legal abortion,[6] the restriction and ultimate abolition of the death penalty[7] and access to life-saving drugs.[8] These are all important legal struggles worthy of attention, but they tend to focus on "leveraging the law"[9] to force high-level policy changes. They leave out of account the way in which law is tied to deep structures of inequality that shape the very terms of what ordinary men and women understand to be a just society, and the way in which those structures facilitate or constrain everyday agency.

The forms and content of property law are a substantial and important case in point. The common law of property creates a complex structure of status hierarchies that overwhelmingly privilege the powers and rights of owners over things, and other people with subordinate rights, or no rights at all. In some cases, these hierarchies privilege one form of ownership over another, as in the case of mortgagors and mortgagees. The pattern is everywhere the same, however: a pattern of domination and control by reference to status. That status is membership of a pre-social common law category that affords its members privileged rights.

The common law reproduces manifold forms of social disadvantage, not the least of which is class-based inequality. When the forms and content of property law change, so too, for better or worse, do the patterns of structural inequality and disadvantage within the society to which it applies. I have illustrated this point by reference to the way in which the property clause and housing clause in the

---

[3] This image is my recollection of a meeting with Isiah just after he relocated to MBV Phase 1, in October 2009. At that time, I formed part of the legal team representing the residents of San Jose in their fight against eviction, and in their relocation to the MBV property, and another property, known as "Old Perm", in Hillbrow, Johannesburg.

[4] T Patterson *Brown v Board of Education: A civil rights milestone and its troubled legacy* (2002).

[5] M McCann *Rights at Work: Pay equity and the politics of legal mobilisation* (1994).

[6] G Rosenberg *The Hollow Hope: Can courts bring about social change?* 2 ed (2008).

[7] C Steiker and J Steiker *Courting Death: The Supreme Court and Capital Punishment* (2016).

[8] S Robbins *From Revolution to Rights in South Africa: Social Movements and Popular Politics* (2008) 100 to 144.

[9] D Schultz (ed) *Leveraging the Law: Using courts to achieve social change* (1998).

South African Constitution have subjected the common law of property to constitutional limitation and control. This has resulted in legal changes that provide enhanced protection to unlawful occupiers, residential tenants and homeowner mortgagors.[10]

These legal changes have enlarged the spaces in which unlawful occupiers, residential tenants and homeowner mortgagors can act to protect their homes, and widen the range of social possibilities available to them. What was once a space of prompt dispossession of a person by state and capital has become, at the very least, a site of negotiation with, and challenge to, the state and capitalist forces. Across a range of cases, that challenge has been successful. Unlawful occupiers have not been evicted, but have strengthened their tenure security. Tenants have restrained rent increases, resisted unfair lease terminations and controlled landlord profiteering. Homeowner mortgagors have redefined their relationships with banks and resisted, sometimes successfully, bank-driven dispossessions of homeownership.[11] The challenge is not limited to habitation rights either. The Constitutional Court has, at least tentatively, suggested that ownership may, in an appropriate case, be limited by any competing constitutional interest.[12]

In this chapter, I conclude the book with two observations. The first relates to the effectiveness of post-apartheid land reform. The second emphasises the dynamic and ongoing nature of the transformation of property law, and how the limited emancipation from the common law hierarchies that has been achieved is potentially quite fragile, and open to challenge.

7.1   THE "FAILURE" OF SOUTH AFRICAN LAND REFORM

Often, the discussion of the transformation of property law in South Africa is reduced to a debate about the progress of large-scale land reform programmes. The weight of international opinion is that these programmes have failed. Thomas

---

[10] Against this approach, scholars such as Joel Modiri have in recent years argued for a radical constitutional pessimism. The Constitution, it is suggested, cannot play a meaningful role in transforming society because it emerges out of, and remains embedded in, colonialist and capitalist power relationships. See J Modiri "Conquest and constitutionalism: first thoughts on an alternative jurisprudence" (2018) 34 *South African Journal on Human Rights* 300. Although there can be no argument with the attention Modiri calls to the colonialist and capitalist roots from which the legal form emerges, the problem with Modiri's critique is that it leaves little room for the subject, and fails to acknowledge the ways in which exercise of individual and group agency can fundamentally alter the structures of domination that the law embodies. My argument in this book is that the open-text, aspirational content of the legal forms adopted in and after the Constitution, is capable of being engaged, and has been engaged, in an effort to restructure property relationships. Property relationships form a key part of the structure of colonialist and capitalist domination. Accordingly, the question is not whether the Constitution can be called upon in aid of an anti-colonialist or anti-capitalist project. Clearly, it can. The question is rather how far that manipulation can be taken. It is only once that question has been answered that we will know the limits of the constitutional project.

[11] Sometimes, these developments have themselves caused shifts in policy. The *Grootboom* community's legal action indirectly brought about the Emergency Housing Policy. The *Jaftha* and *Gundwana* cases caused elaborate changes in judicial policy through changes to judge-made rules of practice. The policy changes were necessary to accommodate the alterations in legal relationships brought about by the *Grootboom*, *Jaftha* and *Gundwana* decisions. The cases opened up the space in which they were possible, but the policy changes were a by-product, and not the purpose of the legal action that caused them.

[12] *Governing Body of the Juma Musjid Primary School and Others v Ahmed Asruff Essay NO and Others* 2011 (8) BCLR 761 (CC) para 70.

Piketty speaks in sweeping terms of the absence of any significant land reforms in post-apartheid South Africa.[13] Samuel Moyn blithely accuses the ANC of having "abandoned" land reform, and sums up the Constitutional Court's *Grootboom* decision as having ultimately resulted in not much more than "copious ink … spilled" in academic discussion of its implications.[14]

Neither Piketty nor Moyn seems interested in South Africa as much more than corroboration of grand theories of capitalist ideology (Piketty) or the inefficacy of human rights (Moyn). Whether or not South Africa supplies the evidence Piketty and Moyn think it does, a more contextual examination of the progress of land reform in post-apartheid South Africa does not justify talk of the absence or abandonment of land reform – and much less of the failure of the *Grootboom* decision.

Talk of the abandonment or the absence of land reform is simply inaccurate. Since the end of apartheid, 3.5 million hectares of land have been transferred to land claimants under the Restitution of Land Rights Act 22 of 1994.[15] The South African state has provided 2.5 million houses and a further 1.2 million parcels of serviced land to housing subsidy beneficiaries since 1994.[16] This has been provided through, or will eventually lead to, the transfer of ownership of large quantities of land to recipients of state housing subsidies.

Of course, in purely statistical terms, the inequalities are still grim, and land reform efforts have not been equal to their task.[17] The statistics depend on the tacit acceptance of a model of land reform that entails the redistribution of traditional property rights. If land reform is simply the redistribution of ownership rights, then the progress has been quite slow.

But if this book has shown anything, it has demonstrated that statistics that quantify the transfer of ownership rights are not the only way to measure the effect of land reform legislation. It is necessary to look at the power relationships encoded in property law, and how these relationships have been altered through tenure reform and through reforms to the deliberative processes through which property rights are characterised in the abstract, determined in the concrete and implemented in practice.

If this is added to the picture, then a more optimistic assessment of the reform of land and property in post-apartheid South Africa is possible. It matters to any assessment of the efficacy of socio-economic rights and to the success of land reform that unlawful occupiers are harder (sometimes impossible) to evict; that residential tenants are protected from exploitation; and that homes may not be

---

[13] T Piketty *Capital and Ideology* (2020) 296–7.

[14] S Moyn *Not Enough: Human Rights in an Unequal World* (2018) 199–200.

[15] South African Government "Land Reform" <www.gov.za/issues/land-reform> last visited 28 August 2020.

[16] "South Africa's Housing Conundrum" in South African Institute of Race Relations @ *Liberty: The Policy Bulletin of the IRR* Issue 20 (2015) 1.

[17] See page 34–35 above. Piketty is closer to the mark when he criticises the South African state for its refusal to embark on any meaningful programme of fiscal reform, by altering economic policy in a manner that leads to more redistributive outcomes. But land reform, whether it succeeds or fails, is just one component of this wider strategy, and land reform has at least seriously been attempted, in a way that fiscal reform has not.

foreclosed against without giving the owner every reasonable opportunity to prevent this through restructuring debt and resisting usurious practices.

In other words, if we concentrate only on the statistical incidence of the transfer of traditional property rights to the poor and the vulnerable, we overlook a great deal that is significant and modestly successful about property law reform in South Africa.

7.2   SUSTAINING TRANSFORMATION

It should be clear from this that the transformation of property law in South Africa that I have sought to emphasise in this book is an ongoing process rather than a past event. It is a process that tends away from status hierarchies, and towards substantive equality. It tends towards the enhancement of widespread individual agency rather than the control of a narrow oligarchy of property owners. It has the capacity to contribute to genuine and lasting social justice in post-apartheid South Africa.

Recognising and sustaining this transformation requires, at the very least, the absorption of four key lessons that can be distilled from the developments that this book describes and analyses.

First, I suggest that the study of law and social change involves more than tracking changes in institutional behaviour, public policy or macro-level statistics on the incidence of social phenomena. More attention ought to be given to the ways in which the legal subject acts in legally constructed social spaces. It is true that one possible outcome of the changes in property law I have set out in this book might be a reduced incidence of eviction, lease termination or mortgage foreclosure across South Africa, but the absence of such a reduction would not, in itself, demonstrate that these legal changes had little or no social effect. There may, for instance, be stronger economic or social phenomena driving incidences of dispossession, upon which legal changes are having an ameliatory effect. In addition, a legally created space does not itself ensure change. It needs to be occupied and acted in.

For this reason, and this is the second lesson, the opening up of a legal space creates a potentiality. It does not necessarily imply that this space is being acted in or exploited in expected ways. Changes in the law need to be studied alongside the exercise of agency at the individual or community level. To exploit changes in the law, individuals and communities need, at minimum, to acquire knowledge of those changes, and the ability, where necessary, to form alliances with courts and legal practitioners in the process of enforcing legal rights. Support structures for legal mobilisation are necessary to maximise the change-making potential of the spaces the law opens up, and to protect those spaces against foreclosure. These support structures are not necessary in every case, because legally created spaces can often be exploited without professional legal assistance, but they are important in sustaining legally structured social change.

Thirdly, the structure of the law itself requires scrutiny. The legally structured changes I have examined in this book have all taken a particular form. They have all required a revision in the very structure of legal reasoning about property.

The common law of property categorises legal subjects by whether they possess certain historically determined common law rights, and by the relative strength of those rights. The constitutional innovations I have set out in this book rely on a fundamentally different conceptual approach, which focuses on the context in which common law rights are sought to be exercised, and the impact of the exercise of those rights on constitutionally protected social interests. This shift, from the categorical to the contextual, has enhanced the capacity of the law to respond to pressing social needs. Instead of "privileging in an abstract and mechanical way the rights of ownership over the right not to be dispossessed" the new property law requires us to "balance out and reconcile the opposed claims in as just a manner as possible taking account of all the interests involved and the specific factors relevant in each particular case".[18] It seems to me that this sort of open-ended, value-based legal reasoning is far more likely to lead to social change than the sorting of legal subjects into categories and hierarchies, which is so often the grist in the mill of the common law.

Fourthly, the transformation of property law requires judges and legal practitioners who are willing to develop and accept arguments and strategies that are likely to create new spaces for action, rather than just focusing on narrow public policy goals, or re-asserting time-worn common law principles.

I address each of these lessons, in turn, below.

7.3   LAW IN ACTION

An agent-centred theory of law and social change focuses on the content of legal rules, and how they influence social action. It asks what kinds of social relationships and action are likely to result from a particular set of legal rules. It seeks to characterise the way in which legal rules enable, and disable, particular forms of social action. The claim is that law structures and patterns social relationships and action in fundamentally important ways. It does so by creating, foreclosing and shaping spaces in which some kinds of action are possible, and others are not. The question is always whether a particular legal form, or the content of a particular legal rule, is likely to constrain or facilitate a particular kind of action.

This concern with the relationship between law, the deep structure of social relationships and the possibilities of individual and group agency has not traditionally been the focus of law and social change scholarship. Brian Ray divides scholars of law and social change into "realists" and "constructivists".[19] Realists accept the limited potential of law to bring about social change under the right conditions, but emphasise that change takes place infrequently, and only once the necessary political mobilisation has happened. Realists are often critical of decisions to turn to legal remedies to achieve social change, because, they argue, the resources

---

[18] *Port Elizabeth Municipality v Various Occupiers* 2005 (1) SA 217 (CC) para 23.

[19] B Ray *Engaging with Social Rights* (2016) 22. Ray attributes the distinction to M Langford, B Cousins, J Dugard and T Madlingozi (eds) in their conclusion to their edited collection *Socio-economic Rights in South Africa: Symbols or Substance?* (2014) 421.

expended in the turn to law could be more effectively deployed to seek change "directly through political channels".[20]

These critiques of the use of law to bring about social change rely on research strategies that seek to match changes in the law with shifts in measurements of broad social phenomena. The most obvious of these strategies grounds the standard critique of socio-economic rights. Scholars tend to juxtapose the adoption of socio-economic rights with increases, or only very small reductions, in statistical indicators of poverty, inequality and unemployment, and the absence of significant social policy shifts. The failure of socio-economic rights to act clearly on these indicators is taken as evidence of their inefficacy.[21] Rosenberg, too, links what he suggests is the limited efficacy of the *Roe v Wade*[22] case to what he argues is the limited impact of the decision on the rate in growth of the number of legal abortions in the United States.[23] Rosenberg concludes that the Supreme Court's decisions legalising abortion are "far less responsible for the changes that occurred than most people think".[24]

All the normal limitations of these types of analysis apply here: the reliability of the data; the way that indicators are encoded; the time scales that are being studied; and the inability to say what would have happened had the event that is being studied not taken place. However, the agent-centred theory of law and social change that I have outlined in this book constitutes a further limitation. "Realist" analyses tend to be located firmly within the instrumentalist approach I set out in Chapter 2. Law is posited as a tool that is applied, through policy change, to the social phenomena to which it is addressed. The efficacy of the tool is defined by reference to the underlying goals and purposes that motivated the adoption of the law in the first place. So, socio-economic rights "succeed" if they reduce inequality, since that was taken to be the purpose for their adoption, and they "fail" if inequality is not perceivably affected by their adoption. Similarly, and more controversially, the legalisation of abortion succeeds if more legal abortions take place, so long as some part of the increase can be attributed to the change in the law.

However, these methods and conclusions look less persuasive if a realist approach is substituted with an agent-centred approach to law and social change. The agent-centred approach denies that law can be wielded as an instrument to achieve an a-contextually defined purpose, and then applied to something called "society" to attain that purpose. Law is society. It is just one of a range of social phenomena that influence behaviour by shaping the social context in which individual agents act. If that is accepted, then the mere fact that socio-economic rights cannot be associated with a significant reduction in inequality, or that *Roe v Wade* cannot be said to

---

[20] Ibid 22.

[21] Ibid 330. Citing R Hischl and E Rosevear "Constitutional Law Meets Comparative Politics: Socio-Economic Rights and Political Realities" in T Campbell (ed) *The Legal Protection of Human Rights: Skeptical Essays* (2011) 220–1.

[22] *Roe v Wade* 410 U.S. 113 (1973)

[23] G Rosenberg (note 6 above) 178–9.

[24] Ibid 201.

have "caused" more legal abortions, does little to illuminate the role law plays in bringing about social change.

On any agent-centred theory, law simply influences one part of the social matrix which, in turn, helps determine the scope of possible action by individuals, groups or institutions. It would be unrealistic to expect law to act directly on indicators of social phenomena. What is important about legal rules is not so much their direct impact on income distributions, poverty levels, the incidence of a particular form of behaviour, or the trajectory of policy reform. The question is rather how law affects the range and texture of the choices available to agents over time. For example, the actual incidence of abortion tells us relatively little about the impact of its legalisation. What matters is how the law enhances or retards the ability of a woman to choose whether, how, where and when to terminate her pregnancy.

Statistical studies are accordingly of very limited use in considering whether and to what extent a particular legal development has brought about a particular set of social changes. Because law is often so subtly embedded in the range of social spaces that shape agents' opportunities for action, it is likely impossible to say what impact, if any, a change in the law has had on large social phenomena like poverty and inequality, because law is but one structurant of action.

Studies of the extent to which legal changes have caused changes to institutional behaviour and policy do better, but only because they tend to focus on the way in which a legal change has acted on a particular agent's behaviour. Usually, though, that agent is the state and the behaviour being monitored is the adoption of a particular set of policies. The state is but one agent upon which law acts, and the adoption of policy is but one kind of behaviour. Nonetheless, matching changes in the law to shifts in institutional policy (including the policies that drive the behaviour of non-state actors) is useful, because it helps characterise how law reshapes the spaces in which those institutions, and those individuals who are subject to them, act.

Still, however, these types of studies tend to share a basic instrumentalist flaw. They conceive of social change as something that happens when law acts on policy which, in turn, acts on people. Law is, again, seen as an instrument, and society the material to which it is applied. A more successful study of the relationship between law and social change would focus on the manifold ways in which law is itself enmeshed with a variety of other social phenomena in a way that structures an agent's opportunities for action.

The agent-centred theory outlined in this book has something in common with what Ray calls the "constructivists". The constructivist approach argues that "understanding whether and how social rights have had meaningful effects ... calls for a much finer-grained examination of their interaction with particular aspects of ... socio-political processes".[25] The constructivists accept that the impact of law is mediated through human agency, and that this agency requires study before

---

[25] B Ray (note 19 above) 332. See also Socio-Economic Rights Institute of South Africa (SERI) *Public Interest Legal Services in South Africa* (2015) for an attempt to capture the manifold ways in which strategic litigation leads to social change.

meaningful conclusions about the relationship between law and social change can be drawn. Constructivists draw attention to "rights-based strategies" or "tactics".[26] The aim here is to study the ways in which rights and law have been self-consciously "used" to achieve specific goals, often concerned with shifts in public policy.

The concept of a "movement", "movement lawyering"[27] or "legal mobilization"[28] is often central to these types of constructivist claims. Both emphasise "the limited instrumental power of litigation to push society in progressive directions".[29] Law's efficacy then depends on its deployment as a strategic tool by organised groups. So central is the "movement" to efficacious deployment of law that authors in the constructivist tradition have warned, in stark terms that "litigation can only catalyse mobilisation that is already taking place, it cannot create a movement where there was none".[30]

The finer-grained attention that "constructivists" call to the way law is mediated by movement-based agency is important, but ultimately insufficient, in characterising the relationship between law and social change. The limits of the position lie in the same basic instrumentalist mistake made by the "realists". Law is more than a "tool" to be "used". It is imbricated in a range of action within and outside movements seeking social change, and its efficacy goes beyond those movements.

This insight of the agent-centred theory is demonstrated by all three of the case studies set out in this book. There are, to be sure, occasions where legal forms and processes have been deployed by housing rights movements to achieve specific goals.[31] However, much more often, the alterations to the law of unlawful occupation, landlord and tenant relationships and mortgage bond executions have been driven by a range of different social actors, often without a self-consciously political project. The clearest case is perhaps the mortgage bond execution cases, in which there has been no "movement lawyering" at all, and relatively little "rights-based strategy". While many of the leading cases have been triggered by public interest legal services organisations,[32] the litigants involved were not seeking changes in public policy or greater equality. Nor did they self-consciously "use" rights "strategically" to do anything other than alleviate their own problems. While their lawyers perhaps saw the potential of their claims to give rise to an important judgment, or to develop the law in some important way, it is hard to imagine that

---

[26] M Langford "Introduction" in M Langford (ed) *Socio-economic Rights in South Africa: Symbols or substance?* (2014) 20. See also J Dugard and M Langford "Art or Science? Synthesising Lessons from Public Interest Litigation and the Dangers of Legal Determinism" (2011) 27 *South African Journal on Human Rights* 39.

[27] S Cummings "Movement Lawyering" (2017) *University of Illinois Law Review* 1645–1732.

[28] See generally, M McCann "Litigation and Legal Mobilisation" in G Caldeira (ed) *The Oxford Handbook of Law and Politics* (2008).

[29] S Cummings (note 27 above) 1729.

[30] G Marcus, S Budlender and N Ferreira *Public Interest Litigation in South Africa: Strategies, Tactics and Lessons* 112.

[31] In particular, the *Abahlali* cases dealt with in Chapter 3 above.

[32] The *Jaftha* case was instituted by the Legal Resources Centre; the *Gundwana* case was litigated, at the Constitutional Court level, by the Socio-Economic Rights Institute of South Africa.

even the most prescient legal representative could foresee all of the developments triggered in a case like *Jaftha* or *Grootboom*.

Almost all of the litigants who pursued the cases examined in this book did so because the law extended the spaces in which they could act to resist the processes of dispossession to which they were subject. In many cases, the success of the litigants itself helped to redefine and extend those spaces for others, who then occupied those spaces and pushed them further. This is clearest in the unlawful occupation cases discussed in Chapter 4, where the law progressed from according unlawful occupiers no rights at all, to being on the verge of allowing many unlawful occupiers to assert a right to remain where they had no right to be, on terms over which they can assert some control. In the landlord and tenant and mortgage bond cases dealt with in Chapters 5 and 6, the spaces occupied and acted in have been more constrained, and have generated less reliable outcomes. Yet, they have still provided important forms of resistance to dispossession which did not exist before.

Legal mobilisation and movement lawyering, and the social struggles in which they are enmeshed, only tell part of the story of law and social change, precisely because they see law in terms that are too instrumental. The agent-centred theory set out in this book, however, allows us to go further. The question is not whether law directly influences key indicators of the social phenomena to which it is addressed. Nor is it limited to whether law can be used as an instrument to pursue consciously political ends. The study of the relationship between law and social change must ask whether, and to what extent, legal action expands the space in which agents can act to resist coercion and pursue their own social ends.

7.4   ACTION IN LAW

Changes in the law reshape social and economic relationships across a wide range of geographical and social contexts. But the change wrought is subtle, complex, contingent and takes time to reveal itself. Often, it takes place against the background of deeply entrenched social and political norms that are fundamentally hostile to it. As the early PIE Act cases demonstrated, changes in legal rules do not automatically lead to the revision of the moral and political value systems in which the law is embedded. Carefully thought-through reform legislation meant to protect unlawful occupiers was initially dismissed as a "servitude of trespass",[33] concepts of "fairness" in landlord–tenant relationships are often fundamentally skewed in favour of the vested interests of landlords and property owners,[34] and concepts of "fairness" in debtor and creditor relationships are often undermined by a fundamental judicial suspicion of the debtor class.[35]

Partly for this reason legal changes seldom have any immediate impact on the structures of economic power to which they are addressed. It is only when legal rules are acted upon that the content of a legal rule passes into the

---

[33] *Betta Eiendomme (Pty) Ltd v Ekple-Epoh* 2000 (4) SA 468 (W).

[34] *Tenants of ERF 69, 70, 71, 72 Fairview v AJ and T Vosloo* Gauteng Rental Housing Tribunal Case No 1560/17 (26 November 2018).

[35] *Kubyana v Standard Bank of South Africa Ltd* 2014 (3) SA 56 (CC).

social world. The mechanism through which this occurs is the way in which changes in legal rules influence individual and group behaviour. But this influence is seldom straightforward. For example, an unlawful occupier may simply be unaware that they cannot lawfully be evicted if their eviction would lead to homelessness. If they do know this, they may or may not act on that knowledge by resisting their eviction. Many unlawful occupiers do not act on that information because they lack the legal resources necessary to contest a court application; because they are afraid of violent reprisal by the landowner or the state; because they are isolated, and unable to draw on the solidarity of a broader community in resisting eviction; or because they genuinely believe that the landowner ought to be able to remove them from the property even if that means they will be left homeless. Even if they know that the law affords them the right to remain in occupation, at least until alternative accommodation becomes available to them, other unlawful occupiers may use the knowledge of the content of legal rules, not to resist eviction, but to enhance their bargaining position in a negotiation for more time, or for some other benefit, such as money, to be given to them before they vacate.[36]

Conversely, the principle that evictions should not lead to homelessness may drive, and has often driven, widespread community-based legal resistance to eviction. If every community under threat of homelessness by eviction responded in this way, there can be little doubt that property relations in South Africa would be transformed overnight. Not every community responds to a threat of eviction in this way. However, to detect and begin to describe a relationship between law and social change, it is enough that some communities do respond in this way, and that the law creates, expands or helps protect the space in which this is possible. Often the difference between action and inaction in legally structured social spaces is the existence of a legal support structure that can enable individual agents to access the processes and institutions necessary to assert legal rights.

All of this is to underscore the common sense, but often overlooked, notion that the intent of a law does not translate neatly into practice, and why a theory for the relationship between law and social change cannot hope to draw a straight line between the intent, or even the plain language, of a legal rule, and its social impact. Laws shape the conditions under which people act, but they do not determine that action. Much depends on the practical availability of legal remedies and the means to access them, the individual choices made in whether and how far to engage those remedies, and how those remedies are then acted on. That is why it is best, as this book argues, to theorise the relationship between law and social change as the creation or destruction of spaces in which ordinary men and women can act for themselves.

Changes in the law create the potential for changes in practice, but they need to be exploited and acted upon. The spaces created by agency-enhancing legal rules need to be pushed to their full extent. Agents need to act in those spaces, to create

---

[36] The tenants in the *Plettenberg* cases eventually brought their long-running disputes with Lewray Investments to an end by accepting a substantial cash payment to move out of their flats.

new opportunities for action, and to expand further the range of possibilities for social change. In other words, law enhances the agency of what Mark Galanter calls "repeat players"[37] who are able to act continuously in legal spaces and tailor them to suit their particular interests. It is no accident that the radical pro-poor changes that I have set out in this book have taken place in legal spaces where poor and vulnerable people have no choice but to be repeat players. Unlawful occupiers cannot avoid eviction applications, any more than tenants and defaulting mortgagors can avoid lease terminations or the sale-in-execution process. Each of these processes can, however, be met with legal action that resists the presumption that dispossession is their inevitable endpoint, and makes agency enhancing claims to alternative outcomes. To have any appreciable social impact, these claims cannot be made once or twice. They have to become a regular feature, and change the nature and the processes of dispossession themselves. One major precedent-setting case is never enough. Follow-up action is always required to exploit the opportunities and potentialities created by that case.

A narrow focus on the remedy ordered and its impact on the parties to the case ignores the profound and far-reaching effect that legal development can have beyond the immediate parties to it. The obvious example is the effect that the *Grootboom* had on eviction cases for two decades after it was decided, which I set out in Chapter 4. It is only through understanding "follow-up" in its wider sense: the sense of exploiting the potentialities created by the logic of a particular decision, and pushing that logic further in agency-enhancing directions, that it is possible to understand fully how specific changes in the law can provide the impetus for significant longer-term change.[38]

A support structure for that action is accordingly necessary to exploit the spaces law creates. The agent-centred theory accordingly acknowledges the importance of what Charles Epp calls "the support structure for legal mobilisation".[39] Rights-driven social change, Epp argues, develops "within a broader political economy of litigation".[40] Epp links what he argues amounts to a "rights revolution" in the United States to the institutional development of organisations and initiatives that expanded access to courts throughout the twentieth century. Epp starts with the rise of large managerial firms that run along a bureaucratic model, and which developed the capacity to characterise and seek to influence the regulatory fields in which they are embedded. He then charts the political economy of litigation through to the advent of non-governmental organisations, which litigate for a cause or particular set of causes. Epp also traces changes in the support structure for legal mobilisation partly to changes in the legal profession. These changes provided economies of scale in large firms that could be used to undertake *pro bono* constitutional rights

---

[37] M Galanter "Why the Haves come out ahead: speculations on the limits of legal change" (1974) 9 *Law and Society Review* 95, 97.

[38] Marcus, Budlender and Ferreira (note 30 above) 46.

[39] C Epp *The Rights Revolution: Lawyers, Activists and Supreme Courts in Comparative Perspective* (1998) 44.

[40] Ibid 69.

litigation, and opened the profession up to a more diverse membership, which was, in turn, more likely to pursue rights litigation.

Epp's basic insight is indisputable: legally structured social action requires a support structure that is willing to fund litigation and other forms of legal action. The agent-centred theory advanced in this book argues that law plays a secondary role in social change by re-shaping the space in which agents act. It is agents themselves who act to secure change. Legal spaces can often only be manipulated and acted in with the support of a specialised class of professionals, which implies the need for agent-centred support for that action.

7.5   THE STRUCTURE OF LAW

One further drawback of the instrumentalist approach to law and social change (both realist and constructivist) is that it pays too little attention to the discursive forms that the law actually takes in any particular case. The law is posited as a black box to which strategy is applied and by which outcomes are generated. Those outcomes are then analysed for their potential to bring about social change. In general, the instrumentalist literature is striking in its general lack of concern with legal doctrine, and how it is constructed and changed. Law and social change scholarship proceeds as if there is a sharp distinction between the forms legal decision making takes, which is seen a pre-eminently the study of law, and the outcome and social impact of particular decisions, which is the domain of the humanities. The literature tends to be written within a functionalist paradigm that emphasises the institutional role of the courts rather than the structure and internal logic of their decisions.[41]

This book argues, however, that the structure of legal reasoning is directly related to social change. The structure of law and legal reasoning not only helps determine the outcomes of particular cases; it determines the scope for future action. The conceptual link between law and social change, I have argued in this book, is the extent to which legal reasoning and outcomes opens, shapes and forecloses spaces in which ordinary men and women can act to give effect to their goals. Both the outcome of a case, and the way that outcome is reached, matter for social change, so defined.

South African property law provides a powerful illustration of this. The common law of property is an authority structure that creates a strict hierarchy defined by reference to whether a legal subject is in possession of a series of clearly defined rights. A person is evicted from property unless they can show that they have one of a closed list of common law rights that are enforceable against the owner of that property. A tenant's lease is inherently temporary, and is terminated once a series of contractual conditions have been shown to be satisfied. A debtor faces execution against their property upon default, which is clearly contractually defined. Social

---

[41] K Calavita *Invitation to Law and Society: An introduction to the study of real law* (2010) 4: "So, jurisprudence is mostly devoted to examining what takes place inside the box of legal logic. Law and society takes exactly the opposite approach—it examines the influence on law of forces outside the box". There are exceptions, however. See B Ray (note 19 above), which draws links between the forms of legal reasoning adopted in social rights cases in the South African Constitutional Court, and the capacity of law to bring about social change.

consequences are determined by reference to categorical reasoning which admits of no degrees. A right either exists or it does not: "the concepts and definitions of private-law rights and relations between them permeate legal reasoning, based on a strict conceptual logic deriving from what is seen as abstract, universal and essential relations between the concepts themselves".[42]

This deep logic of the common law enables dispossession, and forecloses social space, because it generates social outcomes based on an asocial, and in many ways antisocial, conceptual hierarchy. The social consequences of decisions about property rights do not matter so much as the possession of particular forms of abstract right. Under apartheid, the result was that "civil law property principles were developed and extended to create new, profitable and secure property rights for the (mainly white) rich" while property law "in the public sphere was developed especially to exclude the (mainly black) poor from obtaining and securing property rights".[43] What mattered was not just the racist policy outcomes that were achieved, but also the way in which those outcomes depended on widespread dispossession of, and control over, where black people lived, and the receptivity of common law categories and reasoning to that project.

It is not surprising, then, that post-apartheid legal reforms have, at their most effective, relied upon an entirely different internal structure and logic. Unlawful occupiers were by definition subject to eviction under the common law. Now they can only be evicted if it is "just and equitable". Tenants' rights of occupation were subject to termination at any time and for any reason, so long as the relevant contractual conditions were fulfilled and reasonable notice was given. Now the termination must not constitute an "unfair practice". Mortgagors were subject to execution against their homes merely upon default. Now execution is only permitted where it is proportionate. These conceptual changes open up substantial space in which those who are subject to them can act. The certain dispossession that followed the termination or absence of rights has been replaced by a conceptual battleground in which action and resistance are possible.

Accordingly, the very conceptual structure that post-apartheid legal reform has assumed has important consequences for the path of social change. Where the courts were before mandated to order prompt dispossession, they must now make a value judgement based on fairness, equity or proportionality, taking into account social claims on property that were simply not relevant under the common law. This does not mean, of course, that the changes brought about are necessarily progressive or predictable. What is "fair", "proportionate" or "equitable" has sometimes been read as the maintenance of the *status quo*. However, more often, fairness, equity and proportionality have required substantial departures from the common law, which

---

[42] A van der Walt "Tradition on Trial: A Critical Analysis of the Civil Law Tradition in South African Property Law" (1995) 11 *South African Journal on Human Rights* 169, 179.

[43] Ibid 187.

have enhanced the agency of the weaker parties in the proprietary relationships to which those concepts have been applied.

By subjecting common law principles to the tests of equity, fairness and proportionality, this new, contextual, structure of legal reasoning makes power visible. The common law model of law obscures how law clothes the exercise of power by simply asserting a predetermined set of logical categories that become the common sense of a legal system. If legal reasoning is just about sorting people into categories of different kinds of rights, there is little room for considering the way in which those categories favour particular interests, reproduce particular forms of power and subjugation and might result in unfair, inequitable or disproportionately harsh outcomes. But by requiring the exercise of common law rights to be fair, equitable or proportionate, the new constitutional property law makes visible how power is exercised through the bland assertion of common law rights. Once that power is visible, it can be challenged on the terrain of equity, proportionality and fairness. This does not mean that those without common law rights, or those with weaker common law rights will always, or even often, win. But it does open the way for a popular critique of long-established "common sense" legal standards.

In this way, the agent-centred theory of law and social change advanced in this book gives us a way of linking legal reasoning directly to social change. The forms of legal reasoning most likely to lead to social change are those that require a value-based examination of legal relationships that takes into account the social consequences of the exercise of power by one or other party to those relationships. In a transforming society, the value-based reasoning invited by the concepts of equity, proportionality and fairness provides the opportunity for law to help reshape society, or for law to be reshaped to suit social ends.

7.6   AGENT-CENTRED JUDGES AND LAWYERS

These shifts in legal reasoning have issued powerful challenges to the legal profession and the judiciary. They force judges and lawyers to explain why their arguments and decisions are socially justified. Teachers and practitioners of law educated and socialised in the dry conceptualism that characterised property law before the advent of the Constitution, have had to fairly rapidly reorient themselves to a set of value-based inquiries that directly link legal ends to social needs. Before the adoption of the Constitution, the Appellate Division of the Supreme Court had asserted, without apparent irony, that the common law is "itself inherently an equitable legal system".[44] This attitude was no doubt indicative of a wider complacency about the South African common law that relieved lawyers of the need to consider whether particular common law rules were fair or equitable in their social impact. The gift of working within an "inherently equitable" legal system is that it is never necessary to think about whether the rules of the game are fair, and

---

[44] *Bank of Lisbon v De Ornelas* 1988 (3) SA 580 (A) 606A.

few lawyers in South Africa have ever been asked, as part of their professional training or socialisation, to consider that issue.

The Constitution changed all of this. In the context of the law of contract "[t]he Constitution requires that its values be employed to achieve a careful balance between the unacceptable excesses of contractual 'freedom', and securing a framework within which the ability to contract enhances rather than diminishes our self-respect and dignity".[45] In property law, too, the authority structure set up by the common law requires adjustment to ensure that it does not exclude pressing social claims or result in unfair dispossession.

This book has shown that the most formidable opponents of constitutionally driven changes to property law have sometimes been judges themselves, who have sought to react to or foreclose legally structured social change by doing little more than re-asserting outmoded common law principles or understating the true nature of new legal principles that have been derived from the Constitution. Sandra Liebenberg notes that "[a] significant constraining factor on the transformation of common law doctrines under rules under the influence of the normative value system of the Constitution is the nature of legal culture" including "traditional understandings of the 'internal logic' and processes through which common-law development takes place".[46]

In response to arguments that seek to develop the common law, or that are grounded in values located outside the common law, judicial posture is often defensive and conservative. High Court judgments often still bear the hallmarks of outmoded approaches.[47] But the difference the Constitution makes is that conservative judges now have to explain why they have chosen the same outcomes that would have been required by the direct application of the common law. This exposes those judges to criticism, and enables the selection and training of judicial officers who are willing to accept arguments and develop principles that restructure legal relationships. This is not to say that the post-apartheid judiciary is always and everywhere progressive, but it does provide a way to assess the extent to which post-apartheid judges are taking on the task of constitutionally mandated transformation, rather than simply falling back on the lazy conceptualism of the common law.

At least in the cases examined in this book, reactionary judicial impulses have generally been outweighed by progressive ones. But that could easily change. A careful examination of the way judges make decisions, and whether those

---

[45] *Brisley v Drotsky* 2002 (4) SA 1 (SCA) para 95. The quote is from Cameron JA's minority concurrence with the majority's order. The majority's reasoning was, as we have seen, far less supple that this quote suggests.

[46] S Liebenberg *Socio-Economic Rights: Adjudication under a Transformative Constitution* (2010) 339–340.

[47] See, for example, Willis J's judgment in *Emfuleni Local Municipality v Builders Advancement Services CC* 2010 (4) SA 133 (GSJ), which criticises, in stridently personal and emotional terms, the limitations on eviction imposed by the Constitutional Court and Supreme Court of appeal as having unjustifiably limited what the judge called "economic freedom".

decisions enhance or foreclose the agency of socially subordinate groups, is required to continually re-assess the potential and limits of legally structured social change.

Lawyers acting for people whose social claims are given no or inadequate recognition face a similar challenge. They must be able to make arguments that engage with the value-based enquiries now required by law; to sustain cross-class relationships with the individuals and social movements they represent; and to detect and exploit the potential to restructure, rather than simply reproduce, the legal norms into which they have been professionally socialised. They "must be prepared to put time and effort into understanding" the "needs and experiences" of socially subordinate groups "and to give voice to them in pleadings, affidavits and written argument".[48] This entails a set of skills and practices which go much further than placing a client in a pre-determined common law category. A good lawyer "serves the true interests of clients".[49] A useful way of thinking about a client's "true" interests is the client's interest lies in maximising their agency and being able to shape the space in which they act. An agent-centred theory of law and social change requires a lawyer who is able to evaluate the law by reference to constitutionally defined social ends, and to deploy legal arguments that tend to expand the spaces in which their clients can act.

7.7   THE MANY FACES OF LAW

This book started out by quoting Eddie Bruce-Jones's haunting invocation of a two-faced legal form that both kills and cures. The paradox Bruce-Jones evokes is keenly felt and perennial. It speaks powerfully to the painful and confusing way legal norms and practices are experienced in everyday life.[50]

The truth is, though, that the law is not a two-faced god that stands above the people it smites or rewards. It is complex construction that structures everyday life. It is part of the filter through which we experience the social world, and it is one of the constraints on, and enablers of, our action in that world.

Property law shapes the way in which we access and use resources. The point of this book has been to bring to light the manner in which the Constitution has triggered a series of changes in the forms and content of property law. Each of these changes, however small, has, in its own way, triggered substantial effects. But, taken as a whole, the alterations in the relationships between landowner and occupier, landlord and tenant, and debtor and creditor explored in this book have fundamentally altered the terms on which everyone, everywhere in South Africa, can expect to get access to the property they need to live, and to prosper.

The content of property law, perhaps more than any other area of law, determines the opportunity structure of our everyday lives, and our opportunities across an entire lifetime. Small changes in property law, and the processes through which

---

[48] S Wilson and J Dugard "Taking Poverty Seriously: The South African Constitutional Court and socio-economic rights" (2011) 22 *Stellenbosch Law Review* 664, 665–6.

[49] D Linder and N Levit *The Good Lawyer* (2014) 187.

[50] For a classic statement of law as it is experienced in everyday life see H Zinn (ed) *Justice in Everyday Life: The way it really works* (1974).

its content is determined and its principles are enforced, can lead to substantial changes in the social world. The agent-centred theory of property law and social change advanced in this book seeks to draw attention to the manifold ways in which property law integrates itself into society and structures how we think and act about property and human relationships. The picture is complex, and it is unlikely ever to be fully known. But an agent-centred theory of property law nonetheless helps us to locate the power and efficacy of law in the everyday. It also offers a way of building justice there too.

BIBLIOGRAPHY

Books and Articles

R Abel *Politics by Other Means: Law in the Struggle Against Apartheid, 1980–1994* (1995).

C Albertyn "Gender and Public Interest Litigation in Post-Apartheid South Africa" in J Brickhill (ed) *Public Interest Litigation in South Africa* (2018) 185.

R Arnott "Time for Revisionism on Rent Control?" *Journal of Economic Perspectives* (1995) vol 9 (1) 99.

P Bourdieu "The Force of Law: Towards a Sociology of the Juridical Field" (1987) 38 *Hastings Law Journal* 814.

W Blackstone *Commentaries on the Law of England Book 2* (1776).

J Brickhill (ed) *Public Interest Litigation in South Africa* (2018).

R Brits & A van der Walt "Application of the housing clause during mortgage foreclosure: a subsidiarity approach to the National Credit Act" (2014) 2 & 3 *Tydskrif vir die Suid Afrikaans Reg* 228 and 508.

R Brits "Sale in execution of property at unreasonably low price indicates abuse of process: *Nxazonke v ABSA Bank Ltd* [2012] ZAWCHC 184 (4 October 2012)" (2013) 76 *Tydskrif vir Hedendaagse Romeins-Hollandse Reg* 451.

J Brown & S Wilson "A Presumed Equality: State and Citizen in Post-Apartheid South Africa" (2013) 72 *African Studies* 86.

J Brown *South Africa's Insurgent Citizens: On Dissent and the Possibility of Politics* (2015).

G Budlender "Justiciability of the Right to Housing: The South African Experience" in S Leckie (ed) *National Perspectives on Housing Rights* (2003) 207.

J Byne "What we talk about when we talk about property rights – a response to Carol Rose's Property as a Keystone Right?" (1995) 71 *Notre Dame Law Review* 1049.

G Calabresi "Some Thoughts on Risk Distribution and the Law of Torts" (1961) 70 *Yale Law Journal* 499.

K Calavita *Invitation to Law and Society: An introduction to the study of real law* (2010).

G Carpenter "Constitutional interpretation by the existing judiciary in South Africa – can new wine be successfully decanted into old bottles?" (1995) 28 *Comparative and International Law Journal of Southern Africa* 322.

W Chafe *The Unfinished Journey* (1995).

M Chaskalson "Stumbling Towards Section 28: Negotiations Over the Protection of Property Rights in the Interim Constitution" (1995) 11 *South African Journal on Human Rights* 222.

L Chenwi "Democratising the Socio-Economic Rights Enforcement Process" in H Garcia, K Klare & L Williams (eds) *Social and Economic Rights in Theory and Practice: Critical Inquiries* (2015) 178.

L Chenwi "Legislative and judicial responses to informal settlements in South Africa: A silver bullet?" (2012) 23 *Stellenbosch Law Review* 540.

R Coase "The Problem of Social Cost" 1960 (3) *Journal of Law and Economics* 31.

GA Cohen *Karl Marx's Theory of History: A Defence* 2 ed (2001).

D Cole *Engines of Liberty: The Power of Citizen Activists to Make Constitutional Law* (2016).

W Cooper *The Rent Control Act* (1977).

D Davis "The case against the inclusion of socio-economic demands in a bill of rights except as directive principles" (1992) 8 *South African Journal on Human Rights* 475.

D Davis "The Scope of the Judicial Role in the Enforcement of Socio-Economic Rights" in H Garcia, K Klare & L Williams (eds) *Social and Economic Rights in Theory and Practice: Critical Inquiries* (2015) 197.

D Davis & K Klare "Transformative Constitutionalism and the Common and Customary Law" 2010 (26) *South African Journal on Human Rights* 403.

J Dugard & M Langford "Art or Science? Synthesising Lessons from Public Interest Litigation and the Dangers of Legal Determinism" (2011) 27 *South African Journal on Human Rights* 39.

J Dugard, T Madlingozi & K Tissington "Rights-compromised or rights-savvy? The use of rights-based strategies by Abahlali baseMjondolo, the South African shack-dwellers' movement" in H Alviar-Garcia, K Klare & L Williams (eds) *Social and Economic Rights in Theory and Practice: Critical Inquiries* 23.

WJ du Plessis "Protection of traditional knowledge in South Africa: does the 'commons' provide a solution?" in DA Frenkel, (ed) *Public Law and Social Human Rights* (2013).

J Elster *Karl Marx: A Reader* (1986).

F Engel & FW Munger *Rights of Inclusion: Law and Identity in the Life Stories of Americans with Disabilities* (2003).

C Epp *The Rights Revolution: Lawyers, Activists and Supreme Courts in Comparative Perspective* (1998).

R Epstein *Takings: Private Property and the Power of Eminent Domain* (1985).

P Ewick & S Silbey *The Common Place of Law: Stories from Everyday Life* (1998).

J Faris "Rental Housing" in WA Joubert (ed) *The Law of South Africa* 2 ed (1997).

B Fine *Democracy and the Rule of Law: Marx's Critique of the Legal Form* (2002).

O Fiss *Pillars of Justice: Lawyers and the Liberal Tradition* (2017).

S Fredman *Women and the Law* (1998).

M Galanter "Why the Haves come out ahead: speculations on the limits of legal change" (1974) 9 *Law and Society Review* 95.

D Graeber *Debt: The First 5000 Years* (2012).

J Griffin *On Human Rights* (2008).

L Hawthorne "Tenant Protection" in WA Joubert (ed) *The Law of South Africa* (1986).

FA Hayek *The Constitution of Liberty* (1960).

C Heyns & D Brand "Introduction to Socio-Economic Rights in the South African Constitution" (1998) 2 *Law Democracy and Development* 153.

M Heywood "Shaping, making and breaking the law in the campaign for a national HIV/AIDS treatment plan" in P Jones & K Stokke (eds) *Democratising development: the politics of socio-economic rights in South Africa* (2005).

M Heywood "Seize Power! The Role of the Constitution in Unifying Social Justice Struggles in South Africa" in V Satgar (ed) *Capitalism's Crises: Class Struggles in South Africa and the World* (2015).

R Hischl & E Rosevear "Constitutional Law Meets Comparative Politics: Socio-Economic Rights and Political Realities" in T Campbell (ed) *The Legal Protection of Human Rights: Skeptical Essays* (2011).

A Honoré "Ownership" in A Guest (ed) *Oxford Essays in Jurisprudence* (1961).

B Hugo & E du Plessis "Sales in Execution of Immovable Property, the Rules of Court and the Consumer Protection Act Regulations: Back to the Drawing Board" (2014) 25 *Stellenbosch Law Review* 55.

L Juma "Mortgage bonds and the right of access to adequate housing in South Africa: Gundwana v Stoke [sic] Development & Others 2011 (3) SA 608 (CC) (2012) 37 *Journal for Juridical Science* 1.

D Kairys (ed) *The Politics of Law: A Progressive Critique* 3 ed (1998).

J King *Judging Social Rights* (2012).

K Klare "Legal Culture and Transformative Constitutionalism" (1998) 14 *South African Journal on Human Rights* 146.

M Kruger "Arbitrary deprivation of property: an argument for the payment of compensation by the state in certain cases of unlawful occupation" (2014) 131 *South African Law Journal* 328.

P Langa "Transformative Constitutionalism" (2006) 17 *Stellenbosch Law Review* 351.

M Langford "Housing Rights Litigation" in M Langford, B Cousins, J Dugard & T Madlingozi (eds) *Socio-Economic Rights In South Africa: Symbols or Substance?* (2014) 187.

M Langford, B Cousins, J Dugard & T Madlingozi "Concluding Perspectives" in M Langford, B Cousins, J Dugard & T Madlingozi (eds) *Socio-economic Rights in South Africa: Symbols or Substance?* (2014) 421.

B Latour *The Making of Law: An Ethnography of the Counseil d'Etat* (2010).

RW Lee *An Introduction to Roman Dutch Law* 2 ed (1925).

S Liebenberg "Remedial Principles and Meaningful Engagement in Education Rights Disputes" 2016 (19) *Potchefstroom Electronic Law Journal* 1.

S Liebenberg "South Africa's Evolving Jurisprudence on Socio-Economic Rights: An effective tool in challenging poverty?" (2002) 6 *Law Democracy and Development* 159.

S Liebenberg "The Value of Dignity in Interpreting Socio-Economic Rights" (2005) 21 *South African Journal on Human Rights* 1.

S Liebenberg *Socio-Economic Rights: Adjudication under a Transformative Constitution* (2010).

D Linder & N Levit *The Good Lawyer* (2014).

S Maas "Rent Control: A Comparative Analysis" (2012) 15 *Potchefstroom Electronic Law Journal* 41.

T Madlingozi "Post apartheid Social Movements and Legal Mobilisation" in M Langford, J Dugard, B Cousins & T Madlingozi (eds) *Socio-Economic Rights in South Africa*: (2014) 92.

K Marx "Critique of the Gotha Programme" in A Ryan (ed) *Justice* (1993).

K Marx *Capital Volume 1* (1976).

A Mattheus *De Auctionibus* (1680).

M McCann *Rights at work: Pay Equity and the Politics of Legal Mobilisation* (1994).

SS Merry *Getting Justice and Getting Even: Legal Consciousness Among Working-Class Americans* (1990).

F Michelman "Possession v Distribution in the Constitutional Idea of Property" (1987) 72 *Iowa Law Review* 1319.

C Miéville *Between Equal Rights: A Marxist Theory of International Law* (2005).

J Modiri "Conquest and constitutionalism: first thoughts on an alternative jurisprudence" (2018) 34 *South African Journal on Human Rights* 300.

S Moyn *Not Enough: Human Rights in an Unequal World* (2018).

C Murray & C O'Regan *No Place To Rest: Forced Removals and the Law in South Africa* (1990).

T Ngcukaitobi *The Land is Ours: South Africa's First Black Lawyers and the Birth of Constitutionalism* (2018).

R Nozick *Anarchy, State and Utopia* (1974).

EB Pashukanis *Law and Marxism: A General Theory* (1976).

T Patterson *Brown v Board of Education: A civil rights milestone and its troubled legacy* (2002).

O Patterson *Slavery and Social Death: A Comparative Study* (1982).

M Pieterse "Development, the right to the city and the legal and constitutional responsibilities of local government in South Africa" (2014) 131 *South African Law Journal* 149.

M Pieterse "What do we mean when we talk about transformative constitutionalism?" (2005) 20 *South African Public Law* 155.

T Piketty *Capital and Ideology* (2020).

T Piketty *Capital in the Twenty-First Century* (2014).

R Posner *Economic Analysis of Law* (1973).

J Rawls *A Theory of Justice* (1971).

B Ray *Engaging with Social Rights: Procedure, Participation and Democracy in South Africa's Second Wave* (2016).

S Robbins *From Revolution to Rights in South Africa: Social Movements and Popular Politics* (2008).

G Rosenberg "Saul Alinsky and the Campaign to Win the Right to Same-Sex Marriage" (2009) 42 *John Marshall Law Review* 643.

G Rosenberg *The Hollow Hope: Can courts bring about social change?* 2 ed (2008).

RFG Rosenow & MA Diemont *The Rents Act in South* Africa 2 ed (1950).

T Roux "Continuity and Change in a Transforming Legal Order: The Impact of Section 26(3) of the Constitution on South African Law" (2004) 121 *South African Law Journal* 466.

T Roux "Pro-Poor Court, Anti-Poor Outcomes: Explaining the Performance of the Land Claims Court" (2004) 20 *South African Journal on Human Rights* 511.

J Ryan Collins, T Lloyd & L Macfarlane Rethinking the Economics of Land and Housing (2017).

A Scalia "Modernity and the Constitution" in E Smith (ed) *Constitutional Justice Under Old Constitutions* (1995).

S Scheingold *The Politics of Rights: Lawyers, Public Policy and Political Change* (1974).

A Schiavone *The Invention of Law in the West* (2012).

D Schultz (ed) *Leveraging the Law: using courts to achieve social change* (1998).

J Seekings & Nicoli Nattrass *Class Race, and Inequality in South Africa* (2005).

JW Singer *Entitlement: The Paradoxes of Property* (2000).

R Skidelsky *Money and Government: The Past and Future of Economics* (2018).

C Steiker & J Steiker *Courting Death: the Supreme Court and Capital Punishment* (2016).

EP Thompson *The Poverty of Theory and Other Essays* (1978).

EP Thompson *Whigs and Hunters: The Origins of the Black Act* (1975).

K Tissington "Demolishing Development at Gabon Informal Settlement: Public Interest Litigation Beyond Modderklip?" (2011) 27 *South African Journal on Human Rights* 192.

L Underkuffler-Freund "Property: A Special Right? (1996) 71 *Notre Dame Law Review* 1033.

A van Aswegen (ed) *The Future of the South African Private Law* (1994).

A van der Walt "Exclusivity of Ownership, Security of Tenure and Eviction Orders: A Critical Evaluation of Recent Case Law" (2002) 18 *South African Journal on Human Rights* 372.

A van der Walt "The state's duty to protect property owners v the state's duty to provide housing: Thoughts on the *Modderklip* case" (2005) 21 *South African Journal on Human Rights* 144.

A van der Walt "Tradition on Trial: A Critical Analysis of the Civil Law Tradition in South African Property Law" (1995) 11 *South African Journal on Human Rights* 169.

A van der Walt *Constitutional Property Law* (2005).

A van der Walt *Property in the Margins* (2009).

K van Marle "Transformative Constitutionalism as/and Critique" (2009) 20 *Stellenbosch Law Review* 286.

J Voet *The Selective Voet, being the Commentary on the Pandects* (translated Percival Gane) (1955).

J Voet *Commentary on the Pandects* (translated by J Buchanan) (1920).

J Waldron *The Right to Private Property* (1988).

M Wegerif *Still Searching for Security: The reality of Farm Dweller Evictions in South Africa* (2005).

L Williams "Introduction" in L Williams A Kjonstad & P Robson *Law and Poverty: The legal system and poverty reduction* (2003).

G Willie & G Bradfield *Willies Principles of South African Law* 9 ed (2007).

S Wilson & J Dugard "Taking Poverty Seriously: the South African Constitutional Court and socio-economic rights" (2011) 22 *Stellenbosch Law Review* 664.

S Wilson "Breaking the Tie: Evictions from Private Land, Homelessness and a New Normality" (2009) *South African Law Journal* 126.

S Wilson "Curing the Poor: State Housing Policy in Johannesburg after Blue Moonlight" (2014) 5 *Constitutional Court Review* 279, 291.

S Wilson "Litigating Housing Rights in Johannesburg's Inner City: 2004–2008" (2011) 27 *South African Journal on Human Rights* 127.

S Wilson "Planning for Inclusion in South Africa: The State's Duty to Prevent Homelessness and the Potential of 'Meaningful Engagement" (2011) 22 *Urban Forum* 265.

S Wilson "Taming the Constitution: Rights and Reform in the South African Education System" (2004) 20 *South African Journal on Human Rights* 418.

S Woolman *The Selfless Constitution: Experimentalism and Flourishing as Foundations of South Africa's Basic Law* (2013).

H Zinn *A People's History of the United States* (2005).

H Zinn (ed) *Justice in Everyday Life: The way it really works* (1974).

Cases

Abahlali baseMjondolo v Premier of KwaZulu-Natal 2010 (2) BCLR 99 (CC).

ABSA Bank v Mokebe 2018 (6) SA 492 (GJ).*

ABSA Bank v Ntsane 2007 (3) SA 554 (T).

ABSA v Lekuku [2014] ZAGPJHC 244 (14 October 2014).*

All Builders and Cleaning Services CC v Matlaila (42349/13) [2015] ZAGPJHC 2 (16 January 2015).*

Bank of Lisbon v De Ornelas 1988 (3) SA 580 (A).

Beinash v Wigley 1997 (3) SA 721 (SCA).

Baron v Claytile 2017 (5) SA 329 (CC).

Betta Eiendomme (Pty) Ltd v Ekple-Epoh 2000 (4) SA 468 (W).

Brisley v Drotsky 2002 (4) SA 1 (SCA).

---

* The cases in which I appeared as an advocate are marked with an asterisk.

Campus Law Clinic (University of KwaZulu-Natal Durban) v Standard Bank of South Africa Ltd 2006 (6) SA 103 (CC).

Cape Killarney Property Investments (Pty) Ltd v Mahamba [2001] 4 All SA 479 (A).

Chetty v Naidoo 1974 (3) SA 13 (A).

Christian Education South Africa v Minister of Education 2000 (4) SA 757 (CC).

City of Johannesburg Metropolitan Municipality and Others v Hlophe and Others 2015 (2) All SA 251 (SCA).*

City of Johannesburg v Blue Moonlight Properties 2012 (2) SA 104 (CC).*

City of Johannesburg v Changing Tides 2012 (6) SA 294 (SCA).*

City of Johannesburg v Dladla 2016 (6) SA 377 (SCA).*

City of Johannesburg v Rand Properties 2007 (6) SA 417 (SCA).

Daniels v Scribante 2017 (4) SA 341 (CC).

Dladla v City of Johannesburg 2018 (2) SA 327 (CC).*

Du Plessis v De Klerk 1996 (3) SA 850 (CC).

Ekurhuleni Metropolitan Municipality v Dada NO 2009 (4) SA 463 (SCA).

Ekurhuleni Metropolitan Municipality and Another v Various Occupiers, Eden Park Extension 5 2014 (3) SA 23 (SCA).

Emfuleni Local Municipality v Builders Advancement Services CC 2010 (4) SA 133 (GSJ).

eThekwini Metropolitan Unicity Municipality v Pilco Investments CC (320/06) [2007] ZASCA 62 (29 May 2007).

Ex parte Geldenhuys 1926 OPD 155.

Faieza Salie v Ebrahim Kaskar Western Cape Rental Housing Tribunal Case Nos. 21/3/1/21654/S47 &S48 (5 November 2018).

Fernflat Share Block (Pty) Ltd v Willemse [2019] ZAGPJHC 345 (3 October 2019).

First National Bank of SA Ltd t/a Wesbank v Commissioner South African Revenue Service 2002 (4) SA 768 (CC).

Firstrand Bank Limited v Dhlamini 2010 (4) SA 531 (GNP).

Firstrand Bank v Folscher 2011 (4) SA 314 (GNP).

Firstrand Bank v Zwane 2016 (6) SA 400 (GJ).

Fischer v Unlawful Occupiers 2018 (2) SA 228 (WCC).*

Gerber v Stolze 1951 (2) SA 166 (T).

Gien v Gien 1979 (2) SA 1113 (T).

Governing Body of the Juma Musjid Primary School and Others v Ahmed Asruff Essay NO and Others 2011 (8) BCLR 761 (CC).

Government of the Republic of South African v Grootboom 2000 (1) SA 46 (CC).

Groengras Eiendomme (Pty) Ltd v Elandsfontein Unlawful Occupants 2002 (1) SA 125 (T).

Gundwana v Steko Development 2011 (3) SA 608 (CC).*

Herison v South African Mutual Life Assurance Society 1942 AD 259.

Hlophe and Others v City of Johannesburg and Others 2013 (4) SA 212 (GSJ).*

Hudson v Hudson 1927 AD 259.

Jaftha v Schoeman; Van Rooyen v Stoltz 2005 (2) SA 140 (CC).

Jele v Young Min Shan CC Gauteng Rental Housing Tribunal Case No. 909/12 (31 May 2013).*

Joubert v Van Rensburg 2001 (1) SA 753 (W).

Kendall Property Investments v Rutgers [2005] 4 All SA 61 (C).

Kilburn v Estate Kilburn 1931 AD 501.

Komani NO v Bantu Affairs Administration Board, Peninsula Area 1980 (4) SA 448 (A).

Kubyana v Standard Bank of South Africa Ltd 2014 (3) SA 56 (CC).*

Laugh It Off Promotions CC v South African Breweries International (Finance) BV t/a Sabmark International and Another 2006 (1) SA 144 (CC).

Ledlie v ERF 2235 Somerset West (Pty) Ltd 1992 (4) SA 600 (C).

Lewray Investments v Mtunzi [2018] ZAGPJHC 432 (23 May 2018).*

Malan v Nabygelegen Estates 1946 AD 562.

Maphango v Aengus Lifestyle Properties (Pty) Ltd 2011 (5) SA 19 (SCA).*

Maphango v Aengus Lifestyle Properties 2012 (3) SA 531 (CC).*

MEC for Human Settlements & Public Works of the Province of Kwazulu-Natal v Ethekwini Municipality and Others; Abahlali baseMjondolo and Others v Ethekwini Municipality [2015] 4 All SA 190 (KZD).*

Melani v City of Johannesburg 2016 (5) SA 67 (GJ).

Messenger of the Magistrate's Court, Durban v Pillay 1952 (3) SA 678 (A).

Modderfontein Squatters, Greater Benoni City Council v Modderklip Boerdery (Pty) Ltd; President of the Republic of South Africa v Modderklip Boerdery 2004 (6) SA 40 (SCA).

Modderklip Boerdery (Edms) Bpk v President van die RSA 2003 (6) BCLR 638 (T).

Munien v BMW Financial Services (SA) (Pty) Ltd 2010 (1) SA 549 (KZD).

Ndlovu v Ngcobo; Bekker and Another v Jika 2003 (1) SA 113 (SCA).

Nedbank v Fraser 2011 (4) SA 363 (GSJ).

Nedbank v Mortinson 2005 (6) SA 462 (W).

Nino Bonino v De Lange 1906 TS 120.

Nkata v Firstrand Bank Limited 2016 (4) SA 257 (CC).*

Nxazonke and Another v ABSA Bank Ltd and Others (18100/2012) [2012] ZAWCHC 184 (4 October 2012).

Nzimande v Nzimande 2005 (1) SA 83 (W).

Occupiers of 51 Olivia Road and 197 Main Street, Johannesburg v City of Johannesburg 2008 (3) SA 208 (CC).

Occupiers of Saratoga Avenue v City of Johannesburg 2012 (9) BCLR 951 (CC).*

Occupiers, Berea v De Wet NO 2017 (5) SA 346 (CC).*

Oregon Trust v BEADICA 231 CC (74/2018) [2019] ZASCA 29 (28 March 2019).

Port Elizabeth Municipality v Various Occupiers 2005 (1) SA 217 (CC).

Port Elizabeth Municipality v Peoples Dialogue on Land and Shelter 2000 (2) 1074 (SE).

Port Elizabeth Municipality v Various Occupiers 2005 (1) SA 217 (CC).

President of the Republic of South Africa v Modderklip Boerdery (Pty) Ltd 2005 (5) SA 3 (CC).

Quenty's Motors Ltd v Standard Credit Corporation 1994 (3) SA 188 (A).

Rates Action Group v City of Cape Town 2004 (5) SA 545 (C).

Reflect All 1025 CC v MEC for Public Transport, Roads and Works, Gauteng Provincial Government 2009 (6) SA 391 (CC).

Residents of Joe Slovo Community, Western Cape v Thubelisha Homes and Others 2011 (7) BCLR 723 (CC).

Residents of Joe Slovo Community, Western Cape v Thubelisha Homes and Others 2010 (3) SA 454 (CC).

Roe v Wade 410 U.S. 113 (1973).

Rossouw and Another v Firstrand Bank Ltd 2010 (6) SA 439 (SCA).

S v Govender 1986 (3) 969 (T).

S v Makwanyane 1995 3 SA 391 (CC).

S v Zuma 1995 (2) SA 642 (CC).

Sebola v Standard Bank of South Africa Ltd 2012 (5) SA 142 (CC).*

Soobramoney v Minister of Health, KwaZulu-Natal 1998 (1) SA 765 (CC).

Standard Bank of SA Ltd v Snyders and Eight Similar Cases 2005 (5) SA 610 (C).

Standard Bank v Saunderson 2006 (2) SA 264 (SCA).

Tenants of ERF 69, 70, 71, 72 Fairview v AJ and T Vosloo Gauteng Rental Housing Tribunal Case No 1560/17 (26 November 2018).*

Tenants of Plettenberg v Urban Task Force Gauteng Rental Housing Tribunal Case Nos 91/2017 and 182/2017.

The Occupiers, Shulana Court, 11 Hendon Road, Yeoville, Johannesburg v Steele [2010] 4 All SA 54 (SCA).

Thompson v Scholtz 1999 (1) SA 232 (SCA).

Thwala and Another v First National Bank Limited and Others (2015/19201) [2013] ZAGPPHC 514 (11 December 2013).*

Todd v First Rand Bank Ltd and Others [2013] 3 All SA 500 (SCA).*

Treatment Action Campaign v Minister of Health 2002 (5) SA 721 (CC).

Tudor Hotel Brasserie & Bar (Pty) Ltd v Hencetrade 15 (Pty) Ltd (793/2016) [2017] ZASCA 111 (20 September 2017).

Young Ming Shan CC v Chagan NO 2015 (3) SA 227 (GJ).*

Zulu v eThekwini Municipality 2014 (4) SA 590 (CC).*

Statutes and Regulations

Consumer Protection Act 68 of 2008.

Expropriation Act 63 of 1975.

Extension of Security of Tenure Act 62 of 1997.

Gauteng Unfair Practice Regulations, *Provincial Gazette Extraordinary* 124 Notice 4004 of 2001, 4 July 2001.

Interim Protection of Informal Land Rights Act 31 of 1996.

Labour Tenants Act 3 of 1996.

National Credit Act 34 of 2005.

Prescription Act 68 of 1969.

Prevention of Illegal Eviction from, and Unlawful Occupation of Land Act 19 of 1998.

Prevention of Illegal Squatting Act 52 of 1951.

Rent Control Act 80 of 1976.

Rental Housing Act 50 of 1999.

Tenants Protection (Temporary) Act 7 of 1920.

Research Reports and Media Articles

E Bruce Jones "Black Lives and the State of Distraction" *Los Angeles Review of Books* <https://lareviewofbooks.org/essay/black-lives-and-the-state-of-distraction> last visited 4 March 2016.

S Budlender, G Marcus & N Ferreira *Public Interest Litigation in South Africa: Strategies, Tactics and Lessons* (2014).

Z Postman "Huge Shack Demolition in Johannesburg" *GroundUp* (30 April 2019) <https://www.groundup.org.za/article/huge-shack-demolition-johannesburg> last visited on 2 May 2019.

Socio-Economic Rights Institute of South Africa (SERI), *Minding the Gap: An Analysis of the Supply of and Demand for Low-Income Rental Accommodation in Inner City Johannesburg* (2013).

Socio-Economic Rights Institute of South Africa (SERI) *Public Interest Legal Services in South Africa* (2015).

World Bank, *South Africa Systematic Country Diagnostic: an incomplete transition – overcoming the legacy of exclusion in South Africa* (2018).

INDEX

A

Abahlali baseMjondolo 5, 80
abortion 127, 132, 133
accommodation
   alternative 58, 62n29, 64, 70, 71, 72, 73–74,
     75, 100, 101, 136
   personal 47–48
   residential 46, 48, 72, 88
acquisitive prescription 40
agency
   human 10, 32, 133
   individual and group 131
   operation of shaped by law 6
   of the poor 76–77, 81n129
   social 9
agent(s)
   -centred approach to law and social change
     21, 28, 30–33, 131–135, 137, 138, 140,
     142, 143
   centred judges and lawyers 140–142
   with unequal power 19
aggregate social welfare 43
alternative accommodation 14, 46, 58, 62n29,
   64, 70, 71, 72, 73–74, 75, 100, 101, 136
alternative dispute resolution 119
Anti-Privatisation Forum 5
apartheid
   dispossession 43
   economic structure 17
   ending of 1, 3, 6, 11, 16, 34, 52, 53
   evictions 65
   landlord and tenant 48
   lawyers and judges 8
   legacy 53
   legal regime 3–4, 38
   ownership 34, 45–46, 47, 103
   property law 139
   rental housing 86
arbitrary eviction 17, 54, 60, 74
Archimedean perspective 26
attachment and sale of property *see* execution
   against residential property
autonomy 6, 19, 23, 24, 27, 30

B

Black Act 1723 8
building(s)
   derelict 1, 14
   legislation and eviction applications 2–3
   unsafe 68, 75

C

children's rights 5, 66, 67
civil liberties 5
civil rights movement in United States 4, 5, 9
class-based inequality 127
classical economics 20
classical Marxist tradition 20, 21–24, 27–28, 29,
   34
colonialism 4, 16, 17, 43, 47
common law of property
   absolute control 36
   Constitutional interferences 55–56, 127–128
   debtor/creditor 39–40
   development of 141
   dispossession 45, 139
   dominium 36
   equity, proportionality and fairness 140
   evictions 60, 81
   execution against residential property 48–52
   extinction or limitation of owner's rights 39
   good reason 37, 60, 85
   hierarchies of power 38, 39, 43, 45, 46, 48,
     52, 56, 57, 61, 64, 90, 127, 128
   landlord and tenant 46–48, 83, 89–90, 94
   legal subjects 131
   normality assumption 37, 60
   power imbalance between debtor and creditor
     39–40
   presumptions 55, 56
   public good 37–38
   real security 41, 49, 50
   remodelling 37, 38
   rights against owners 39
   Roman-Dutch 11–12
   social exclusion 39–43
   transformation 3–4

unlawful occupation of land 44–46
consciousness 29, 30
conservative theories of law 19–20
Constitution
   blueprint for social transformation 16, 33
   economic transformation 3
   egalitarian social transformation 3
   social change desired in 16
   transformative 16–19
constitutional negotiations 53–54
constitutional state 22, 24
constitutional supremacy 16
constructivists 131, 133–134, 138
consumer credit, rules of 10
contract, classical Marxist tradition 22
contractual freedom 141
controlled premises 84
credit agreement, reinstatement of 123–124
credit legislation *see* debtor/creditor
creditor(s) *see* debtor/creditor
cross-class relationships 142
customary law rights 61

D
death penalty 8, 27
debt
   acceleration of 51, 107, 116, 117, 119
   counsellor 119
   enforcement procedures 125
   execution against residential property 48–52,
      107–114
   forgiveness 49
   interest 49
   right to collect 49
   value of 49
debtor/creditor
   alternative dispute resolution 119
   common law 125
   creditors rights vs ownership rights 48–49
   delivery of s 129 notice 119–124
   evasion argument 121–122
   fairness 135
   meaningful engagement 122–123
   non-compliance with credit legislation
      118–124
   notice requirement 119–124
   power imbalance 39–40
   real security 49–50, 105–106
   relationship between 18, 49
   remedy of default in 119
   reshaping of law 7

social change 124–125
social power relations 103–107
declarations of rights 24
deductive reasoning 45
demolition of structures 44, 77, 80
deprivation
   of liberty 4
   of property 55, 60, 65, 69, 72, 73n94
derelict buildings 1, 14
desegregation 9, 27, 127
dignity 6, 16, 31, 66, 76, 77, 141
discrimination 16, 54, 85, 86, 88
dispossession
   common law of property 45, 139
   of poor and vulnerable 4, 14
   property law and 33–35
dominium 12, 36, 37, 38–39, 42, 43, 44, 47, 55,
   56

E
economic relationships 18–19, 21, 23, 135
economic theories of law 20
economic transformation 3
economics 8, 20
education 3, 16, 44
efficiency 20, 41, 43
egalitarian social transformation 3
electricity charges 97–98
emergency housing
   policy 68, 73, 75, 78, 128n11
   housing shelters 75
English law 13
Enlightenment revolutions 42
equality 8, 16, 23, 28, 37, 130, 134
equity in eviction proceedings 66–74
estoppel 12, 40
evictions
   alternative accommodation 14, 58, 62n29,
      64, 70, 71, 72, 73–74, 75, 100, 101, 136
   arbitrary 17, 54, 60, 74
   building legislation 2–3
   children's rights 66, 67
   commercial farmlands between 1994 and
      2004 34
   common law of property 60, 81
   compensation for right to exclusive posses-
      sion 70
   Constitution 57–59
   cost of executing order 69
   customary law rights 61
   development of constitutionalised law 60–74
   due to renovation of property 99–100

duty to act reasonably 67
emergency housing
    and basic shelter 70, 73
    policy 68, 73, 75, 128n11
equity in proceedings 66–74
expropriation and 64
farm workers 61–62
holders over 64, 65
homelessness 18, 71, 73, 136
housing rights 60–74
inner-cities 2–3, 35
in interests of safety 14, 46
just and equitable 63, 64–65, 72–73, 139
land invasions 66, 67–68, 70, 71, 74, 77
last resort 80
mass 3, 4, 75, 80
meaningful engagement 62–63, 80
PIE Act 62–74
prevention of illegal 62–74
proceedings 59, 63, 64, 66–74, 75, 78, 79,
    80, 92, 98
reasonable housing policy 67
refusal to move 79–81
rental housing 87, 88, 90, 92, 94, 98–101
retaliatory 98, 99, 101, 102
right
    not to be arbitrarily evicted 3, 72
    to remain on land 59
San Jose 1–2, 14
school 40–41
state's failure to assist in giving effect to order
    69–70
temporary shelters 67, 75
tenant from rental housing 85
tension between property and housing rights
    clause 60–61
exceptio non adempleti contractus 83
execution against residential property
    abuse of process 115
    alternatives to 7, 107, 116, 118, 121, 123
    arrear amount or overall debt claimed dispro-
        portionately low 117–118
    balancing exercise 108–109
    common law of property 48–52
    fair and proportionate 18
    infringement of rights 108
    judicial oversight 109–111, 113, 114,
        115–116
    limitation of right of access to adequate hous-
        ing 108
    mortgage bonds 109–113
    personal service 117

primary residence 111, 114–115
process of obtaining judgment 51
proportionality inquiry 107–114, 115, 116,
    118, 124
qualified right to a reserve price 124
refusal of 112
stages of 50–51
wide judicial discretion 115–116
expropriation
    evictions and 64
    just and equitable compensation 3, 17, 54
    ownership rights 40
    public interest 54, 55
    public purpose 54, 55
    social claims 42
    unlawful occupation of land 59, 74, 78

F
fairness
    apartheid 8
    common law of property and 37
    debtor/creditor 40, 135
    eviction 60, 66
    execution against residential property 52, 106
    landlord and tenant 88, 91, 92, 93, 95, 135
    legal reasoning 140
family law 23, 28
farm workers 61–62
freedom 8, 10, 11, 12, 16, 28, 141
Freedom Charter (1955) 3
freedom of expression 5, 16

G
gay marriages 27, 30
gentrification 14, 85, 92, 96, 97, 101, 102
good reason 37, 60, 85
Griffin, James 30, 31, 32
group areas 46, 48

H
habitation rights 41, 128
healthcare 3, 5, 16
healthy environment 3
homelessness 12, 14, 18, 44, 58, 67, 69, 70, 71,
    73, 75, 102, 111, 136
housing
    backlog 77
    clause 14, 54–55, 58, 60–62, 64–67, 69–73,
        85, 106, 108, 111, 113, 127–128
    crises 68

emergency
   policy 68, 72, 73, 75, 78, 128n11
   shelters 75
formal delivery 77
progressive realisation of right to 3, 33, 54
reasonable policy 67
reasonableness 62n29, 67, 71, 72, 73, 79
refusal to be relocated 79–81
relocation 74, 75–77, 79, 80
rental *see* landlord and tenant; rent; rental
   housing
rights
   access to adequate 3, 5, 14, 17, 33, 54, 67,
      70, 71, 80, 85, 108, 111, 113
   clauses 52–56, 60–61
   struggles 74–81
   vs right to exclusive possession 70
unlawful occupation of land 77–78
human agency 10, 31, 32, 133
human dignity 16, 31, 66
human rights, philosophical justification of
   9–10
human standing 30, 31

I

inequality 5, 6, 7, 11, 13, 14, 17, 37, 43, 47, 82,
   85, 127, 132, 133
influx controls 1, 48
informal settlement upgrading 59, 74–75, 79–80
inner-city regeneration 3, 35
institutional behaviour and policy 127, 133
instrumentalist approach to law and social
   change 24–27, 132, 138

J

Johannesburg inner city 1, 2, 35, 93
judges
   agent centred 140–142
   apartheid 8
judicial oversight
   execution against
      primary residence 115–116
      residential property 109, 110, 113, 114

L

labour practices 3
labour tenants 61–62
labour unions 5
laissez-faire economic policies 43
land invasions 66, 67–68, 71, 74, 77, 78
land occupations *see* unlawful occupation of
   land

land reform
   failure of 128–130
   progress 129
land restitution and redistribution 3
land tenure, rules of 10
landlord and tenant *see also* rent
   bare power of landlord 13, 48
   bargaining power 46, 47, 88, 102
   common law of property 46–48, 83, 89–90,
      94
   constitutionalism 82
   duty of good faith 88
   exploitative practices 97
   failure to effect maintenance 85, 89–90
   fairness 135
   interest of tenants 82
   landlords' rights
      compensation for damage 86
      recovery of rent 86
      rental payments 86
   owner's power of dominium 48
   power imbalance 101
   reciprocal obligations 94, 95
   relationship between 18
   reshaping of law 7
   residential property 46, 47
   tenants
      associations 82, 85, 87, 97, 98
      protection 47–48, 85
      right to organise 83, 102
law
   action in 135–138
   economics and 8, 20
   as epiphenomenon 6, 21–24
   equal application 4
   at every bloody level 29
   form of social practice 6
   as instrumentality 6, 24–27
   is malleable 6
   justice 4
   paradoxical quality of 4
   places "effective inhibitions on the exercise of
      power" 6
   power of 8
   preservation rather than alteration of social
      relations 19–20
   shapes spaces within which agency operates
      6
   social change and 19–21
   as social structurant 6, 27–33
   structure of 138–140

lawyers
    agent centred 140–142
    apartheid 8
    to serve true interests of clients 142
leases *see also* landlord and tenant
    common law 12
    fair termination 18
    service charges 97–98
    termination of 13, 19, 47, 84, 85, 86, 90, 91,
        92, 98, 102, 139
    terms of 86
    written 86
left politics 28–29
legal innovations 7
legal mobilisation 130, 134, 135, 137
legal realism 128
legal reasoning 42, 54, 102n123, 130, 131, 138,
    139, 140
legal relationships 7, 21, 22, 42, 128n11, 140,
    141
legal rules 27, 131, 133, 135–136
legal spaces 130, 137, 138
legal subjects 130, 131, 138
legal support structure 136
letting *see* landlord and tenant
liberal approach to law 28, 34
liberal tradition 9, 20, 24–27
liberty 4, 29, 30

M
mandament van spolie 13, 61
Marikana informal settlement 77
market exchange 20
Marx, Karl 21–23, 27–28
meaningful engagement
    debtor/creditor 123
    evictions 62–63, 80
minimum level of resources and capabilities 30
moral rights 31
morality 29, 30, 31, 105
mortgage bonds
    default notice 119–124
    executions 50–52, 109–113, 114
        arrear amount or overall debt claimed
            disproportionately low 117–118
        proportionate 139
        qualified right to a reserve price 124
    real security 50
    reinstatement of loan agreement 123–124

right to
    accelerate debt and demand full amount
        116–117
    demand repayment 116–117
    execute 116–117
    specific performance 123
mortgage property
    adequate housing 111, 113
    execution against 50–52
mortgagees, common law 12
movement lawyering 134, 135
multi-racial urban tenant class 48

N
National Housing Code 68, 78, 79
neo-liberal economic orthodoxy 3
new left theories 28
normality assumption 37, 60
normative relationships 8
Nozick's theory of rights 31–32
nuisance 12, 36, 40, 85

O
owner/occupier relationship 18
ownership
    alienation of 11
    bundle of rights 41
    common law 12
    as *dominium* 38, 42, 43
    limitations on rights 11, 40
    model of property law 6, 7, 10, 11, 14
    right of 53
    rights vs creditors rights 48–49
    social claims on 11

P
Pashukanis, EB 22
paterfamilias 36
personal accommodation 47–48
personal service requirement 117
personhood 30, 31, 32
political disputes 5
political traditions 20–33
politics of rights 24, 25
post-Marxist theories 28
poverty 5, 11, 29, 43, 132, 133
power relationships 6, 8, 63, 106, 125, 129
prescription 11, 13, 40
privacy, right to 76, 86
progressive realisation 3, 33, 54

property
  acquisition of significant 37
  clause 52–56, 60–61, 127–128
  common law of property *see* common law of
    property
  constitutional negotiations 53–54
  deprivation of 55, 60, 65, 69, 72, 73n94
  distributive outcomes 34
  dominium *see* dominium
  execution against residential 48–52
  inherent inequality of 37
  insiders 7, 12
  law
    class relationships 6–7
    classical Marxist tradition 22
    constitutionally driven changes to property
      141
    dispossession 33–35
    forms and content 22, 127, 142–143
    models of 13
    ownership model 6, 7, 10, 11, 14
    purpose of 10
    rules of 10
    shapes terms of accessibility of resources
      6–7
    social practice 10–11
    transformation of 130–131
  as medium of participation in collective 53
  non-arbitrary deprivation 55
  outsiders 7, 13, 14
  power structures 4
  private law conceptualism 52–53
  public good 36, 37, 38
  rights
    contemporary struggles 11–14
    distribution of 11, 17
    redistribution 17–18
    social consequences 139
    transfer of 18
  social claims on 11, 40, 42, 139, 141, 142
  structured equity 74, 75, 77, 78, 80, 81, 95
  subsidiary rights 37
  proportionality in debt execution process
    107–114, 115, 116, 118, 124
provincial Rental Housing Tribunals 84, 86
public good 36, 37, 38
public law 22–23, 28, 118
public policy 24, 25, 27, 83, 127, 130, 131, 134

R
real security 39, 41, 49, 50, 105, 106
realists 131–132, 134, 138

reasonableness 3, 62n29, 67, 71, 72, 73, 79
redistributive claims 11
rei vindicatio 12, 44, 45, 46
relocation
  last resort 79
  management 75–77
  terms and conditions 74, 80
rent
  control 19, 40, 47–48, 83–85, 88, 92, 99,
    101–102
  controlled premises 84
  determination 83, 90, 93–97
  increases 47, 82, 83, 84, 85, 86, 90, 96, 99,
    101, 102, 128
  interference by Rental Housing Tribunal 87
  market conditions 83
  order for reduction of 89
  reasonable rental 85
  remission of 83, 89
  withholding of 46, 82, 101
Rent Boards 47, 48, 85
rental housing
  community's multiple interactions 92–93
  complaints 86–87
  court decisions 88–92
  discrimination 86, 88
  evictions 85, 87, 88, 90, 92, 94, 98–101
  legislation 82, 84–92
  market conditions 91, 101
  notice to vacate 99–100
  pending renovation 93–94
  privacy 86
  provincial regulations 87
  remedial powers of Tribunal 87
  renovation of property 99–100
  specific performance of landlord's obligations
    89
  stimulation of supply 85–86
  subsidy programme 86
  unfair practices 84, 86, 87, 88–92, 93–94, 95,
    97, 98, 99, 101–102, 139
  value-based reasoning 95, 102
Rental Housing Tribunals 16, 84, 86, 92–101,
  102
repeat players 137
reserve price, execution against residential
  property 124
residential accommodation 46, 47, 48, 72, 85, 88
residential property 46, 47, 50, 52, 56, 106
rights
  declarations of 24
  liberal approach to law 24–25

politics of 24, 25
revolution 137
theory of 31–32
Roman-Dutch common law of property 11–12
Roman law 36, 42
rule of law 8, 28, 45, 48

S
sale in execution, common law of property 52
San Jose 1–2, 14, 126
sectional title units 34
service charges 97–98
servitude of trespass 65, 72, 73, 135
shelter regime, emergency 75–76
slum clearances 2
slumlording 89
social agency 9
social change
  conceptual foundations of legal rights 9–10
  debtor/creditor 124–125
  desired by Constitution 16
  development of law 7–10
  extent to which law can structure and direct 4–7
  law as agent of 8
  lawyering 9
  paradox of law and 4–7
  relationship between law and 19–21
  role of law in 6
social disadvantage 127
social justice 130
social life 34
social needs 7, 11, 12, 39, 40, 42, 48, 53, 56, 81, 131, 140
social order 3, 16, 20
social outcomes 31, 32, 139
social participation 10
social practice, property law and 10–11
social relationships 8, 19–20, 24, 29, 30, 43, 131
social security 3
social services, access to basic 31
social transformation 3, 4, 15, 20, 21, 31, 33, 102n123
socially subordinate groups 8–9
socio-economic rights 3, 5, 31, 53, 129, 132
state of independence 75
statistical studies 133
structured equity, property 74, 75, 77, 78, 80, 81, 95
subtraction from the dominium 12, 36
suitable alternative accommodation 62n29
support structure 136, 137, 138

T
temporary shelters 67, 75
tenants *see* landlord and tenant
theory of rights 31–32
transformation
  common law of property 3–4
  social 3, 4, 15, 20, 21, 31, 33, 102n123
Treatment Action Campaign 5
trespassing 65, 66, 72, 73, 135
tribunals, equity and fairness 93

U
unemployment 13, 107, 132
universal adult suffrage 3, 16
unlawful occupation of land
  agency 59
  apartheid legislation 44
  arbitrary deprivation of property and 60, 65, 69, 72
  common law of property 44–46
  Constitution 57–59
  criminal offence 44
  customary law rights 61
  demolition of structures 44, 77, 80
  expropriation 59, 64, 74, 78
  farm workers 61–62
  housing rights and 77–78
  marginalisation of non-ownership rights 44
  meaningful engagement 62–63, 80
  needs and vulnerabilities of occupiers 59
  occupiers in desperate need of shelter 69
  prevention of illegal evictions 62–74
  purchase of property 78
  rei vindicatio 44, 45, 46
  reshaping of law 7
  right to remain on land 59
unsafe buildings 68, 75
unsafe living conditions 14, 46
urban freehold land 34
usufruct 12, 37

V
value-based reasoning 45, 54, 95, 102, 131, 140, 142
violence 3, 4
voting system 3

W
welfare states 11